2-19
22/12
N/F

So what are our euroleaders giving us? A European single market where independent countries cooperate for the benefit of their people? Or an authoritarian, meddlesome and undemocratic superstate obsessed with increasing its own power?

And are we, Europe's 495 million citizens, enthusiastic supporters of our leaders' great European project? Or are we being dragged into our rulers' dream of a United States of Europe by an arrogant, out-of-touch euro-elite who contemptuously ignore the opinions of the voters who pay for their secure, luxury lifestyle?

In *The Great European Rip-off* David Craig and Matthew Elliott reveal the shocking story of how the eurocrats have tricked us into giving them ever-increasing control over our lives. And the authors ask whether we are going to subserviently allow our unelected eurorulers to run almost every aspect of our lives or whether we are prepared to fight back to protect our individual freedoms and democratic rights.

David Craig has spent most of his career as a management consultant working for and competing against some of the world's best and worst management and IT systems consultancies. He has helped to sell consulting to almost 100 organisations in 15 countries across Europe, Asia and the US, as well as the British public sector. He is the author of the controversial bestsellers *Rip-Off! The Scandalous Inside Story of the Management Consulting Money Machine*, *Plundering the Public Sector*, and, most recently, *Squandered: How Gordon Brown is Wasting Over One Trillion Pounds of Our Money*. He has an MA from Cambridge and an MBA from Warwick Business School.

Matthew Elliott is Co-Founder and Chief Executive of the TaxPayers' Alliance, the UK's most high-profile campaign group. He is a Fellow of the Royal Society of Arts and sits on the Advisory Committee of the New Culture Forum. His last book was *The Bumper Book of Government Waste 2008* (Harriman House).

Praise for *Squandered*

'It is no exaggeration to say that if the right people read it, take it seriously, and take appropriate action, this book could not only save the taxpayer billions, it could save lives . . . This is a terrifying book, but a brilliant and necessary one. Please read it.'
Daily Telegraph

'The most illuminating political book to date this year'
Nick Cohen, *Evening Standard*

Praise for *Plundering the Public Sector*

'The first serious work to deal in a thorough fashion with the incompetence, nepotism and waste that have defined New Labour in government . . . David Craig and Richard Brooks have performed an immense public service, and this horrifying book deserves a wide readership.' *Spectator*

'This is a good topic and Craig knows his stuff. He writes with passionate disgust and with rich detail.' *Management Today*

'Racy yet well-researched . . . gripping and important'
New Statesman

Praise for *Rip-Off!*

'David Craig has now done for consulting what [Oliver] Stone did for investment banking' *New Statesman*

One of Danuta Kean's books of the year in the *Independent on Sunday*: 'The most shocking book of the year . . . It is a must-read for anyone in business or on the receiving end of consultants' advice.'

THE GREAT EUROPEAN RIP-OFF

RIP-OFF

How the corrupt, wasteful EU is taking control of our lives

David Craig and Matthew Elliot

BOOKS

Published by Random House Books 2009

2 4 6 8 10 9 7 5 3 1

Copyright © David Craig and Matthew Elliott 2009

David Craig and Matthew Elliott have asserted their rights under the Copyright,
Designs and Patents Act, 1988, to be identified as the authors
of this work

This book is sold subject to the condition that it shall not, by way of trade
or otherwise, be lent, resold, hired out, or otherwise circulated without the
publisher's prior consent in any form of binding or cover other than that
in which it is published and without a similar condition, including this condition,
being imposed on the subsequent purchaser.

First published in Great Britain in 2009 by
Random House Books
Random House, 20 Vauxhall Bridge Road,
London SW1V 2SA

www.rbooks.co.uk

Addresses for companies within The Random House Group Limited can be
found at: www.randomhouse.co.uk/offices.htm

The Random House Group Limited Reg. No. 954009

A CIP catalogue record for this book
is available from the British Library

ISBN 9781847945709

The Random House Group Limited supports The Forest Stewardship
Council (FSC), the leading international forest certification organisation.
All our titles that are printed on Greenpeace approved FSC certified paper carry
the FSC logo. Our paper procurement policy can be found at
www.rbooks.co.uk/environment

Mixed Sources
Product group from well-managed
forests and other controlled sources
www.fsc.org Cert no. TT-COC-2139
© 1996 Forest Stewardship Council

FSC

Typeset by
SX Composing DTP, Rayleigh, Essex

Printed and bound in Great Britain by
CPI Bookmarque, Croydon, CR0 4TD

CONTENTS

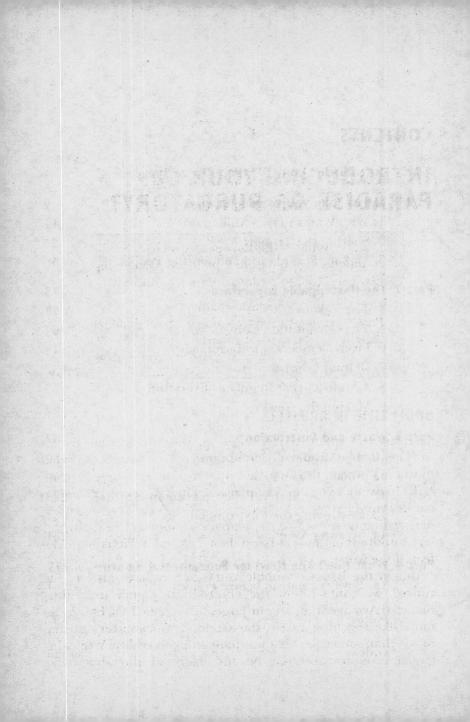

INTRODUCING YOUR EU: PARADISE OR PURGATORY?

> **What is the European Union?**
> A unique economic and political partnership between 27 democratic European countries.
>
> **What are its aims?**
> Peace, prosperity and freedom for its 495 million citizens – in a fairer, safer world.
>
> EU website, 2009

BOOM TIME IN BRUSSELS

The last few months have been an interesting time to be working in the European Union's capital city, Brussels. Outside, in the real world, the global economy seemed to stagger from crisis to catastrophe and then back again. Our most reputable banks crumbled to dust, shares across the world went into a hair-raising nosedive, major companies became close to worthless, hundreds of thousands lost their jobs and millions of others feared the worst.

But in the Brussels bubble you'd hardly have known. Of course, we could follow the entertainingly gory unfolding financial Armageddon on our large, flat-screen TVs, but it was more like watching a new, star-studded, blockbuster disaster movie than something that was happening in reality. While the global economy tottered on the brink of the abyss, the

European parliament passionately debated such issues as new rules for timeshares, the tropical timber agreement, a European licence for online music sales, a special strategy for mountain farming, human rights in Vietnam and whether 2009 should be declared the 'European Year of Creativity and Innovation'. And while we watched with horror as our savings and pensions seemed to evaporate before our eyes, the European Commission issued over ten new laws a day covering every conceivable area of our lives, including increasing customs duties to put up the price of many imported foods, mandating that slaughter-houses should employ a full-time person to look after animals' welfare in the last few minutes before they were killed and launching an anti-dumping investigation into whether China had been falsely declaring shipments of footwear with a protective toecap as coming from Macao in order to avoid import restrictions.

Then, after their busy days debating weighty subjects and making new laws, the Brussels euro-elite continued to go to lavish champagne-fuelled receptions in the evenings, as if unaffected by the financial crisis, before taking taxis to highly rated restaurants to feed themselves at the taxpayers' expense; continued to flit from city to city to attend important meetings; continued to fly around the world on crucial fact-finding missions; and continued to think of ever more new rules and regulations to help organise the lives of the EU's almost 500 million citizens.

FOR US OR AGAINST US?

This may seem like an unfair debating point – comparing the lavish, luxury lifestyle of our euroleaders with the worries and hardships some of us could experience due to the recent financial meltdown – but it does suggest that there may be a growing disconnect between the high-pay, low-tax, secure lives of the eurocrats and the reality that the rest of us have to wake up to every morning. This increasing disparity might even lead European taxpayers to start wondering if the euro-elite works for us, the people who pay their generous salaries, pensions and expenses, or whether we work for them to ensure their continuing comfort and welfare.

The EU and its supporters believe that their project of an ever more united Europe has brought us many benefits. They claim that the EU has played an important political role both in maintaining peace in Europe after centuries of war and in providing a centre of stability on the continent that has promoted democracy and freedom, at first for countries emerging from dictatorship like Portugal, Italy, Greece and Spain (often colloquially referred to as the PIGS) and then for those escaping from communism, the BEES (the Baltic and eastern European states). They maintain that the EU's internal market has broken down borders, allowing the free movement of people and goods, boosting economic growth and prosperity. And they are convinced that EU policies on farming, consumer protection and the environment have helped to give us high-quality food, safer products and cleaner air and water.

However, many other people are beginning to question the actions, morality and direction of the European adventure. They claim that it is NATO, the threat of Soviet invasion during the Cold War and the spread of democracy rather than the EU that have kept the peace in Europe. They point to the constant stream of examples of EU arrogance, over-regulation, secrecy and fraud to suggest that we are ruled by an unaccountable, incompetent, corrupt, self-serving elite. And some even subscribe to a view (generally attributed to former Soviet leader Mikhail Gorbachev) that we are, possibly unwittingly, 're-creating the Soviet Union in western Europe' (see Figure 1).[1]

All this has led to an entertaining game, which we could call 'Euromyths', that is played out in the media. On the one side, the eurosceptics treat us to case after case of 'stupid EU laws' and seemingly endless incidents of shocking EU financial waste

Figure 1 There are some strongly conflicting opinions about the EU

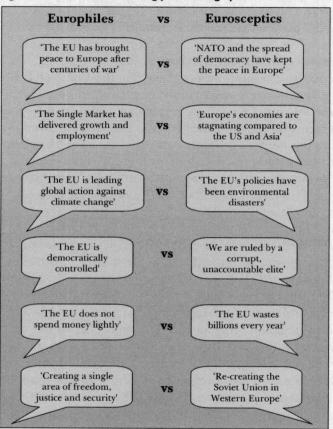

Europhiles	vs	Eurosceptics
'The EU has brought peace to Europe after centuries of war'	vs	'NATO and the spread of democracy have kept the peace in Europe'
'The Single Market has delivered growth and employment'	vs	'Europe's economies are stagnating compared to the US and Asia'
'The EU is leading global action against climate change'	vs	'The EU's policies have been environmental disasters'
'The EU is democratically controlled'	vs	'We are ruled by a corrupt, unaccountable elite'
'The EU does not spend money lightly'	vs	'The EU wastes billions every year'
'Creating a single area of freedom, justice and security'	vs	'Re-creating the Soviet Union in Western Europe'

and fraud. This leads the EU to bemoan the fact that it is apparently misrepresented in the press:

> Most of us rely on our national newspapers, television and radio news to find out about what is going on in the EU. Unfortunately, amongst the clear and informative reports lie a large number of stories based on twisted facts or even

lies. The stories can make entertaining reading, but many people believe them and often come away with a picture of the EU as a bunch of mad eurocrats.[2]

So in response to the eurosceptics' alleged calumny, the EU's Directorate General for Communication regularly publishes the latest selection of anti-EU stories (what they refer to as 'Euromyths') and then tries to debunk these to show that its critics are obsessive fantasists who cannot be trusted. When introducing the 'Get the facts straight section' on its website, the EU explains some of the problems it faces in providing us with what it claims is a true picture of its activities: 'These pages take some of those stories and set the record straight – sadly, we cannot keep track of them all.'

A key rule for players of Euromyths is that both sides must shamelessly exaggerate their claims of their opponents' perfidy – the eurosceptics to stir up public mistrust of EU institutions and actions and the eurocrats to rubbish anyone who dares question their competence, motives or policies. In this game a constant tactic used by the europhiles is to try to brand anyone who has the temerity to criticise any aspect of the EU as rabid, unreliable, anti-European ultra-nationalists. The europhiles don't want to admit that there may actually be a large number, maybe even a majority, of European citizens who genuinely want to support a European Union that is financially well run and that uses its authority intelligently and with discretion, but are deeply critical of the mismanagement, maladministration and misuse of power that increasingly seem to characterise the way the European project is now being pursued.

DELIVERING A BETTER LIFE FOR EVERYONE?

There is no denying that the European Union has achieved some important successes for its citizens. Perhaps the europhiles' claims that the EU has brought peace to Europe have been exaggerated (arguably NATO achieved this), but certainly it's unlikely that democracy and stability would have spread so quickly and so effectively to the PIGS and then to the BEES if the EU's influence and money had not been there to help prevent political and economic breakdown. Moreover, the removal of borders and the creation of the Internal Market have transformed Europe beyond all recognition, even though countries like France, Italy and Spain constantly and contemptuously undermine free trade in order to protect their own uncompetitive industries. EU consumer legislation has probably given us safer, higher quality products. And European environmental rules have pushed many countries to significantly clean up their industries, water, rivers and beaches. So the EU has definitely had a constructive role in helping solve some of Europe's problems from the last century.

But as a new century gets underway, some people have become concerned by how the EU keeps finding new reasons to aggressively increase its authority and control. Each year the EU takes and spends more of our money without EU auditors being able to reliably confirm where much of this money has actually gone. The number of EU bureaucrats rises ever upwards. Ever more bureaucrats seem inevitably to lead to ever more rules and regulations, allowing the EU to expand its influence to almost every area of our lives. Stories of fraud, waste and a widespread culture of financial dishonesty have led to questions about the motives and morality of our euroleaders. Each time the EU produces one of its treaties, it seems to grab more power for itself, making our elected governments increasingly unable to oppose often costly EU legislation with which they may disagree. And whenever Europe's citizens dare to vote against the EU's growing power, the eurocrats derisively ignore public opinion and press on with their project regardless.

There are certainly many talented and fundamentally honest people working within the EU's halls of power. But unfortunately for us, the EU has also become an irresistible magnet for the over-ambitious, the dogmatic, the self-righteous, the rapacious, the lazy, the profligate, the self-serving, the incompetent and the morally corrupt. And there are strong indications that the whole European Union project has been increasingly hijacked by an ever more isolated, arrogant and overbearing ruling class who are convinced they know what's best for us; who consider themselves above the law; and who are disdainfully uninterested in the wishes of those whose interests they are supposed to represent. Even when capable people of apparently good character enter the EU institutions, they seem to quickly go native and get sucked into the EU culture of arrogance, avarice and amorality.

In *The Great European Rip-off* we have tried to break through the EU's secrecy and misinformation to reveal what is really going on in our name in the three EU capitals – Brussels, Luxembourg and Strasbourg. We will look at the kind of people who go to work in the European parliament, the Commission and other EU institutions; how they behave once they have become members of the exclusive EU club; how they use their power; how much of our money they spend on the European project; and what we European citizens get from their efforts.

The EU was a unique and probably necessary experiment to try to prevent the seemingly endless series of European wars that twice have dragged most of the rest of the world into Europe's bloody and destructive internecine squabbles. As we Europeans put our violent history behind us, many in the EU institutions see themselves as having an historic responsibility to preserve peace and prosperity through introducing, often against our wishes, what some EU insiders call an 'empire of good intentions'. So some eurocrats may genuinely believe the EU's claims that we need not worry about their continually increasing control of our lives, because we are all 'better off in Europe' and the EU is 'delivering a better life for everyone'.[3] However, many ordinary citizens instinctively sense that something is not right in the way we are now being governed and feel a growing unease at the way the EU seems to be trying to transform itself from being an innovative, reasonably effective way for free, independent countries to cooperate for the benefit of their citizens and instead appears intent on becoming a monolithic, authoritarian and censorious superstate that mainly serves the interests of those fortunate enough to be members of the ruling euro-elite.

PART I

LET US TAKE YOU TO
YOUR LEADERS

CHAPTER 1

WHO WANTS TO BE A MILLIONAIRE?

DROWNING IN MONEY

A good way to start gaining an understanding of who the EU works for is to examine how much of our money is given to the people paid to represent us there, the members of the European parliament (MEPs), and how diligently and honestly they use this money for our benefit. MEPs' salaries are not especially high. On the surface, it all seems fair enough. Until changes after the June 2009 European elections, their salaries were fixed at the same level as members of parliament in their country of origin. This allowed Italian MEPs to take home over £127,000 a year while some MEPs from the eastern European countries got little more than a tenth of that.[1] British MEPs were paid around £61,180 in 2008, which has now risen to £63,291 (see Figure 1).

However, this is to reckon without MEPs' overly liberal expense allowances. Becoming an MEP is a bit like joining a millionaires club – you can easily live like royalty and still walk away with over one million pounds or euros saved up in your bank account from serving just one five-year term at the European parliament. Get elected twice or more and you can become a multi-millionaire. In Britain there has been quite a lot of press attention paid to how MEPs use and abuse their allowances, and this has led to some British MEPs publishing how much they have claimed. Occasionally, the German media have also picked up on stories of MEPs allegedly abusing their

Figure1 Top 20 MEPs' salaries for 2007/2008

Country	Salary in £*
1. Italy	127,670
2. Austria	102,120
3. Ireland	84,990
4. Germany	80,060
5. France	75,850
6. Netherlands	75,820
7. Greece	69,940
8. Belgium	68,110
9. Denmark	67,240
10. Luxembourg	66,210
11. Sweden	61,930
12. Britain	61,180
13. Finland	60,430
14. Hungary	54,270
15. Slovenia	47,830
16. Portugal	46,220
17. Spain	39,800
18. Cyprus	35,100
19. Poland	27,100
20. Czech Rep.	25,730
	*(at £1=€1.10)

expenses. But in most EU countries members of the press have remained remarkably and worryingly silent on the issue of MEPs lucratively and sometimes fraudulently pocketing tens of millions of our money. Journalists' surprising acquiescence in the issue of our MEPs' incredible generosity to themselves is something we will return to later (see Chapter 9, Making the News). Fortunately, largely thanks to the British press revealing many years of widespread plundering of our money by MEPs, the European parliament has been pushed screaming and kicking into supposedly tightening up on

MEPs' expenses in order to improve transparency and reduce excessive payments. But before looking at these would-be reforms, it might be worth just briefly summarising the main ways that MEPs can legally help themselves to our cash.

In most businesses – and even in many national parliaments – there is normally some kind of relationship, no matter how vague, between what politicians spend in expenses related to their work and the amounts they can claim in reimbursement. For example, British MPs at Westminster are required to provide proof that they are using their £22,000 a year accommodation allowance and that they actually are employing the staff they claim to be employing. In the European parliament, until the introduction of the new Members Statute after the June 2009 EU elections, no such link existed: expenses were paid on a so-called 'flat-rate' basis regardless of whether the person claiming them ever used the money in the first place. Thus MEPs have been able to pocket more than considerable tax-free sums from the virtually control-free and audit-free expenses procedures that they have magnanimously granted themselves.

The biggest pot of money MEPs can dip into is for employing staff. Currently this stands at about €202,968 per MEP per year. This allowance has increased by an inflation-busting 34 per cent in the last five years. There are no guidelines regulating how much an assistant should be paid, and MEPs are permitted to pay a large portion of their allowance to just one person. Some even do this, creating the absurd situation where MEPs' assistants are apparently paid much more than the MEPs for whom they work. There are even cases where several MEPs will share the services of one or two assistants, potentially allowing each of them to make massive profits from claiming the full assistants' allowance. Many MEPs use this allowance to pay members of their own family. The amount is so generous that an MEP can easily afford to slip their partner or offspring £50,000 to £60,000 a year for the occasional helping hand and still have enough loose change to employ more than one full-time secretary and a few researchers.

Some MEPs dispense with the formality of handing the cash to a family member and just pay some of it to themselves. One MEP, for example, was claiming over £36,000 a year for a research assistant to whom he paid just over £6,000 a year. In the 13 months this went on, by adding on a few extra bits and pieces the MEP stashed away over £39,100 tax free – the rest of us would have to earn around £60,000 before tax to get a similar amount. This was actually breaking even the generous rules imposed by Brussels, yet the MEP kept his seat in the EU parliament. Normally, any MEP careless enough to get caught fiddling their expenses in a system where almost anything goes will not be subject to any investigation or disciplinary action. In fact, MEPs are remarkably forgiving to those members of their own club who stray from the path of righteousness. An MEP, who was jailed while in office after being convicted of making more than €70,000 of fraudulent benefit claims in his home country prior to his election and who was described by a judge as 'thoroughly dishonest', was still paid his MEP salary all the time he was in prison, and rejoined his colleagues for the good life in Brussels after finishing his nine-month jail sentence. According to the European parliament's rules, prison sentences of less than one year are not considered a hindrance to retaining one's MEP seat, salary and other benefits.

Each MEP is provided with two fully furnished, rent-free offices in the European parliament building, one for themselves and one for their secretaries and assistants. However, they are also given an office allowance of €48,624 a year for having an office in their constituency. Here too no receipts are required to get this money. As one MEP said, 'There is no need to present receipts for office expenses and there's no audit. You could use the allowance for any purpose you like.'[2] Many MPs claim that their constituency office is in their own home. This allows them to rent out a room in their homes to themselves, which they pay for with EU taxpayers' money. Some even take all the money without bothering to have a constituency office at all. At almost €250,000 tax free over five years, this is probably a welcome addition to many MEPs' household budgets. In some EU countries it's enough to buy a home, or it could be used to pay for a nice holiday flat near the Mediterranean.

MEPs can also claim a subsistence allowance of €287 tax free a day for every one of the 40 or so weeks of European parliamentary sessions without having to provide any receipts. This gives MEPs up to €57,000 tax free a year extra. British MEPs call this the SOSO (sign on and sod off) allowance, because all you have to do to get it is to sign in. There is no requirement to attend a single debate or committee session. What you do for the rest of the day is up to you. On Fridays at seven o'clock in the morning there is usually a queue of MEPs with their luggage waiting to sign in to get their allowance before rushing off to the nearest airport or station. In 2008 a German TV company caused panic by filming MEPs signing in before disappearing off home. One MEP, spotting the film crew, turned around and sped away so fast that she appeared to run into a wall. Others tried to shield their faces, hide in lifts or cover the camera lens with their hands. Some were so angry at being caught red-handed and red-faced that they rang for security guards to throw the news team out of the building.[3] When we tried to get the European parliament to reveal the names of MEPs who signed in on Fridays, we received an almost surreal letter back explaining that as there were no meetings on Fridays, there were no lists of who had claimed their Friday allowance in order to attend the non-existent meetings.

This subsistence allowance is meant to pay for things like MEPs' accommodation and meals in Brussels and Strasbourg. However, it is probably substantially more than adequate. A few years ago, some MEPs slept in their offices in order to avoid paying for hotels. This is now discouraged by the parliamentary authorities. However, a reasonable three-star hotel near the European parliament buildings costs no more than about €125 a night, including breakfast, leaving about €162 a day for lunch and dinner. Yet there are subsidised canteens and restaurants in the parliament buildings, and on many days there are free breakfasts, lunches and evening buffets organised by lobbying groups, parliamentary committees and political parties. In the evenings these typically serve unlimited quantities of champagne and canapés with caviar, smoked salmon and other treats. There are so many of these free meals available to MEPs that one commented, 'In these times of economic crisis what sort of image are we portraying? Every corner of the parliament is filled with receptions and buffet dinners while our constituents are being thrown out of their homes, losing their pensions or having difficulty paying their food and energy bills.' This means most MEPs can easily pocket over €100 a day tax free from their inappropriately named 'subsistence' payments.

One place that seems to benefit from the many allowances we pay to our MEPs is the rue de Parnasse, a street about 50 metres from the European parliament's imposing Brussels buildings. You just go out of the parliament towards the Place de Luxembourg, turn left into the rue de Trèves and then take a first right at the flower shop on the corner. Here there are no fewer than three buildings advertising studios for rent. However, these are not for tired, overworked MEPs to spend the night after long days legislating on our behalf. They are called *studios intimes* and are available to be hired by the hour from a mere €16 an hour, with the price depending on what facilities are required. Most provide large double beds, full-wall mirrors, normal X-rated porn films, S&M films in some of the more expensive rooms and many other extras for the discerning guest. Belgians colloquially call these studios *les cinq à sept* (five to sevens) because people using them are known for leaving work at five but arriving home to their wives and families at seven. These *studios intimes* are an old Belgian tradition but one that seems to have been enthusiastically adopted by some MEPs who like to take their beautiful young research assistants for a bit of daytime jiggery-pokery.

In addition, MEPs get very generous travel expenses. They can claim weekly flights from their constituencies. Here they do actually need to provide some proof that they have travelled. However, they just have to submit the stub from the boarding pass – they are not asked for any information about how much they have paid for their ticket. They are then reimbursed for a fully flexible economy class ticket, plus an extra payment for distance travelled of over €100 for every 500 kilometres, all usually adding up to comfortably more than a business class fare. By buying cheap weekend return tickets or by travelling on budget airlines, many MEPs can rake in more than €300 a week tax free. German MEPs living in Berlin, for example, could, according to one report, make a profit of around €800 each time they travelled to Brussels and over €1,000 for every trip to Strasbourg, giving an annual profit of over €35,000 tax free just from their weekly trips to work. [4]

MEPs also get an annual travel allowance of €4,000 a year to go anywhere in the world as long as this travel is connected with their work as an MEP. The Caribbean and the Far East seem to be popular destinations, with one MEP justifying a trip to exotic Thailand on the basis of a half-hour meeting at the EU's Bangkok offices. Perhaps the MEP wasn't aware that he could have considerably reduced the cost to the taxpayer and saved himself a lot of unnecessary travelling time by making a conference call.

As MEPs preside over a worsening pensions crisis that will leave most private-sector workers in poverty in their old age, they have made sure that they have one of the best pensions schemes in Europe. Typically, government employees across Europe would have to work for around 40 years to get a pension worth about half their final salary. Politicians in the British parliament have a much better deal and have to work for only 20 years to achieve an inflation-protected pension for them and their partner of half their final salary. Any other British worker would have to pay about £50,000 a year into their pension scheme to get similar benefits to their MPs. Until the June 2009 European elections, MEPs got the same pension benefits as their national politicians, and in addition they could save for an additional voluntary EU pension. For every €1,000 they paid per month into their pension scheme, the EU would pay double that amount. MEPs were allowed to pay this extra €1,000 from their €48,624 office expenses. In theory, they were then supposed to reimburse this money from their own bank accounts. However, everything relies on the MEPs' honesty. Unsurprisingly, a few years ago MEPs voted down a proposal that EU parliament auditors should check whether any of them actually did repay this money. All this meant that an MEP would have to work for only around 15 years to get a pension of half their final salary. The rest of us would have to save about £70,000 a year to get the same level of pension as our lucky MEPs.

MEPs could claim their full pension any time after they reached 60, although it appears that this will become 63 after June 2009.[5] However, they also have the option of getting their pension paid out at a reduced rate as soon as they are 50.

Adding all this up, a typical British, French or German MEP will be getting over €460,000 a year in salary, pension and expenses – more than €2 million for each five-year period in Brussels. With a bit of judicious financial management, they can probably get by on around €230,000 a year. This means they can save about €230,000 each year by, for example, buying a flat in Brussels with their daily allowance or even just staying in two- or three-star hotels, paying up to half of their staff allowance to a family member (or themselves), booking cheap weekend return airline fares, paying themselves rent for their constituency offices and using their office allowance to top up their pensions (see Figure 2).

Figure 2 MEPs can easily save over €230,000 a year out of the more than €460,000 a year they can claim

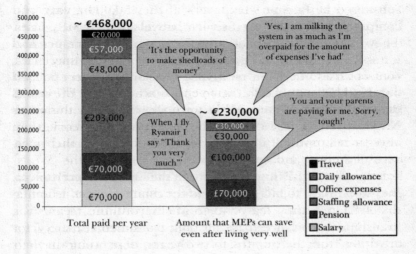

In 2008 one British newspaper sent an undercover reporter to Brussels to pose as a student on work experience, and she recorded a British MEP, Tom Wise, explaining how, if you claimed what was lawfully available, it was impossible not to make money from the MEPs' expenses system.[6] In a response to the newspaper report Tom Wise wrote, 'I claim that which is made available to me, I do not fiddle, embezzle or otherwise operate any scam for the purposes of unlawfully extracting more than this. I believe that the system is disgraceful and should be changed.'[7] Many Brussels insiders privately admit that the majority of MEPs are similarly benefiting from the generous expense allowances for which we pay. If you are the EU candidate for one of the main political parties, you have about a one in three chance of scoring your EU millions – all in all, much better odds than winning the EuroMillions lottery or else correctly answering all the questions on *Who Wants to be a Millionaire?*

The benefits of being an MEP don't stop here. MEPs also have a huge list of other entitlements that are generously subsidised by Europe's taxpayers. If they take language and computer courses we pay their fees, travel and living expenses. They have full, free accident insurance, travel insurance and life assurance. They and their families get money for spectacles, contact lenses and dental treatment. One British dentist pointed out that MEPs could claim up to four times more for the cost of dental work than he could get for doing that work under his National Health Service contract. MEPs and their families can also get full payment for things like hydrotherapy, mud baths, aerosol therapy and acupuncture.

Even when MEPs lose their seats in the European parliament, they don't have to bid goodbye to the financial benefits immediately. Once they leave office MEPs continue to enjoy a 'transitional allowance' (basically their parliamentary salary) for anything from six months to two years, depending on their length of service. They can also keep on using the parliament's subsidised restaurants and cafeterias, libraries and telephone facilities in Brussels, Strasbourg and Luxembourg. Moreover, once they start drawing their EU pensions, these are subject to special, low EU tax rates and not the, usually much higher, tax rates in whichever country they may retire to.

Usefully, being an MEP gives immunity from prosecution unless your colleagues vote to suspend your immunity – which they never do. In several EU countries rich fraudsters, feeling the hot breath of the forces of law and order on the backs of their necks, have quickly 'bought' themselves seats as MEPs by making large contributions to local political parties. Thus, as long as they maintained their lucrative but legal Brussels 'jobs', they could stick two fingers up at the police and at those they had defrauded. In many cases, by the time they eventually left the European parliament, local statutes of limitations meant they could no longer be prosecuted for the crimes they perpetrated before hurriedly decamping to the well-paid safety of Brussels.

DO YOU WANT TO KNOW A SECRET?

In 2008 yet another story concerning MEPs' financial shenanigans hit the headlines. Unfortunately this was only covered by the media in just a couple of EU countries and totally ignored by the press in most EU member states. A report by the EU's Internal Audit Service found evidence of what looked like widespread abuse in how MEPs used the €160 million that they could claim each year in assistants' allowances. However, only the few MEPs on the parliament's budget control committee were allowed to see the report, and to do so they had to apply to enter a special room protected by biometric locks and security guards. Moreover, they were not allowed to take notes and had to sign a confidentiality agreement confirming that they would not tell anyone what was in the report. When a British MEP revealed the existence of this report, he was criticised by a colleague: 'Passing information to the press is a misuse of information and a misuse of parliamentary obligations.'[8] One British MEP indicated the seriousness of what was in the audit report when he said: 'I think if names were attached to some of the cases of malpractice highlighted, then prison should follow.'[9]

The parliament's media director seemed to have a different opinion, however. He claimed: 'It did not look into individual MEPs' transactions and did not reveal cases of fraud.'[10] While it is true that the final, published version of the report did not name names, the auditors producing the report knew exactly which MEPs had done what. So if the parliament had actually been interested in stamping out possible dishonesty, it could easily have acted against the more financially creative MEPs instead of straining every sinew to protect them. Questioned about the report by the press, an EU official denied that it was in any way secret: 'The document is not secret. It is confidential. It can be read by Euro-MPs on the budget control committee, in the secret room but not generally. That is not the same as a secret document nobody can read.'[11]

Fortunately, the eurocrats are not always effective at preventing outsiders finding out how our money is being siphoned off by EU insiders. Since the fall of the discredited Santer Commission in 1999, the EU has worked hard to tighten its control over any information that might lead voters to lose confidence in EU institutions. There is an ever-growing EU security service, which has access to all EU staff's emails, phone calls and correspondence and which aggressively investigates any suspected leaks. Moreover, when sensitive documents like the audit report on MEPs' assistants' allowances are produced the paper used is often watermarked differently for each copy, the recipient of each copy is registered on a list and slight changes are made to the text and layout of each copy. This means that any EU staff, who might be tempted to let us know what was really happening with our money, would be afraid to pass any documents to journalists as they would know that any leaked document could be quickly traced back to its original source. Under EU staff regulations, any employee found betraying the trust of their employer by revealing sensitive information would normally be disciplined, even if the leak was in the public interest. The other effect of having slightly different versions of sensitive documents is that journalists are afraid to quote from them as any quote could risk revealing the identity of the source who had handed over the document.

In February 2008 the MEPs on the budget control committee voted by a majority of 21 to 14 not to publish the results of the audit into MEPs' use of assistants' allowances. Two months later the European parliament voted by a majority of 442 against 209 to prevent us, the taxpayers, from finding out what was in the report. Various reasons were given for this decision. One MEP claimed that the report 'cannot be published because of internal rules'. Another defended keeping the report from the public: 'This is a matter of work effectiveness, not an issue of transparency.'[12] But one MEP admitted: 'We want reform, but we cannot make this report available to the public if we want people to vote in the European elections next year.'[13]

The audit report into MEPs' payments to their assistants was originally written at the end of 2006 but was not finally published until the start of 2008. In the intervening 14 months it circulated back and forth between various parts of the EU bureaucracy before the MEPs' budget control committee even became aware of its existence. The report is commonly known as the Galvin Report, as the name and contact details of Robert Galvin, a member of the parliament's Internal Audit Service, are given on the cover page. Unfortunately, even if we had seen this report and even if we had a copy, we would not be able to tell you what's in it. The report is classed as 'a confidential audit report within the meaning of Article 4 (2) of Regulation 1049/2001'. This means that if we had the report the European parliament could take legal action against us and force us to reveal our source (if such a source existed) as the document would have been 'disclosed without authorisation'.

Fortunately, one MEP on the budget control committee has released a summary of what is in the Galvin Report. According to their summary, the report looked at a representative sample of MEPs' parliamentary assistants' allowances and found widespread evidence of what could be breaches of the rules, tax avoidance, illegality and possible fraud. If an EU specialist's investigations are to be believed, the MEPs' countries of origin which came up most frequently in the sample of MEPs whose assistants' allowances were reviewed, were the UK, Greece, Italy and Ireland.[14]

According to the MEP's summary, many MEPs use so-called 'paying agents' to administer the €202,968 they can get each year for paying their assistants. The audit apparently found that not one of these had provided the minimum details required for a valid invoice for their fees, and about 80 per cent of agencies used by MEPs to pay their assistants did not register for VAT (which is in breach of EU rules). Moreover, around 65 per cent of paying agents didn't provide any statements detailing to whom they had paid money and what services they had received, meaning that it was not possible for auditors to establish that our money had gone to the right people. Some paying agents had little or no relevance to the provision of parliamentary assistance – one turned out to be a firm responsible for providing day care for an MEP's children and another was a wood-trading company. The official filed accounts of one paying agency showed no activity, even though it had received hundreds of thousands of pounds of our taxes. The directors of some of the more profitable paying agents were found to be MEPs and members of their families, so that any profits made by the paying agency could go straight into the pockets of the MEPs and their families. The auditors concluded that the majority of funds transferred to paying agents could not be properly accounted for. The German Bundestag helpfully offers a free paying agent service to all German MEPs. This service is highly regarded by EU auditors as it provides good, transparent information, allowing auditors to trace exactly how our money is spent. Strangely, although this service is free, convenient, open and efficient, over two-thirds of German MEPs choose not to use it.

According to the MEP who released the summary of the report, the auditors also found potential problems with travel expenses that were paid to assistants. Several assistants were getting a regular travel allowance paid each month, and in one case this was three times the assistant's salary. Yet around half of assistants receiving reimbursement for travel had no receipts or other documentary evidence showing they had ever travelled anywhere. By getting large amounts paid as 'travel expenses' the assistants avoided having to pay any income taxes or social security charges on these supposedly 'legitimate' expenses.

According to the MEP's summary of the report, it was discovered that a large number of MEPs were making end-of-year bonus payments to their assistants. These bonus payments ranged from three to almost 20 times the assistants' monthly salaries. Curiously, the size of the payments often exactly equalled the amount of each MEP's assistant's allowance that had not been used up by the year end. This made it look as if MEPs were using the bonus payments to get their hands on any unclaimed allowance rather than these payments being directly linked to the quality of the assistants' work. The audit found that in over 80 per cent of cases there was no supporting evidence to explain the payment of the bonuses, that the payments were disproportionate compared to the work done and that in some cases the payments were made into bank accounts in countries that were not even the ones in which the assistants' normal salaries were paid.

Another oddity occurred in what are called 'lay-off' payments. If an MEP is not re-elected they are allowed to pay their assistants 'lay-off' payments for three months after losing their seat. In some cases, assistants were found to have received salary increases of between 71 and 117 per cent just for their last three months in employment. In these cases the salary increases were sufficient to exhaust the balance of money available to the MEPs for assistants' salaries. We talked to some assistants, who had worked for MEPs who had lost their seats. They didn't even know about the existence of these lay-off payments. This could indicate that some MEPs have just pocketed them for themselves.

The audit also apparently revealed that in around 90 per cent of payments there was no evidence of any social security charges being paid, and over 80 per cent of assistants officially working in Brussels had not registered with the Belgian authorities (which is in breach of Belgian law).

THE BRITS HIT THE HEADLINES

In mid-2008 the British public were privileged to witness one of the more farcical of many entertaining spectacles provided by the EU when a string of British Conservative MEPs were revealed to be showing admirable generosity to themselves and their families in the way they – quite legally – obtained considerable quantities of our EU money.

The first to gain notoriety was Giles Chichester, the Conservative leader in the European parliament. Following a series of press stories in Britain, about how Westminster MP Derek Conway had paid his son more than £40,000 as a researcher while he was a student at Newcastle University, Chichester had been asked by Conservative party leader David Cameron to make sure that the party's MEPs were not abusing their expenses. However, we soon found that David Cameron's supposed sleaze-buster was humiliatingly far from being squeaky clean himself. In June 2008 a newspaper reported that since 1996 Chichester had paid around £445,000 to a company, of which he was a paid director, for services 'in connection with secretarial and assistant services for the European parliament, constituency and committee work'.[15] Over the same period the company was reported to have paid out £158,938 to its directors, including £47,792 since 2002, a period when Chichester and his wife were the sole directors.[16] The company also paid about £5,000 a year to rent an office in a house that was the registered home address of Chichester and his wife. By paying money to a company from which he was a beneficiary, Chichester seemed to have broken a rule introduced in 2003. Chichester admitted that it was all a bit unfortunate: 'It is embarrassing not least because I have introduced a new code for my Conservative colleagues for expenses . . . and – whoops a daisy – I am shown up to have made a mistake.'[17] Chichester said it had all been an innocent oversight: 'I was informed that there had been a change in the rules relating to service providers, a change that took effect in 2003. This had not been brought to my attention when I renewed the contract in 2004.'[18] But here we had a man who presumably had been elected on the basis that he was the right person to help pass often complex laws governing the lives of almost 500 million people, and yet apparently he was unable to follow a few simple rules regarding his own lavish expenses.

Faced with this embarrassing situation, David Cameron made much of the fact that Chichester stepped down as leader of the party in the European parliament. Chichester was, however, allowed to keep his lucrative MEP job. The European parliament later cleared Chichester of any wrong-doing.[19]

The day after Chichester slipped out of the limelight, it was the turn of Den Dover, the Conservatives' chief whip in Europe, to take centre stage. It was revealed that since his election in 1999 he had paid around £750,000 of our money to a company, MP Holdings, for providing office services.[20] The company was owned by his wife and daughter, but because Dover himself was not a director of the company, he had not broken the new 2003 rule that tripped up Chichester. Dover explained: 'I am totally within the rules. I am not a director, have no shareholdings, have no payments from any outside company.'[21] Den Dover had been paying his wife between £30,000 and £40,000 a year, and his daughter between £20,000 and £30,000, but, he explained: 'Both are required to work very unsociable hours.'[22] As with Chichester, Dover's company paid rent for the use of office space in his own home, and in 2001 and 2002 the company paid nearly £22,500 for repairs on his homes – all of this, of course, within the rules. However, the day after Chichester stepped down, Dover was replaced as chief whip, although naturally he kept his MEP job and the many benefits associated with it. Towards the end of 2008, to many people's surprise, the European parliament seemed prepared to take action and ordered Dover to repay €600,000.[23] It remains to be seen whether we taxpayers will ever see any of our money again or whether, as is much more likely, Dover, who will be over 70 by the next EU elections, will be allowed to retire gracefully at the June 2009 elections, with his pension and leaving allowances intact, and the parliament will magnanimously decide to let the matter drop.

Next up was MEP John Purvis. He was alleged to have paid up to £120,000 a year in staffing allowances to a financial consultancy firm called Purvis & Co.[24] Because Purvis was a paid director of the company with a share of the profits, it is possible that he had broken the 2003 rule. Purvis said that he had asked the European parliament for clarification about whether his payments were within the rules 'as far back as January 2007', but had not received a response.[25] In 2008 Purvis changed his declaration of interests, confirming that he still used Purvis & Co. as his 'service provider' but removing himself from the list of partners in the firm. His spokeswoman explained: 'He has got rid of his interest. He has no connection with the company any more.'[26] When she was asked if Purvis & Co. employed any of the MEP's relatives, she replied 'he has nothing further to say'.[27]

Several other Conservative MEPs also attracted some press attention although everything they did was within the EU parliament's rules. David Sumberg, MEP for the Northwest, revealed that he had paid his wife £54,000. Sir Robert Atkins, who paid his wife Lady Atkins between £30,000 and £40,000 a year for her secretarial services, was reported to have spent £2,500 of our money on a trip to New York, which fortuitously fitted in with the date of his son's marriage in America. He explained: 'It was a happy coincidence that my son was getting married . . . I have done nothing illegal. The European parliament approved the expenses.'[28] On his website Sir Robert noted that there had been a 'constant stream of tendentious publicity about MEPs' expenses', and he claimed that it was officials at the parliament rather than MEPs who were at fault: 'Many of the recent problems have come about because the advice from the parliamentary authorities has often been culpably weak and invariably contradictory.'[29]

Meanwhile, a document alleged to be a memo to David Cameron from a Conservative MEP was reportedly left on a photocopier at the European parliament. This memo warned the Conservative leader that trying to impose rules about expenses on his party's increasingly wealthy MEPs was 'a direct breach of the rules of the European parliament', which stated that 'members shall exercise an independent mandate: they shall not accept instructions'. The rules of the European parliament were actually intended to ensure MEPs' political integrity and were not aimed at allowing them almost unlimited access to our money. The memo went on to advise Cameron to stop his campaign to clean up the expenses system: 'We will also find that far from buying off criticism, the more we publish, the more questions will be asked . . . The press storm over MEPs' expenses is blowing itself out. We should not be resurrecting it'.[30]

AS TRANSPARENT AS MUD

There have been repeated attempts by a very few more responsible MEPs to have the expenses system changed to a more honest and transparent one by which MEPs would be reimbursed only for legitimate expenses. Time and again these get voted down, and their supporters are shunned by their Brussels colleagues. In some cases they are even expelled from their parties. In 2004 one such effort – to grant MEPs large salary increases in return for them agreeing to just getting reimbursed for expenses actually incurred – got blocked by the German and French MEPs on the basis that the timing was wrong. They did not want voters in the 2004 EU elections to see their MEPs being effectively 'bribed', with large amounts of taxpayers' money, to give up one of the world's most easy-going and lightly policed expenses reimbursement schemes.

In April 2005 MEPs rejected a proposed reform to their travel expenses whereby they would be paid only for actual expenses incurred and would have to provide valid receipts. However, in June 2005, under pressure to clean up their act, MEPs did finally agree to move to a new Members Statute by which they would all get the same salary and would be reimbursed for the real cost of their weekly travel expenses. Curiously, when the EU brings in new regulations that apply to normal people – legislating on the size of kiwi fruit that can be sold or the labelling of cheese, for example – the regulations usually come into immediate effect in all member countries. This means that we EU citizens are committing a criminal offence if we do anything in breach of such regulations as soon as they are introduced. But when it came to MEPs bringing in new, tighter rules for the payment of their weekly travel expenses, they decided (in 2005) that the changes should not come into effect until after the 2009 European elections – around four years after the changes were agreed.

Following the 2005 vote MEPs hoped there would be no more controversy over their salaries and expenses. But the leaking of the existence of Robert Galvin's report into assistants' allowances at the beginning of 2008 and then the series of stories throughout the year of MEPs' generosity to themselves reopened the 'gravy train' can of worms. The Bureau of the European parliament was once again forced to act, and it approved a tightening of the procedures for paying the annual €202,968 assistants' allowances. One of the members of the Bureau assured the press: 'This is a huge step forward for transparency in the European parliament.'[31] One MEP claimed that 'MEPs have made real progress by putting the reputation of the European parliament before their personal financial interests', and another said that the changes in the payment of assistants' allowances was a 'crucial element promoting full transparency and accountability within our institution'.[32]

However, the changes to MEPs' salaries and expenses are

complex, and unfortunately they may not be quite as 'open' and 'transparent' as the EU might like us to believe.

From July 2009 all MEPs will receive the same salary, which will be fixed at 38.5 per cent of the salary of a judge at the European Court of Justice. When this idea was first agreed in 2005 it was thought that MEPs would earn about €7,000 a month. Due to inflation it is currently estimated that MEPs will be paid around €7,665 a month. This will give most MEPs from the wealthier EU countries a large pay rise (see Figure 3).[33]

Figure 3 Most MEPs will get a very large pay rise in June 2009

Country	% Change
1. Italy	same
2. Austria	- 21%
3. Ireland	- 5%
4. Germany	+1%
5. France	+6%
6. Netherlands	+7%
7. Greece	+17%
8. Belgium	+19%
9. Denmark	+20%
10. Luxembourg	+22%
11. Sweden	+30%
12. Britain	+32%
13. Finland	+34%
14. Hungary	+49%
15. Slovenia	+69%
16. Portugal	+75%
17. Spain	+100%
18. Cyprus	+130%
19. Poland	+200%
20. Czech Rep.	+214%

However, MEPs from some of the PIGS and the BEES will receive an absolutely massive pay rise. The lowest paid MEPs in countries like Malta, Lithuania and Estonia will get more than five times what they were previously taking home. The only group who could have seen their pay significantly cut are Italian MEPs, and they managed to block the reform package until their government agreed to compensate them for their salary decrease with Italian taxpayers' money. Austrian and Irish MEPs also look as if they could have been losers. But according to Article 25 of the Members Statute, MEPs are free to choose whether they wish to remain on the pre-2009 salary and pension scheme or move to the new one. This creates a 'heads I win, tails I win' situation for MEPs, because they can take whichever salary and pension option gives them the most money. Moreover, all MEPs who move to the new salary scheme will no longer have to pay national income taxes in their countries. Instead they will pay a special European Union tax, which for most should be between 13 and 17 per cent, depending on their family circumstances. For MEPs from the high tax member countries, like Germany, Austria, France, Denmark, Belgium and Sweden, this will mean a massive reduction of about two-thirds in their taxes and a corresponding – and no doubt welcome – increase in how much they can bank every month. Even MEPs from low-tax countries, such as Britain and Ireland, will see their income taxes almost halved. So if you hear MEPs claiming that the new system is fairer for all and that they will not benefit from its introduction, you just need to look at the figures to see that most will do very nicely indeed from the changes.

The new system does allow MEPs to voluntarily pay the difference between the very low EU tax and their usually much higher national taxes. However, it is far from clear whether many will be sufficiently selfless to make this gesture of solidarity with their voters. The rise in MEPs' earnings from moving to EU taxes is so embarrassingly large that the Dutch government has decided to impose a special income tax on its

MEPs to bring their salaries back into line with those of their national politicians.[34]

Of course, the one group that really loses out from this shameless plundering of their money are European taxpayers, who will see the costs of their MEPs' salaries and pensions leap impressively upwards.

There will also, theoretically, be considerable changes to the way assistants' allowances are paid. From July 2009 there are new rules stating that those who work in Brussels should be paid through the European parliament or through approved paying agents. However, MEPs may be free to choose whether assistants who were in employment before 2009 join the new scheme or remain outside the European parliament's scrutiny. The rules will also require that assistants working in the EU countries must be paid only through paying agents approved by the European parliament. However, the pre-June 2009 rules appear to have been casually ignored by around 90 per cent of the cases said to be included in the Robert Galvin audit report without any action being taken against the MEPs involved. So it remains to be seen whether the new rules manage to significantly reduce the vast amount of financial misman-agement and possible fraud that have been said to be the hallmark of the extraordinarily rewarding assistants' allowances system for the last 30 years or whether MEPs' lucrative lives continue much as before, with the authorities mostly turning a blind eye to even the most flagrant abuses. Anyway, even if MEPs are caught breaking the new, supposedly tighter rules, they could always just say 'whoops a daisy' and claim they were unaware they were doing anything wrong. In the past, that's usually been enough to avoid even a gentle slap on the wrist.

MEPs have also voted to ban the hiring of close family members as assistants. However, any family member employed as an assistant in July 2008 may be able to remain on the EU payroll for another five years until the 2014 European parlia-ment elections.

After the 2009 elections MEPs' weekly travel expenses will be paid out only against actual expenses incurred, which could cut down on many MEPs making huge profits. But experience suggests that the more enterprising MEPs will find that it's easy to get friendly with a travel agent, buy a full-price airline ticket each week, take the last (receipt) page out of the ticket, get a full refund from the travel agent, change the ticket to a low-price alternative and hand in the original expensive, full-price receipt to the parliament bean-counters as part of MEPs' expenses claims.

As far as the payments for subsistence and constituency offices of over €105,000 a year are concerned, these will continue as before with no need to produce any proof that any money was actually spent, allowing MEPs to legally make many tens of thousands of euros or pounds a year tax free thanks to the generosity of the parliament's still enviably lax expenses payment procedures.

Chapter 2

SHARING THE TROUGH

'NOT A BLOATED BUREAUCRACY'

The next group of people who can shed an interesting light on the morals and behaviour of our euro-rulers are the EU's tens of thousands of employees. Traditionally, the EU Commission has claimed that the EU institutions had just over 20,000 employees and that this was 'fewer than the number of staff employed by a typical medium-sized city council in Europe'. However, some commentators have pointed out that the staff of a city council will normally include employees such as police, doctors, nurses, garbage collectors and many others who do useful work, whereas virtually all the staff employed by the EU institutions spend their time pushing paper and sitting in meetings. As EU staff numbers have tended to increase significantly every year, the EU has had to change its story slightly, and on a webpage entitled 'The EU administration: much smaller than you think' the EU now writes:

> The EU is sometimes accused of being a bloated bureaucracy. In practice the total staff of all the institutions of 40,000 is much the same as that of a single government ministry in many member states. Indeed, many member state ministries are larger, even though they generally do not have to work in more than one language.[1]

In the middle of 2008 an entertaining round of our favourite game, Euromyths, was played out in the media between the think-tank Open Europe and the EU Commission. Open Europe produced a study claiming that the total number of EU employees was nearer to 170,000 than 40,000, and it expressed its dismay that this number was almost twice as large as the number of people in the British army. Open Europe commented:

> The Commission desperately tries to play down just how many people are working for the EU. They are extremely secretive about the number of people who are working to churn out regulations.[2]

The Commission spokesman fought back, explaining:

> Open Europe are being duplicitous about figures here . . . They have achieved their fantastic figures by lobbing in nearly every possible facet of the workings of the European Union and then allude that all the participants somehow work in an extremely crowded European Commission.[3]

Actually, the true figure for the number of people on the EU payroll is probably about halfway between the Commission's 40,000 and Open Europe's 170,000. In the 2009 budget there are 44,547 people working directly for the Commission, the parliament and various other EU bodies. These include hundreds of people beavering busily away in organisations most of us probably never knew existed and whose value to our lives could be questioned. There are, for example, 101 at the European Foundation for the Improvement of Living and Working Conditions, 99 at the European Centre for the Development of Vocational Training, 57 at the European Union Agency for Fundamental Rights, 43 at the Community Plant Variety Office, 20 staff at the Gender Institute and an impressive 654 at the European Union Publications Office.

However, the EU believes that its army of a mere 44,547 employees is insufficient to provide the expertise it needs to fulfil its ambitious legislative programmes, and so it frequently uses committees and groups of experts working part time to help out with producing specific laws. The EU lists about 247 committees, involving around 7,000 contributors, and at least 1,047 specialist groups that are often consulted by the EU and call upon the services of more than 40,000 appointed or self-appointed experts.[4] Some insiders claim that there are over 3,000 expert groups. The way the Commission uses its 247 committees and many expert groups to help draft new legislation has led to the appearance of a new word, 'comitology', and the EU even publishes a Register of Comitology of the European Commission to help insiders find their way around this system of lawmaking.

All this gives us something approaching 100,000 individuals employed on a full- or part-time basis in order to produce new laws and regulations to make our lives better.

Housing this euro-multitude seems to be quite a major logistical and financial exercise. Over the years the EU has spent almost €4 billion buying around 87 buildings within the European Union countries to accommodate its employees. In addition, it pays around €476 million a year in rent for another 20 or so buildings. The two most important EU offices are in Brussels: the massive European parliament complex beside the Parc Léopold and the nearby EU Commission Berlaymont building close to the Parc Cinquentaire, which is excellent for a lunchtime jog, should you wish to work off some of the extra kilos gained while eating in the many fine restaurants in Brussels. As well as these, the EU's external services (its diplomatic service) have bought over 40 ambassadorial residences and rent almost 100 more throughout the world. One of the most splendid is apparently the EU representative's residence in Washington. Built for a steel and railway tycoon in 1923, it was renovated in 2005 at a cost of about €1.7 million. It has 16 bedrooms, a grand dining room and a spacious living room in which up to 150 guests can be entertained. The hall is covered with polished marble, and at the back there is an Italianate garden with classical statues in bronze. The EU ambassadors in Moscow, Tokyo and many other capitals also live in similar luxury at our expense, even though the rejection of the EU Constitution and the Lisbon Treaty means that there is no agreed legal basis for the EU to have a diplomatic service at all.

LA DOLCE VITA

People at the EU seem to have a relatively comfortable existence thanks to our generosity. For a start, we EU taxpayers fork out about €130 million a year to pay for the running of 14 European schools. These schools are situated in the main European cities – Brussels, Frankfurt, Alicante, Luxembourg, Munich, Bergen and so on – where there are EU institutions. At around €9 million a school a year, they make sure that eurocrats' offspring receive probably the best multilingual education in the world. This is provided completely free of charge and allows the children of eurocrats to spend their childhood almost completely insulated from the uncouth progeny of the countries where their parents work. These private and exclusive schools also enable the eurocrats' children to establish networks and friendships with other eurocrats' children. Their excellent multilingual education, their own networks and their parents' connections put them in an advantageous position to get well-paid eurojobs themselves. This is starting to create a self-perpetuating euro-elite that becomes ever more remote from – and uninterested in – the lives of those whose taxes so philanthropically support it.

Belgium, where most eurocrats are stationed, has some of the highest income tax rates in Europe. Belgian citizens earning £50,000 a year would normally pay around 60 per cent of their salary in taxes and social costs. Fortunately for EU employees, they are exempt from the local tax systems in the countries where they are stationed. Instead, they pay a special EU tax, which is around one-third of what they would pay if they were taxed in a high-tax European country such as Belgium, Germany, France, Italy, Denmark, Finland or Sweden and around half what they would pay if they were subject to the relatively low income tax rates of Britain, Ireland, Malta or Cyprus (see Figure 1).

Figure 1 Most UK taxpayers could halve their income taxes by paying the special EU tax

Salary	UK tax	EU Tax
£20,000	14%	6%
£30,000	16%	7%
£40,000	20%	9%
£50,000	24%	11%
£60,000	26%	13%
£70,000	28%	15%
£80,000	30%	20%
£90,000	31%	21%
£100,000	32%	23%

EU employees also get an expansively wide range of benefits in addition to their low taxes. When they start work with the EU their moving expenses are reimbursed, and they also get two months 'installation expenses to help you settle at a new place of employment'.[5] They benefit from VAT exemption for any household goods and for a car bought during their first year of employment. There are tax-free allowances for each child, for their children's education, for their household and for living in a different country from their country of birth, and a vast list of medical benefits, covering all aspects of their health, from glasses, contact lenses and dental treatment through to more exotic medical interventions, such as acupuncture, mud baths, hydrotherapy and massage. Similarly, when they leave EU employment they are given both their moving expenses and a tax-free resettlement allowance should they return to their country of origin or retire to their villas in the south of France or in Tuscany. They can take up to four days sickness leave at any one time without having to provide a medical certificate, subject to a limit of 12 days in any 12-month period, and they get 20 weeks maternity leave in the case of either a pregnancy or an adoption. If they are fired for incompetence, they can automatically get a dismissal allowance, their household allowance and their family allowances paid for up to 12 months. In addition, the EU pays around €47 million each year for its employees' Christmas travel. As many have lived in Brussels for years and no receipts need to be submitted, it is believed that a significant number just take the money as an extra tax-free Christmas present without bothering to do the travelling.

WE WANT MORE

One might have thought that most eurocrats would be pretty happy with their big salaries, low taxes, generous tax-free allowances, guaranteed pensions, short working days and all the other benefits of their jobs. But this doesn't seem to be the case. Every year almost 150 EU staff hire lawyers in order to take legal action against their employers, the European institutions. This means that there are about three eurocrats suing their employer every week. Any private-sector company similar in size to the EU probably gets sued by about one employee a year. Many of the claims against the EU by staff may be valid, but the sheer number of cases and judgements and appeals and new judgements for which we have to pay might make some outsiders think that our euromanagers are unbelievably incompetent and hopeless at leading their staff and that our eurocrats are uniquely privileged.

One gentleman, for example, objected to being reassigned from sunny Algiers to rainy Brussels. He sued the EU to have the transfer annulled and to get €300,000 in compensation 'in respect of the material and non-material damage suffered as a result of that decision'. Another litigant was unhappy with a decision that 'she did not satisfy the requirements of physical fitness for the performance of duties with the European Commission'. She and her lawyer apparently felt that she should get compensation 'for the pecuniary and non-pecuniary damage suffered by the applicant provisionally and fairly estimated at €170,900' plus interest. Many of the court cases concern fairly trivial matters, such as employees who believe they are entitled to extra allowances. One, for example, wanted an education allowance for his daughter, and another claimed for an increase in his household allowance.

Legal action, rather than hard work, also seems to be a popular means to get a larger pension. The Court of Auditors, which should be experts in the proper application of staff procedures, was taken to court by an employee who wanted an increase of €1,232.32 a month in his pension, plus compensation for supposed 'non-material loss suffered by the applicant during more than 14 years'. Quite a few litigants rush to their lawyers because they possibly haven't been either sufficiently intelligent or hard-working to pass the exams that make them eligible for the lucrative and lazy EU lifestyle. On finding that they have failed to be offered a job, they sue the EU in order to have their grades improved. Many of the lucky ones who do get EU jobs later sue because they are convinced they should have been promoted, even though their presumably high opinions of their own value were not shared by their superiors.

TIME FOR A JOLLY

One of the financial highlights of thousands of eurocrats' lives is their monthly trip to Strasbourg to support the European parliament's Plenary Sessions. Twelve times a year between 3,000 and 4,000 staff travel from Brussels or Luxembourg to Strasbourg. In addition to their travel expenses, they get over €1,000 a week to pay for hotels and meals without having to provide any receipts showing the money was actually used. This privilege of getting flat-rate expenses, rather than having to show real receipts, is something the employees' union SGPOE (Syndicat Général du Personnel des Organisations Européennes) is proud of having fought for, as they wrote in an email sent in late 2008: 'Up to now the EP [European parliament] enjoyed a special opt-out from the staff regulations – something the previous SGPOE-led staff committee fought hard to achieve – so EP colleagues benefited from a flat-rate system. Better for us all'.[6]

Hotels in Strasbourg can be expensive. But then, many staff don't actually use them. They either stay with friends or at hotels in the German part of the town, where a reasonable room with breakfast costs about €40 . During one dinner, a German hotel owner who charged only €38 a night (including breakfast) boasted about how many very senior EU officials regularly stayed in his hotel. Moreover, many people will stay in Strasbourg for only three nights – Monday, Tuesday and Wednesday. They travel home on Thursday afternoon because they get a so-called 'free Friday' as compensation for the hardship of spending almost four whole days away from home. When you also consider that there are subsidised restaurants in the parliament buildings, most eurocrats can easily pocket more than €600 tax free from their Strasbourg four-day week. Over a year, this extra €7,200 is probably almost enough to pay for the eurocrats to take their families on their annual skiing holiday and a long summer holiday, all paid for by us, the EU taxpayers.

However, some eurocrats do actually spend part of their generous allowances, but not necessarily only on food and hotels. Some of our money seems to go to the many, mostly east European, prostitutes who work in Strasbourg. The majority of them live on the German side of the river that divides the town because providing prostitutes is illegal in France but legal in Germany. They wait in the safety of Germany until they are summoned to visit their clients in both the French and German districts. One insider explained:

> The parliamentarians are not interested in street prostitutes. They prefer escort girls, call girls of a slightly higher level. They find little adverts and make telephone calls. That's how they take care of business.[7]

The use of prostitutes by MEPs and eurocrats had become so marked that in late 2008 a group of Nordic MEPs proposed that EU staff should be allowed to patronise only those hotels that pledged not to tolerate the use of prostitutes. It seems unlikely that this call to sexual abstinence will be widely supported, and so the good ladies who service the eurocrats' physical needs can look forward to many more years of satisfying their well-paid eurocustomers – all at our expense.

FOLLOW YOUR LEADERS

The people who really influence how effective or ineffective, how efficient or inefficient and how honest or corrupt the army of eurocrats will be are their leaders, the members of the EU Commission, which is directly responsible for the management of most of the EU's massive workforce. As the EU's senior managers, the commissioners set an example to their staff as to whether they should spend our money wisely and carefully or just stuff their own pockets with as much as they can get hold of. It's the commissioners who ultimately decide whether staff who are serially incompetent should be promoted or removed. And it's the commissioners who say whether employees caught committing fraud or theft should be vigorously pursued and punished for their sins or whether financial and other transgressions should be hastily covered up to prevent anyone outside the institutions from discovering that their taxes are being plundered and wasted by EU insiders.

In 2009 there are 27 commissioners, one from each member state. Like the MEPs, the Commission serves for a five-year term, and a new Commission is appointed within six months of the European parliament elections. In most commercial companies you would normally appoint the number of managers required to run the business, rather than trying to create top jobs for everyone you knew. However, the number of commissioners is now equal to the number of member countries. Each time new countries join, jobs are created so that each new country has a commissioner with an impressive title, well-staffed offices and something extremely important to do. A management team of 27 is rather unwieldy, expensive and hardly likely to be effective, but in the EU each country has to have a commissioner, because national pride has always taken precedence over effectiveness and concern for the wise use of our money. The French have helpfully suggested a solution to the problem of an excessively large Commission: countries that share the same language (like Britain and Ireland) and smaller countries should have just one commissioner between them, while France would, of course, always retain its own commissioner. Unsurprisingly, this typically Gallic proposal was rejected by the countries that would lose a place on the Commission high table.

The EU commissioners have been granted what many outsiders might consider to be a very attractive package of salary and benefits (see Figure 2). For a start, there's a salary of around €206,000 a year. In addition, there are other allowances for living in Brussels totalling over €44,000, including a €7,200 allowance for representation, even though all representation expenses are reimbursed. There are also allowances for each child, presumably to help pay for the education that is provided completely free of charge by the EU's own schools.

Figure 2 EU Commissioners' salary and benefits

Basic salary	€206,000
Allowances:	
– Residential	€31,000
– Household	€6,000
– Representation	€7,200
(plus representation expenses)	
(plus allowances per child)	
Total per year	**€250,200**
Taking up duty:	
– Installation	€38,507
(plus all moving and family travel expenses)	
Leaving office:	
– Resettlement	€19,254
(plus all moving and family travel expenses)	
– Transition	€103,000
(paid per year for 3 years)	
Total for one 5-year term	**€1,617,761**
(plus pension depending on length of service)	

When they take up office, commissioners quite reasonably have their moving and family travel costs fully reimbursed. However, they also receive an extra €38,507 tax free, presumably as compensation for the inconvenience of having to move. Similarly, when they leave office, they once again have all their costs fully refunded and, in addition, get €19,254 tax free to help with the move back to their homeland. Moreover, after leaving office they get around 50 per cent of their salary paid to them each year for an incredible three years. This huge wad of money must be a great solace to those commissioners who are suffering from withdrawal symptoms after their departure from their luxury EU mandarin lifestyles.

All this comes to over €1.6 million for a five-year term. Then, when you add in the costs of their assistants, researchers, secretaries, spokespeople, offices, large pensions plus sundry costs like entertainment, travel expenses, chauffeur-driven cars and all sorts of other goodies, the cost of a commissioner is probably well above €5 million for five years – around €135 million for each 27-member Commission. Like most organisations, the EU could probably be most effectively run by a team of 10 to 12 people. So, more than half the 27 commissioners are getting extremely nice salaries and benefits for jobs that were artificially created and never actually necessary in the first place.

THE GOOD, THE BAD AND THE UGLY

For at least the last 15 years or so the Commission has, unfortunately, not exactly done much to earn the respect and trust of the EU's citizens. When the Jacques Santer Commission took office for the period 1994–9, Santer launched a reform programme to improve the performance and image of the EU. This consisted of three main streams of work: 'Sound and Efficient Management', 'Modernising the Administration and Personnel Policy' and creating the 'Commission of Tomorrow'. However, following numerous revelations of maladministration and fraud within the Commission and the complete failure of the Commission president and his commissioners to take action against those responsible for wasting and stealing our money, the Santer Commission resigned in disgrace, even though a majority of our MEPs consistently voted to protect Santer's much-criticised team.

Next up was the Romano Prodi Commission. This contained four members of the discredited Santer Commission. One of these four was the British commissioner Neil Kinnock, whom Prodi put in charge of cleaning up maladministration and corruption in the EU institutions. While there are no suggestions of wrong-doing by Kinnock personally, sceptics might wonder whether a member of a severely tarnished team really was the best person to drive through a programme of fundamental reform. Unlike its predecessor, the Prodi Commission did manage to serve its full five-year term in office, but to some outsiders its most distinguishing characteristics were probably its efforts to cover up a series of financial scandals and to persecute the people courageous enough to blow the whistle on the EU administration's incompetence and corruption (see Chapter 10, The Cradle of Corruption?).

In 2004 the former Portuguese prime minister José Manuel Barroso became the new president of the Commission. Barroso's Commission was interestingly different from most previous Commissions in that at least three of his commissioners had already been involved in financial or political controversy even before they became EU commissioners.

Every time a new EU parliament is elected, the MEPs have the chance to interview each commissioner-designate before approving or rejecting the proposed Commission. Once the Commission is approved by the parliament the commissioners can start work. What is possibly depressing for us taxpayers is that the vast majority of MEPs seemed to have had absolutely no qualms at all about approving those of Barroso's commissioners-designate who had rather eventful pasts, yet rebelled in outrage against the proposed appointment of one commissioner who had expressed rather politically incorrect views about the family, the role of women and also homosexuals.

The commissioner-designate with possibly the most colourful curriculum vitae was Frenchman Jacques Barrot. As far as we understand the situation, under French law it might be unwise for us to go into too much detail about aspects of Jacques Barrot's career. When one eurosceptic MEP did find out about Barrot's past and subsequently questioned the Frenchman's suitability for high office it caused quite a rumpus. However his objections were overwhelmingly rejected by the huge majority of his fellow parliamentarians. In 2004 Jacques Barrot became commissioner for transport. Four years later, following the departure of Italian commissioner Franco Frattini, Barrot became commissioner for justice and home affairs. At the time an MEP voiced his concerns about the propriety of this appointment:

> In the current climate in which the financial probity of some colleague MEPs is in question, not to say the auditors once again refusing to sign off the EU books due to corrupt handling of funds, is this not a most untimely and inappropriate appointment?[8]

But his worries do not seem to have been accepted by a large majority of his colleagues in the European Parliament.

Another interesting character is Siim Kallas. While he was president of the Bank of Estonia in 1993 about $10 million was transferred from the bank to a company with a bank account in Switzerland for what were reported to be 'highly improbable dividends from the oil trade'.[9] The money went missing. About three years later details of the missing millions began to seep out. Four years of legal proceedings and appeals followed, during which Kallas was first Estonia's minister of foreign affairs and then minister of finance. Kallas was cleared of all charges and consistently maintained his innocence, later saying: 'Back then I was under serious investigation for four years at the end of which I was completely exonerated'.[10] In 2004 Kallas was approved to become commissioner for the 'three As': administrative affairs, audit and anti-fraud. He promised to crack down vigorously on any dishonesty and fraud and to improve the Commission's tainted image from being an 'unpleasant mixture of arrogance and inefficiency'.[11]

The British commissioner Peter Mandelson also appeared to have an exotic history. While working for Tony Blair's New Labour government, Mandelson resigned twice. In 1999 he went following the revelation that he had borrowed about £373,000 from a fellow minister and had also reportedly been less than forthcoming to a mortgage lender while obtaining a further loan to buy a house. He soon returned to government but went again in 2001 following allegations that he might have assisted an Indian billionaire who had applied for a British passport. Throughout both resignations, Mandelson denied that he had ever done anything wrong. However, his credibility was so damaged in the eyes of some of the British press that journalists have since vilified him.[12] Few people in British political life have ever been the subject of such deliberately vitriolic insults. Mandelson became Barroso's commissioner for trade with nary a bleat of concern from the MEPs assessing his suitability for the post.

The flexibility and consideration that had been accorded to Barrot, Kallas and Mandelson were distinctly lacking when MEPs came to review the Italian commissioner-designate Rocco Buttiglioni, who had been put forward as commissioner for justice, freedom and security. The 'crime' committed by Buttiglioni, a Catholic and close friend of Pope John-Paul II, was that he was alleged to hold excessively conservative views on gay people and women's role in society. During his interview he told MEPs, 'I may think homosexuality is a sin, but this has no effect on politics unless I say homosexuality is a crime', and he was adamant that he strongly opposed discrimination of any kind.[13] But the majority of MEPs were in agreement that Buttiglioni's personal opinions could not be tolerated in a supposedly open and tolerant institution like the European parliament, whose motto is 'United in Diversity'. So, for the first time in the parliament's recent history, they rejected the commissioner-designate's appointment, forcing the Italian prime minister Silvio Berlusconi to replace him.

Our MEPs no doubt felt a great sense of moral self-righteousness and satisfaction at preventing Buttiglioni's appointment. One MEP summed up the mood just before the Italian's withdrawal: 'The game is almost up for Buttiglioni . . . Most MEPs don't want this man to be put in charge of defending human rights, civil liberties and the EU's anti-discrimination laws'.[14] When Buttiglioni was replaced, much of Europe's press celebrated. Germany's *Die Welt* proclaimed: 'This is an important victory for parliamentarianism'; in Spain *El Pais* trumpeted that the crisis showed the EU was 'alive and kicking'; and France's *Libération* wrote that MEPs had 'laid a foundation stone for the future'. Germany's *Frankfurter Allgemeine Zeitung* was one of the few papers to question whether the European parliament had really scored such a victory: 'It was not to the credit of Europe's diversity and tolerance that a candidate was rejected because of his religious beliefs'.[15] Meanwhile, many outside the Brussels bubble might have felt more than slightly queasy at the way a man like Buttiglioni was rejected by MEPs because of his personal beliefs, while three individuals with arguably questionable incidents in their careers failed to attract much detailed scrutiny from MEPs. The issue is not whether any of these men had ever been proved to have done anything wrong, but rather that the European Parliament may not have been as assiduous in assessing their suitability for high office as we voters might have expected.

SO WHAT DOES IT ALL COST?

When the EU published its 2008 budget of €129 billion, it stressed how little the EU actually cost us and that it offered good value for its people: 'At some €270 per citizen per year and around 1 per cent of the EU's national wealth each year, the investment in our future represented by money spent by the EU is one which delivers a great deal'.[16] In 2009 the EU budget increased by €5 billion to around €134 billion. But the clever people in Brussels managed to reword their statements so that at first glance it actually looked as if the EU was magically getting much cheaper in spite of it actually costing us more: 'A small amount – around 1 per cent of the Union's national wealth, which is equivalent to about €235 per head of the population – comes into the EU's annual budget and is then spent mainly for its citizens and communities'.[17]

Most people in the EU are well aware of how much they pay each week or month for things like petrol, bread, butter, their homes, taxes and so on, and as prices and taxes seem to spiral ever upwards we can clearly see the effect on our finances. However, because we do not pay directly for the EU in the same way we pay for so many other things, many of us probably don't have such a clear sense of what the EU actually costs us.

The annual cost of the EU's 44,500 or so employees and European politicians is about €7 billion or around €14 a year for every man, woman and child in the 27 member countries. In addition to their costs, the politicians and the 44,500 eurocrats manage to spend around €127 billion of our money each year, which is around €256 a year taken from every person in the EU. The €127 billion consists of about €58 billion given to EU farmers under the Common Agricultural Policy and Rural Aid and €69 billion for Regional Aid to help the poorer areas of the EU catch up with those that are more prosperous as well as things like education, grants to future members, various research projects and Third World humanitarian aid. This money comes from payments linked to each country's GNI (Gross National Income), from the EU being given a cut from our governments' VAT receipts and from the heavy import duties imposed on products from outside the EU.

But the cost of the EU is much higher than just the money spent on and by the politicians and the tens of thousands of eurocrats. They are only in the business of making new laws and regulations in Brussels, Strasbourg and Luxembourg, they are not actually out in the 27 member countries working to implement and police the more than 2,000 new rules and regulations that the EU issues every year. This is done by national civil servants and other authorities in the member states. It's almost impossible to calculate how many officials are actually being paid out of our taxes to make sure that we all obey the eurocrats' dictates. Every single working day hundreds and sometimes thousands of civil servants from the EU's 27 countries pour into Brussels to take instructions from their European masters. Although there is no exact figure, there are some data that allow us to make a guestimate of the cost of officialdom in the 27 countries. For example, the European Commission spends about €38 million a year administering the Common Fisheries Policy, and that figure compares with over €350 million that the various EU countries use to police and enforce the policy – Britain alone spends almost €36 million a year on fisheries policy enforcement. There is an even more extreme situation with the Common Agricultural Policy. The EU administration costs are around €130 million, and it employs around 1,000 staff, but about €250 million are spent on over 4,200 bureaucrats just in Britain on administering agricultural and rural payments.[18]

This suggests that the cost of officials running EU policies in the 27 countries must be at least ten times the €7 billion cost of eurocrats producing the policies. But if we play extremely safe and assume that the costs of administering and enforcing EU regulation out in the 27 countries is only five times the cost of producing it (and this is certainly a huge underestimate), this would give us about another €35 billion a year to pay for the privilege of being ruled by the eurocracy.

It's not just bureaucracy that costs us money. The huge

import tariffs that the EU puts on products from the rest of the world massively increase the prices we pay in the shops. Three studies from the World Bank, the British Treasury and the consumers' association Which? have all estimated that on food alone Europeans pay over €50 billion a year more than we would if we could buy from outside the EU at world prices.[19] Moreover, complex and unwieldy EU tax rules and widespread corruption allow crooks to siphon off somewhere between €60 billion and €120 billion a year, mostly from customs duties scams and VAT fraud.[20] The EU estimates the figure at €100 billion a year.[21]

A further way the EU takes our money is that we have to pay for both the administrative and compliance costs of EU legislation. In general, compliance costs will be much greater than just the administrative costs. For example, when slaughterhouses had to employ inspectors to look after animals' welfare in the moments before they were killed, the time these inspectors spent doing paperwork would count as administrative costs, while the time and expense associated with them carrying out their job would fall under compliance costs. Similarly, if a company has to employ more staff because of new health and safety regulations most of the cost will be for the new employees' work and only a small part will be administrative. A detailed study by the EU's own statisticians of the administrative costs of national and EU red tape on business has come up with the figure of around €600 billion a year in lost earnings for EU companies.[22] Assuming that only half of this amount is due to EU red tape, that still adds €300 billion a year to the total cost. In addition, complying with some pieces of EU regulation will cost billions more each year. Different studies have estimated the cost of compliance at anywhere between 2 and 12 per cent of EU GDP, between €250 billion and €1.5 trillion a year.[23] If we take a low estimate and assume that the cost of compliance is about twice the administrative cost, this adds at least another €600 billion to our bills.

So if we add up the EU administration costs (€7 billion), the money spent by the EU (€127 billion), the costs of officialdom in the member states (€35 billion), higher food prices (€50 billion), EU tax fraud (€100 billion), red tape (€300 billion) and regulatory compliance (€600 billion) this brings the cost of the EU for us, its citizens, to around €1,219 billion a year, about €2,400 a year for each person in the EU, close to ten times the €235 figure quoted in 2009 by the eurocrats (see Figure 3).

Figure 3 The real cost of the EU may be about ten times higher than Brussels admits

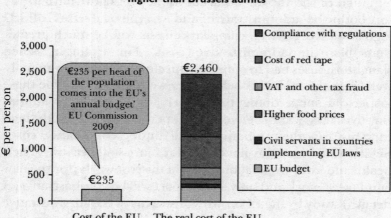

Of course, some of the above figures are rough estimates. But two things are clear from this brief exercise in number-crunching. First, the EU has a tendency to brazenly play down its real cost to its citizens; and second, the real costs are many times higher than the EU likes to admit.

IS IT WORTH IT?

Reports on the financial benefits the EU has brought should usually be handled with extreme care. Either they are produced by pro-EU think-tanks and so tend to exaggerate hugely the advantages of belonging to this expensive club. Or they are published by eurosceptic pressure groups, which seem to find eurobashing one of life's most worthwhile and enjoyable sports. However, a few years ago the Commission produced a report that tried to calculate the value the EU had brought to its citizens. The Commission's conclusion was that the implementation of the Internal Market had boosted EU output by about 1.8 per cent, equivalent now to a little under €225 billion a year.[24] This is comfortably above the direct cost of the EU's €134 billion annual budget. But it is embarrassingly far below the real cost of somewhere near to €1,219 billion a year.

Of course, the financial value or cost of EU membership can look very different depending on which country one comes from. Over the last thirty years or so, if you were from one of the PIGS or Ireland, joining the EU must have seemed like winning the lottery – you got given an awful lot of other people's money without having to do anything in return, except for remembering to spend all the cash so effortlessly coming your way. However, if you were Dutch, Swedish, British or German, you had to work pretty hard and pay your taxes diligently so that there was plenty of money available for those countries that prefer to receive rather than to give. In the current budget period 2007–13, it looks like the greatest beneficiaries will be the new members like Hungary, the Czech Republic and Poland. From the older members, Greece and Portugal are still scooping up mountains of our cash. So if you're sitting in one of these countries, you almost can't get enough of the EU as more EU means more money for you. The Spanish and Irish, on the other hand, will do less well in the future than they have in the past. This might partially explain the diminishing enthusiasm for the EU shown by the Irish. The good folk in the Netherlands, Denmark, Sweden, Austria and Germany will be paying more per person into EU funds than the citizens of any other country (see Figure 4).

Figure 4 In the 2007–13 EU budget, the Dutch, Danish, Swedes, Austrians and Germans will be the most generous contributors

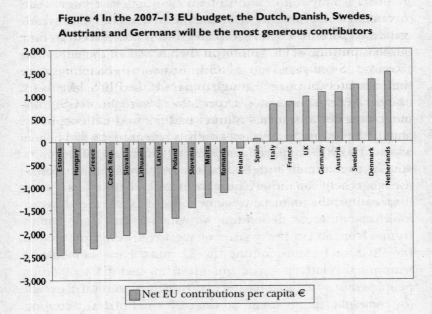

Net EU contributions per capita €

As they were the largest contributors to the EU budget for the period 2000–6 and will continue to be so for the period 2007–13, the Dutch and the Swedes will have magnanimously given more into the EU per citizen than the citizens of any other country for almost one and a half decades. When it comes to controlling EU expenditure, those who contribute the most naturally tend to be more enthusiastic about proper management of our cash. However, there are so many countries that are scooping up large amounts of our money that the more frugally minded can never gather sufficient supporters to tighten the EU's spending.

Looking forward a few years, it seems as if Germany may have to make a much larger contribution than it does currently. While the Germans have prudently kept their country's borrowing under tight control, several of the PIGS have ratcheted up massive levels of public debt. Moreover, their overstaffed, inefficient public sectors and their unaffordably generous pension schemes will cause their debt levels to go even higher, putting severe strains on the survival of the euro. The Danish, Swedish, Dutch and Austrian economies are unfortunately not large enough to pay for the PIGS' largesse to themselves. So one could expect that when the PIGS' ever-increasing debt eventually causes a collapse in confidence in the euro, the French, enthusiastically supported by a herd of clamouring PIGS, will demand that 'in the interests of solidarity' and 'to preserve the benefits of a strong EU' the long-suffering Germans help bail the PIGS out from the consequences of their financial profligacy.

Chapter 3

MAKING FRIENDS AND INFLUENCING PEOPLE

THE LAND OF THE FREEBIE

MEPs and eurocrats live a life of luxury that most of us could hardly dream of but that we have been volunteered to pay for – huge salaries, low taxes, little work, almost unlimited expenses, long holidays, early retirement, generous pensions, a tsunami of fine food, champagne and expensive wines and an encyclopaedic list of other benefits. Yet there are further sources of vast amounts of money swilling into the pockets of the euro-elite. These are the thousands upon thousands of lobbyists who are employed to throw money at our eurorulers in order to ensure that new laws and regulations serve the interests of their paymasters.

Estimates of the number of lobbyists working in Brussels vary widely. Representatives of the two main lobbyists' professional associations, EPACA (European Public Affairs Consultancies Association) and SEAP (Society of European Affairs Professionals), have claimed that there are only about 1,500, but on its website the European parliament stated in 2008 that 4,951 accredited lobbyists were registered. All these almost 5,000 individuals are allocated a badge that gives them unlimited access to parliament buildings, while the rest of us have to go through elaborate security checks before being permitted inside.

These 4,951 lobbyists are, however, probably just the tip of a rather substantial and extremely influential iceberg. For a start, while each lobbying organisation can only have up to four permanent access passes to the European parliament buildings, many of these organisations may have 20 to 30 employees. Moreover, the passes apply only to organisations based in Brussels, Luxembourg and Strasbourg – there are thousands more lobbyists working for organisations situated in other European cities who may not be included in the official figures. According to the EU's own estimates, there are about 2,600 different interest groups employing about 15,000 lobbyists whose only goal in life is to ensure that EU laws are made to their benefit. This number is already triple the 'official' number, and there are indications that even the higher figure may be understated. For example, a Chinese government website containing guidance for Chinese companies exporting to the EU suggested that there are closer to 20,000 lobbyists targeting EU movers and shakers.[1]

The EU's 15,000 or more lobbyists face off against 785 MEPs, so there are at least 20 lobbyists for each politician. This is a similar ratio to Washington D.C., often considered the birthplace of lobbying, where about 11,600 lobbyists work to influence the decisions of 435 members of Congress and 100 members of the Senate. All these lobbyists are eager to wine and dine MEPs, pay for them to go on junkets and give them all kinds of other freebies to recruit them to the lobbyists' causes. One MEP estimated that over three years about 500 lobbyists had visited him in his office, around one for every single day he was in Brussels and Strasbourg. Another approach to estimating the overwhelming strength of the lobbying industry is to say that if there are a couple of thousand eurocrats with real power to make or break new laws, then there are around seven to ten lobbyists for each key eurocrat, disbursing all kinds of gifts and favours in return for the 'right' kinds of legislation.

Organisations are spending an awful lot of money on influencing EU lawmakers. Including salary, secretarial support, office costs and expenses, it probably costs at least

£100,000 a year to keep a lobbyist in one of the main EU cities, with a senior well-connected lobbyist easily costing over £500,000 year. This means that with 15,000 EU lobbyists, more than £1.5 billion a year is being spent by various groups with the sole purpose of shaping legislation to their benefit. Lobbyists have often sought to downplay their part in governing the EU, and the vice-president of one professional association claimed: 'There is a fundamental misconception that money equals influence'.[2] But it seems unlikely that so many large, successful and smart organisations would spend this vast amount of money if they didn't feel they were getting some very tangible bangs for their lobbying bucks.

It's impossible to know how much of this £1.5 billion finds its way directly into the pockets of MEPs and eurocrats. The most widely quoted estimates are that somewhere between £60 million and £80 million is being spent on helping MEPs and eurocrats get a better understanding of lobbyists' views. So, if we assume that most of the lobbying efforts are concentrated on MEPs plus the key couple of thousand eurocrats, that gives £15,000 to £20,000 spent on each person a year in treating them to meals, sporting events, entertainment, travel and other goodies. One can say with confidence that with so many lobbyists swarming around the euro-elite and dispensing and seeking favours, most key EU insiders are probably hard-pressed to find the time for all the dinners, freebies and junkets being thrust upon them.

HORSES, DONKEYS, DENTISTS AND GUNSHIPS

Lobbyists have several different, commonly used techniques for influencing EU decisions. One of the most popular is the 'Trojan horse'. Because the majority of EU laws come from 247 advisory committees and around 1,047 EU-sponsored expert groups with specialist knowledge in the relevant legislative areas, these committees and groups are key targets for the lobbyists. 'Trojan horse' lobbying involves getting your own people on to the relevant committees and expert groups so that they can work from the inside, ensuring the legislative proposals suit your particular interests. Although around 70 per cent of Brussels lobbyists are paid by commercial companies, the EU Commission has claimed that big companies have limited influence over EU lawmaking because only about 20 per cent of experts on the committees represent industry.[3] However, many of the committees are not dealing with issues that affect large companies. Some detailed studies of committees and expert groups drafting key new regulations that are of interest to big companies have found that lobbying groups are skilled at identifying the committees and groups that matter and often manage to place their own people in a majority on those that are working in areas that affect their business. On one expert group, for example, the CBAG (Competitiveness in Biotechnology Advisory Group), there were 20 industry representatives, six academics and nobody at all from non-governmental organisations (NGOs). The CBAG's recommendations were in favour of encouraging biotechnology, claiming that it offered 'opportunities to address many of the global needs relating to health, ageing, food and the environment' and recommending that 'entrepreneurship in biotechnology needs to be encouraged if Europe is to remain competitive'.[4] The CBAG also warned against excessive regulation: 'The regulatory framework for all areas of bio-technology must not be over-stringent'.[5] Following the CBAG's fine work, one of the EU Commission's vice-presidents outlined the EU's positive attitude to encouraging biotechnology when he said: 'Biotechnology is an important means to promote growth, jobs and competitiveness in the EU.'[6] Similarly, a climate change panel was found to be made up of 30 industry experts, 13 Commission officials and only seven members from NGOs and universities.

One of the EU's leading lobbyists has held seminars on

effective lobbying where he explained the importance of getting into these committees in order to influence legislation: '80 per cent of the dossiers we deal with are finalised in comitology.' He went on to stress how influencing technical committees is preferable to trying to get to people at the top of the EU food chain: 'The bottom-up approach is much more effective than the top-down – lobbying ministers and commissioners; in the bottom-up approach you deal with experts behind the scenes.'[7]

If lobbyists don't manage to dominate or otherwise influence the relevant legislation with their 'Trojan horses' they can try the 'donkey' technique. With the 'donkey' you get decision-makers to make the 'right' decisions through a combination of carrots and sticks. Lobbyists have plenty of carrots – free trips, help with careers, gifts, job offers and even bribes. On its training courses one lobbying firm reportedly explained that the 'donkey' is a 'combination of stick and carrot approaches to key decision-makers that usually stopped short of bribery'. If they claimed that lobbyists 'usually stopped short of bribery', then it cannot be unreasonable to infer that bribery might sometimes be used. If the carrot approach doesn't give the right outcome, as many MEPs and eurocrats have received extensive benefits from lobbyists and are often compromised by their excessive closeness to some lobbyists, this gives the lobbyists considerable scope for using a stick to beat legislators into submission.

In the event that both the 'Trojan horse' and the 'donkey' don't give the required results, another much-used strategy is the 'dentist', by which a lobbying organisation tries to pull out the worst teeth from any legislation that threatens its interests. So even if the legislation eventually goes through, it is more or less toothless by the time it reaches the statute book.

This strategy was demonstrably and effectively used by lobbyists out to protect their own interests. In 2005 the EU started to look at ways to exert better control over lobbyists and to establish some transparency into the names of their clients and the amounts of money used to influence lawmaking. The

Commission's first proposal was to create a compulsory register in which lobbyists would have to give information about who they worked for and how much their clients spent on lobbying each year. When the register was finally introduced in 2008, after years of discussion, delay and the painful removal of a considerable number of teeth, it was completely voluntary – there was no requirement for lobbyists to participate at all.

Finally, if all else fails, the lobbyists send in the 'gunship', a strategy that is mainly used to benefit the largest corporations and industries. Only they have the financial clout to threaten EU lawmakers that if some specific regulation is introduced that they feel will harm their business, the companies will have to take drastic steps, like firing workers or relocating out of the EU. This was deployed when the EU tried to introduce its REACH initiative, which would have required the testing of around 30,000 chemicals to ensure they were safe to use. A bit of 'gunship' lobbying by the large chemical companies resulted in the number of chemicals needing detailed testing being reduced to 10,000. Similarly the German car industry successfully sent in a 'gunship' when a proposal to set a limit on carbon dioxide (CO_2) emissions from cars particularly threatened the German manufacturers because of their reliance on larger and more powerful models.

BEHIND THE SMOKE AND MIRRORS

Because lobbying is a fairly secretive affair, it's quite difficult to establish who is doing what, how much they're spending doing it and what results, if any, they are achieving. However, thanks to the assiduous efforts of some groups trying to get some limited transparency into the EU lobbying business, occasionally we do get a glimpse of how lobbyists work to craft EU regulations to suit their own commercial ends.[8] One technique used by many businesses and their lobbyists is to create organisations and pressure groups which can assist them with their lobbying. The names of these pressure groups often seem as if they are designed to suggest that the front organisation is aiming to do the exact opposite of what it is really out to achieve.

The software giant Microsoft, for example, which has been fined almost €1.7 billion over four years for what the competition commissioner called its 'failure to comply with an anti-trust decision', was one of the largest funders of a pressure group perhaps surprisingly called Initiative for Software Choice (ISC).[9] The goal of the ISC was to oppose government efforts around the world to give preference to open-source or open standards-based systems, which might weaken Microsoft's dominance of the global software market. (Microsoft is currently appealing against part of its €1.7 billion fine, calling it 'excessive and disproportionate'.[10])

Moreover, what MEP or eurocrat could be cold-hearted enough to refuse to listen to the views of the trendily named C4C (Campaign for Creativity), which encouraged its members to email MEPs on its behalf? On its website C4C says it represents 'artists, musicians, designers, engineers, software developers and anyone else whose livelihood depends on their creativity' because 'creativity, like a butterfly, is fragile and needs to be nurtured and protected'. C4C was sponsored by companies like Microsoft and the German software giant SAP, and it was campaigning for the EU to give them greater patent protection.[11]

Drugs companies have been particularly active in setting up and supporting supposed campaign groups. Cancer United, which was launched in October 2006, claimed to represent doctors, nurses and patients campaigning for equal access to cancer care across the EU. Its promotional material claimed: 'Cancer United brings together for the first time under one banner all parties concerned with the care of all cancer patients in Europe'. In fact, its secretariat was run by a PR company working for the Swiss pharmaceutical giant Roche, the maker of Herceptin for breast cancer, Avastin for bowel cancer and Tarceva for lung cancer. As it became clearer that Roche was the main sponsor, several dignitaries withdrew from Cancer United's executive board. One leading campaigner for improved cancer care who found herself listed as a member of the executive board without her consent asked for her name to be removed. 'We have reservations about the transparency of the Cancer United initiative, which appears to have only one funder,' she said.[12] Moreover, some leading cancer specialists were scathing in their criticism of Cancer United's campaign. One stated: 'Governments will no doubt be pressed to fund a big increase in expenditure on cancer drugs – on the entirely spurious grounds that such an increase has been proven to increase survival rates.'[13] Roche, however, denied that Cancer United was just a front to help sell their products: 'The Cancer United Campaign is about cancer care for patients. It is not about marketing for Roche.'[14]

The campaign group European Women for HPV Testing managed to get positive headlines, including 'European women's group calls for human papillomavirus testing', in medical publications such as the *British Medical Journal*,[15] but it seems to have had similar credibility problems to Cancer United. This group campaigned for increased screening of women for cervical cancer, and it was funded by the Digene Corporation, a company that 'develops, manufactures and markets proprietary DNA and RNA tests for the detection, screening and monitoring of human diseases' and, in particular, a test for cervical cancer.[16] It sent letters to high-profile women, trying to enlist their support, stating: 'Each year 12,800 European women die needlessly from cervical cancer, a slow-growing cancer that is 100 per cent detectable and 100 per cent treatable if detected early enough.'[17] The letter was sent from a PO box near the European parliament, and although post office staff refused to reveal the identity of the organisation behind the letters, the signatory was eventually found to be a full-time lobbyist working for the Brussels office of a leading PR company. When contacted, several of the celebrities listed as supporters on the group's website and in articles in medical journals said they had never heard of it. One leading cervical cancer specialist criticised what she called 'celebrity selling' of medicines:

> It is outrageous and potentially dangerous. We have seen it in prostate cancer, osteoporosis and in the marketing of other expensive drugs. It is a way the drugs companies can bypass the authorities and medical profession and take their lobbying straight to the public.[18]

A spokeswoman from the Digene Corporation denied that the campaign was just a marketing ploy: 'It is simply not true. This is not a cloak-and-dagger operation. We make sure everything is very transparent and we clearly state that Digene funds the campaign group.'[19]

But it's not just big business that is spending billions to influence EU lawmakers. In order to balance the lobbying power of commercial companies, the EU gives over €1 billion a year of our money to hundreds of so-called 'public interest groups', including Friends of the Earth and the World Carfree Network. In one year about half of Friends of the Earth's budget for running its 25-person Brussels office came straight out of our pockets.[20] The head of fundraising for Friends of the Earth Europe explained: 'There has to be some EU funding for groups like ours otherwise industry and big business would just have their own way.'[21] In some cases, this does perform a valuable role by providing some counterbalance to the massive financial power of the large commercial companies. However, most of the recipients of our EU money are strongly pro-EU and so are being paid out of our taxes to lobby EU institutions in favour of greater EU integration.

DEPLOYING THE GREAT AND THE GOOD

To have influence with EU decision-makers it helps to have a few members of the euro-elite working for you. This is acknowledged by many of the leading lobbying firms and is used as a way of encouraging targeted clients to buy their services. One company, for example, claims that it believes in 'pro-active lobbying' to promote its clients' interests, and it makes great play of the importance of employing former EU people on its staff: 'Our firm combines former top EU officials and politicians and high-profile EU attorneys.'[22] The firm explains the significance of such people's connections within the EU government: 'Many important political ties were forged from our professionals' earlier government and parliament experience.' All of which means that: 'The professionals of Alber & Geiger know the decision-makers, understand their political histories and current positions and are able to work shifting alliances and priorities to benefit client positions.'[23]

While it is clearly beneficial for lobbying firms to employ former EU officials and politicians, the number of eurocrats walking straight out of their eurojobs into well-paid employment with lobbying firms has caused concern among organisations that are advocating greater transparency in EU decision-making. The worry is that an official might be influenced in favour of a lobbying firm's clients if that official is also in the process of negotiating their next job with that lobbying firm. Some countries have so-called 'cooling-off' periods during which politicians and officials shouldn't take jobs with private-sector companies, but eurocrats can join any firm they choose the day after they leave their EU jobs. Some of the moves from the EU to lobbying firms have raised eyebrows even in the relaxed 'anything goes' atmosphere of Brussels. For example, a European Commission official chosen to lead the anti-trust case against Microsoft left to work for a consultancy that had the software company as a client.[24] A leading Brussels diplomat and a lawyer working on protecting consumer rights also went to work for Microsoft. One MEP even managed to leave the EU, move to a lobbying firm and then get back into the EU as a special adviser while working as a lobbyist.

A few years in Brussels are so valuable on the job market that a leading French newspaper recently published an article titled *Bruxelles: la ligne de CV qui vaut de l'or* (Brussels: the line on your CV that's worth a fortune).[25] Many senior politicians have also done very nicely by jumping from politics to lobbying their previous colleagues. When Germany's EU representative retired, he went on to become the chief Brussels lobbyist for the German industrial giant Siemens, and the chief EU lobbyist for the German car industry is a former German transport minister.[26] In an article two leading lobbyists explained how lobbying was attracting former politicians: 'Lobbying is no longer seen as an annex to PR only, but rather as a high-end management discipline dealt with by lawyers and former politicians.'[27]

A recent estimate suggested that about 50 EU officials leave the EU each year to work for the private sector, usually in areas where they have the most value, which are obviously those most closely connected with the work they were doing while supposedly in public service at the EU. One PR agency was even set up by four previous Commission officials and so can use its extensive insider experience and contacts to market its services. It states about one of its founders that his 'ten-year stretch as an official working for the European Commission has given him first-hand experience of all the major developments in EU policy over the last decade', and about another that he has 'built up considerable experience of the EU while working at senior political level in the European parliament and Commission'.[28]

WE DON'T WANT NO REGULATION[29]

Following a spate of corruption scandals in the US, the American authorities moved towards drastically increasing the regulation of the lobbying industry by introducing a series of measures ranging from the US Lobbying Disclosure Act in 1995 to the Honest Leadership and Open Government Act of 2007. A 600-page book of rules now requires that lobbying firms list in great detail whom they contact and for which client as well as giving their income and its sources. It also demands that politicians provide exhaustive information about any gifts, meals and other benefits they receive. Until 2005 the European parliament was the only EU institution with a register of lobbyists. There was, however, one catch: the register was entirely voluntary.

In 2005 the EU Commission finally responded to concerns about the power and opacity of the lobbying industry, and Siim Kallas, commissioner for administration, audit and anti-fraud, announced the European Transparency Initiative (ETI) because: 'People [should be] allowed to know who [lobbyists] are, what they do and what they stand for.'[30] The stated objective of the ETI was: 'To increase the transparency with which the EU handles the responsibilities and funds entrusted to it by the European citizen.'[31] At the time it seemed as if a tough compulsory registration and a code of conduct, similar to the one in the US, might well be on the way. Siim Kallas certainly made his views clear. For example, he expressed his belief that lobbyists needed to be regulated and that he had a negative opinion of voluntary systems of regulation:

> Self-imposed codes of conduct have few signatories and have so far lacked serious sanctions. Lobbyists can have considerable influence on legislation . . . But their transparency is too deficient in comparison to the impact of their activities.[32]

A year later Kallas wrote an article for a US newspaper in which he reiterated the need to regulate the activities of lobbying firms:

> Brussels and Washington are widely recognised as the two lobbying capitals of the world. In both places legislation is being drafted affecting the lives and economic interests of hundreds of millions of citizens . . . It would be arrogant,

and indeed a sign of ignorance, to claim that European
politicians can't be corrupted.[33]

For three years the ETI slowly moved towards a conclusion,
with dentists pulling out a lot of teeth along the way. In May
2008 the European parliament voted to introduce a compulsory code of conduct and registration of lobbying firms and
their clients. But a few days later the Commission appeared to
come to the opposite conclusion when it announced its
decision. Campaigners who had hoped that the ETI would
deliver transparency were to be disappointed. The
Commission's decision was that in July 2008 it would set up a
code of conduct and register for lobbyists. However, these
would both be voluntary, and there would be no requirement
for any lobbying firm to sign up or to reveal any information
about themselves, their sources of income or their clients.
Having previously disparaged voluntary systems of regulation,
Kallas appeared to have changed his mind: 'We think a
voluntary system can be more efficient than a mandatory
system.'[34] Moreover, although the commissioner had once
written about the similarities between lobbying in Washington
and Brussels, his spokeswoman now seemed of the opinion that
lobbying in the two lawmaking capitals of the world was really
'radically different' because the EU 'gives subsidies, but it's not
like a government giving contracts – there is no business money
financing politics'. In saying this, she may have been forgetting
both what her boss had written a couple of years earlier about
the need to regulate lobbyists in the EU and the fact that the
way EU laws were drafted could make or break major
companies and even industries.

Critics of the new voluntary scheme argued that it was a
'token gesture' of 'less than no value' because: 'When you
compare it to other tested systems, such as in the United States,
its voluntary nature and distortion in fact make it look like one
of the world's weakest registers.'[35] Others even claimed that it

would allow companies to hide much of their lobbying. Corporations could, for example, conduct their 'clean' lobbying through a registered lobbying firm, thus appearing to be transparent in their dealings. At the same time they could carry out their 'dirty' lobbying, such as setting up bogus campaigning groups, distributing freebies, handing out bribes and offering jobs to MEPs and eurocrats, through lobbying firms that hadn't registered with the voluntary scheme.

Faced with a barrage of criticism from transparency campaigners, the Commission announced that it would review the functioning of the register in 2009 to assess how effective it had been. The suggestion was that the Commission might then consider making the register compulsory if a voluntary system proved ineffective.

By the beginning of 2009 only about 20 per cent of interest groups had felt it worth their while to sign up with the EU Registry of Interest Representatives and most of these were NGOs and non-commercial pressure groups. Only a few of the large commercial firms had joined, and almost all the major law firms had refused to do so, rightly claiming that the disclosure requirements would break their obligations of confidentiality to their clients. The Commission and parliament have now set up a joint working group to propose how they could create a common register for lobbyists. Given that the parliament's register is mandatory, it looks as though this new initiative will eventually lead to plans for a compulsory register of some kind. However time is short. To be sure of being implemented, the group's proposals would need to be presented and adopted before a new Commission takes office after the June 2009 EU elections, because a new Commission might have other priorities.

AND THE WINNER IS . . . .

Every year for the last few years a group of organisations that have campaigned for open and transparent lobbying have organised the Worst EU Lobbying Awards. The awards are aimed at discouraging controversial lobbying practices by exposing some of the worst offenders, and they are given to the lobbyist, company or lobby group that the organisers and voters believe 'has employed the most deceptive, misleading or otherwise problematic lobbying tactics in order to influence EU decision-making'.

In 2005 the 'proud' winner was the Campaign for Creativity (C4C), which, as noted above, turned out to be representing the world's largest software suppliers out to gain greater patent protection for their products. In 2006 Exxon-Mobil received the top award for its efforts to influence EU policies on global warming. In 2007 three German carmakers (BMW, Daimler and Porsche) won the competition for their effective lobbying to delay and dilute the introduction of lower CO_2 emission limits. By using the 'gunship' (the threat that thousands of German jobs would be lost), the lobbying campaign helped get the planned EU target of 120 grams of CO_2 per kilometre by 2012 increased to 130 grams per kilometre, and larger cars exempted from the planned targets altogether for at least another seven years.[36] Second place in 2007 went to EPACA (European Public Affairs Consultancies Association), an association of lobbying firms, for their campaign to ensure that the register of lobbyists being introduced by the EU Commission would 'preserve lobbying secrecy' by being voluntary rather than compulsory. A special 'Greenwash' prize was also given in 2007 for what the organisers called 'the most audacious attempt to gain unjustifiable green credentials'. This went to the German Atomic Forum for its campaign to improve the image of nuclear energy through a series of advertisements featuring happy farm animals grazing in beautiful countryside beside supposedly environmentally friendly nuclear power plants.

In 2008, in addition to the worst lobbying award, there was also a special Worst Conflict of Interest Award for 'the MEP, commissioner or Commission official whose background, side-jobs or other liaisons with special interests raised the most serious concerns about their ability to act in the public interest'. The 2008 nominations for Worst Lobbying Award included IATA (the International Air Transport Association) for its campaign to persuade MEPs and commissioners not to include air transport in the main EU CO_2 reduction scheme; two PR agencies that acted for Russia and Georgia during their 2008 spat; and the European Alliance for Access to Safe Medicines (EAASM) whose objective is 'fighting against counterfeit medicines and promoting patient safety around Europe'.[37] The 2008 joint winners were PR agencies working for Malaysian and Brazilian producers of agrofuels. More details about the awards can be found on the organisers' website.[38]

THE WORST IS YET TO COME

As for the future, according to one leading EU lobbyist who also held seminars teaching lobbying techniques, lobbying activities will become more intense and will use ever more suspect methods: 'I think that in the future . . . we will move to ever harder lobbying strategies, towards ever more sophisticated approaches to economic intelligence probably involving practices such as manipulation, destabilisation or disinformation.' When asked why this would happen, he replied: 'Because the stakes are higher, because Brussels is the number one centre of power in Europe, because Brussels will become the permanent theatre of heavy industrial warfare.'[39]

PART 2

THE UNSTOPPABLE SUPERSTATE

Chapter 4

THE TAKEOVER

SUPERMARKET OR SUPERSTATE?

Perhaps the most important question about the EU is: what are our leaders actually giving us? Are they working to deliver a single European market in which independent countries voluntarily cooperate for their common economic benefit, or are they constructing a single European superstate in which members' freedom of action is severely constrained by rules that are formulated by the central EU authorities? A clue to the answer can be found in the way our leaders have altered the name of their pet project. At first it was called the European Economic Community (EEC), also known as the Common Market. Then, around 1967, the word Economic started to be dropped from official documents and the name changed to the European Community (EC), suggesting that it now dealt with matters that were broader than just economic issues. In the pre-amble to the 1986 Single European Act the concept of the European Union (EU) started to appear alongside the EC, and by the 1991/1992 Maastricht Treaty the EU had entered the main text, replacing the EC as the official name. It should be fairly clear that the word 'Union' represents rather more than a voluntary trading alliance.

So, if the euro-elite is intent on creating something resembling a single monolithic superstate, are we, the EU's 495 million citizens, all enthusiastic participants in this great project or have we somehow been railroaded into a situation in which our individual countries have unknowingly and possibly unwillingly lost their sovereignty and independence? In this chapter we will review how we were taken from the EEC to the EU. In doing this, we will try to assess whether we have been clearly informed about our single European destiny or whether we have been misled by the members of an elite that were keen to do what it considered was in our (or at least their) best interests, whether we liked it or not. Unfortunately, the evidence strongly suggests that our leaders have not always been totally honest about the superstate into which they were intent on leading us.

THE SIX STEPS TO HEAVEN

The EU has been built up through a series of treaties, beginning with the Treaty of Rome in 1957 and culminating in the Lisbon Treaty in 2008–9. There are six main treaties that have swept us along the one-way road towards a European superstate. Most of these treaties are drafted in a completely impenetrable mixture of legalese and eurospeak that is incomprehensible to all except a few expert insiders. Several treaties don't make any sense in themselves because they are just verbose, legalistic amendments to previous treaties, and to understand them you would have to read more than one treaty simultaneously. We don't have the space to provide a detailed explanation of each of these dire documents here. Instead, we'll focus on a few vitally important features that are common to all these treaties and look at the role each treaty has played in herding us into the superstate that the euro-elite has been planning for the last 50 years.

Although the six main treaties have all been drafted by different groups of people over the last half century, there are some worryingly consistent characteristics that can be found in every one of them:

- Each treaty suffers from 'eurocreep' by going much further in giving power to the EU central institutions than the supposed aim of the treaty suggests should be necessary.

- Each treaty is cumulative and irreversible, always giving more power to the EU institutions and thus taking power away from national governments, police, civil services, judiciaries, armed forces and even health services.
- Each treaty has significantly increased the number of areas where the EU has accorded itself the authority to regulate and has reduced the number of areas where member countries could use their veto to block policies that were to their disadvantage.

Many national politicians have not fully understood and, indeed, have often not even read the treaties that they were signing in our name. Politicians have seldom admitted the full extent of each treaty and instead have tended to present them to us as just a bit of 'tidying up', 'streamlining' and making the EU 'more efficient'. At the same time, the public's right to vote on these treaties has increasingly been restricted, and when any country has rejected any treaty their votes have usually been ignored. In addition, the EU institutions have usually begun implementing the conditions of each treaty long before the treaties have been ratified by the EU member countries, as if they didn't really care if the EU countries and voters wanted the treaties or not.

Step 1: Treaty of Rome 1957

The first major treaty was the Treaty of Rome, signed by the original six members of the EEC, Belgium, France, West Germany, Italy, Luxembourg and the Netherlands. This treaty established the EEC, basing it around what were called the 'four freedoms': the free movement of goods, services, capital and labour. Curiously, although the Treaty of Rome was portrayed by the politicians as just building a tariff-free trading area, it set up three powerful central institutions that are completely absent from other free trade organisations, such as the European Free

Trade Association (EFTA), which was formed in 1960, the Association of Southeast Asian Nations (ASEAN), founded in 1967, or the North American Free Trade Agreement (NAFTA), signed by the USA and Canada in 1988 and by Mexico in 1992. These three central institutions were the European Council, the European Commission and the European Court of Justice.

The Treaty of Rome defined in detail the role and authority of these three new institutions, in some cases giving them considerable executive powers over member countries. Article 189, for example, stated that 'a regulation shall be binding in its entirety and directly applicable in all member states'. This meant that any regulation issued by the European Commission automatically became law in all member countries and that national parliaments had surrendered any authority to examine, debate or even question any regulation emanating from the centre. The European Court of Justice (ECJ) also did quite nicely from the treaty when it was accorded supremacy over all the members' national courts. This meant that the highest courts in all the member countries had to accept any judgement made by the ECJ and that there was no right of appeal.

In addition, the Treaty of Rome established the European Investment Bank. None of the other free trade areas saw any need for their own, centrally-controlled investment bank, suggesting that the EEC was intended to be something more than an EFTA, ASEAN or NAFTA.

Step 2: Single European Act 1986

Although there were a few more treaties and declarations after the Treaty of Rome, the next significant step forward towards the superstate came with the Single European Act of 1986. This Act came about mainly because insufficient progress had been made towards creating the common market that had been promised by the Treaty of Rome 29 years earlier. The European institutions identified about 300 measures that had to be implemented to enable the single market to function as planned, and the Act committed the now 12 members of the EC to have completed these measures by December 1992.

Although ostensibly aimed at finally allowing the single market to operate effectively, the Single European Act successfully eurocrept its way into many areas that could be considered well beyond the normal scope of a simple free trade area. For example, the Act added some new policy areas to what the EC called its 'areas of competence'. (Here the word 'competence' meant only that the EC gained the power to regulate these areas; it in no way implied that the EC was actually competent to use this power in an intelligent way.) The new areas were monetary cooperation, social policy, cohesion (the power to distribute money to the EC's poorer regions), research and development and environmental standards.

Adding new competences every time there is a new treaty is a crucial part of the EU's power-grab. Whenever the EU issues a new law or rule it has to justify taking action by showing that it has the legal authority ('the competence') to regulate. Therefore, the more competences it can slip into each treaty, the more areas it can take away from member countries' control.

The Act also set up the basis for member countries to cooperate on foreign policy and policing, and in its preamble it set the goal of a single European currency. So, although the Single European Act was presented to us citizens as ensuring a well-functioning European market, it actually moved the EC considerably further along the road leading from a free market to a centrally-controlled single state. This shift was eloquently identified by the EU Commission president Jacques Delors when he said in 1988 that within ten years '80 per cent of our economic legislation, perhaps even fiscal and social as well' would come from the EU rather than individual countries' parliaments.[1] This was actually quite an accurate prediction – in 2007 the German president calculated that about 84 per cent of all legislation passed by the German parliament came from the EU.[2]

Step 3: Maastricht Treaty 1991/1992[3]

A total of 29 years went by between the Treaty of Rome and the Single European Act, but now the treaties seemed to be coming thicker and faster. Just six years after the Single European Act, the Maastricht Treaty was foisted upon us. The purpose of Maastricht was to prepare the EU for monetary union and the introduction of the euro, and it set a timetable for the participating countries to align their economies so that the single currency could replace national currencies in January 2002.

But once again this treaty eurocrept its way into a wide range of areas that had nothing at all to do with the single currency. For example, Maastricht extended the EU's so-called 'competence' to consumer protection, public health, education and vocational training, culture and what were named Trans-European Networks (TENs) – that is, any energy or transport links that crossed national borders. Not only did Maastricht manage to eurocreep its way into many other aspects of our lives, it also gave the EU a guiding role in leading inter-governmental discussions on deciding a common foreign and security policy and matters of justice and home affairs. Perhaps more ominously, Maastricht set up the European Central Bank (ECB), in the process giving the bank control over the financial reserves of the countries that would participate in the single currency – an extraordinary abandonment of national economic independence that was never even considered by any of the world's other trading organisations.

However, even this massive extension of the EU's powers was not sufficient to satisfy the euro-elite. Deep within the Maastricht Treaty was the delightfully flexible Article 308:

> If action by the Community should prove necessary to obtain, in the course of the operation of the common market, one of the objectives of the Community and this

Treaty has not provided the necessary powers, the council
shall take the appropriate measures.

In plain language, this infinitely flexible 'rubber article' said
something like 'we, the happy, well-paid Brussels bureaucrats,
have given ourselves power over everything we can think of for
the moment, but if there's something we've missed out or
forgotten that has anything at all to do with the operation of
the common market, we've also got power over that too'. Article
308, which remains with us to this day, appeared to give the EU
almost unlimited authority over any area of our lives in which
it chose to intervene, yet there were not many politicians at the
time who seemed particularly keen on informing their electorates of the extent to which national governments were giving
up their authority to the unelected euro-elite.

Step 4: Treaty of Amsterdam 1997

Only five years passed until the next treaty came along. The
Treaty of Amsterdam was a relatively modest document that
was intended to implement the Schengen Agreement, which
removed all border controls between EU countries. This meant
that once someone entered the EU they would not have to show
their passports to travel to any other EU country except for
Great Britain and the Republic of Ireland, which opted out.

Although this treaty was primarily and supposedly aimed at
enabling the free movement of people within the EU, our
euroleaders added a few little extras, all intended to further
extend their power over member countries. For example, the
treaty created the post of High Representative for the Common
Foreign and Security Policy, basically an EU foreign minister,
who, it was planned, would eventually take foreign policy
negotiations and decisions away from individual countries'
foreign ministers. So eager was the EU to move ahead with its
great plans that it appointed a commissioner with 250 staff to

deal with foreign policy long before the Amsterdam Treaty had been ratified. The treaty gave the EU authority over member countries' asylum policies, employment legislation and discrimination laws, and it imposed a legal obligation on members' police forces to cooperate more closely against racism, xenophobia, terrorism, people-trafficking, drug-trafficking, corruption and fraud. In the interests of supposedly improving decision-making, the treaty also removed the national governments' right of veto in any EU policies concerning employment, social exclusion, equal opportunities, research and public health, thereby giving the central EU institutions free rein to regulate in all these areas.

All this meant a huge increase in the power of the EU and a correspondingly enormous decrease in the independence of members' parliaments.

Curiously, the thousands of politicians in the member country parliaments failed to notice that, as ever more of their legislation came directly from Brussels and had to be implemented without any discussion in national parliaments, there was a decreasing need for so many politicians in national parliaments. In fact, by 2008 the number of domestic politicians in member countries could easily have been reduced by 80 per cent to match the transfer of power from national parliaments to Brussels. This would have saved a massive amount of money for European taxpayers. When one politician in the British House of Commons did suggest that the number of MPs should be drastically reduced to match their greatly reduced workload, he found that his colleagues weren't very enthusiastic about his proposal.

Step 5: Treaty of Nice 2001

It was a mere four years before the Treaty of Nice in 2001. The purpose of the treaty was to prepare the EU for enlargement as it planned to allow eight eastern European countries together with Malta and the Greek part of Cyprus to join. The treaty also included such administrative changes as setting a limit on the number of members of the European parliament at 732 and fixing the number of commissioners at 27, which meant that the larger states had to give up one of their two commissioners.

However, as usual the treaty was used to allow the EU to eurospread its way to granting itself even more power. Its main territory grab was over foreign policy and defence, but perhaps the most significant lurch towards a superstate came with the linking of the Charter of Fundamental Rights of the European Union to the Treaty of Nice. This charter included such basic rights as the right to marry, freedom to hold opinions and the right to life, but it also gave Europe's citizens some more politically charged rights, including consultation guarantees to workers, the right to strike and equality between men and women in all areas, while at the same time allowing positive discrimination in favour of 'the under-represented sex'.

One British Minister for Europe claimed that 'the EU Charter of Fundamental Rights will be no more binding than the *Beano* or the *Sun*',[4] but the charter soon started creating havoc in member states. Countries that had a higher pension age for women to reflect the fact that they tended to live longer had to bring the retirement age for men and women into line. Some criminals, especially murderers who didn't want to spend the rest of their lives in prison, managed to have their sentences reduced on the basis that long sentences represented an infringement of their rights. Other criminals used the charter to prevent themselves being deported back to their countries of origin, even when these countries were members of the EU. Convicted terrorists used the charter to avoid being deported to prison in the USA. Even schoolchildren were able to jump aboard the human rights bandwagon by using the charter to claim that their rights were being horrifically abused when they weren't allowed to wear supposedly religious jewellery in school. Whatever the rights and wrongs of individual issues and cases, overall the charter often ruled against the policies of democratically elected governments, and it cost ordinary taxpayers billions as EU countries' police, schools, local councils, hospitals and other public services had to implement a large number of extra controls and bureaucracy to ensure they were not infringing the new, wide-ranging rights of some of the most demanding but sometimes least deserving members of our society.

Step 6: Constitutional Treaty 2004

Just three years after the Treaty of Nice we were presented with the European Constitutional Treaty of 2004, which metamorphosed into the Lisbon Treaty of 2008–9 after it was rejected by French and Dutch voters. This treaty is such a major leap towards the EU superstate that it deserves a chapter of its own, but the key point to note here is that it will sadly be the last European treaty we voters will ever see. Our leaders have got wiser over the years and have realised that it is pointless to go through the hard work of agreeing treaties that some countries might try to opt out of or that the electorate (if given a choice) might reject. With the Constitutional Treaty and its offspring the Lisbon Treaty, therefore, the euro-elite has avoided the need for any further treaties. Both versions of the new treaty are what are called 'self-amending'. This means that they can be changed in order to grant new powers to the EU without having to use further treaties. At the same time they are conveniently also irreversible, so that nothing in them can be rescinded or removed. They truly are a one-way street to the EU superstate and are thus the treaties to end all treaties. Our euroleaders must be kicking themselves that they didn't think of the self-amending trick years ago.

WE WERE WARNED

For those of us who want our countries to be merged into a bureaucratic, centrally-run, single superstate, the success of the six main treaties in moving us towards the one-nation goal should be extremely satisfying. For the rest of us, who see our national independence being inexorably taken away, slice by painful slice, the degree to which we are now ruled by Brussels might come as an unwelcome surprise. However, we have been warned many times that there was only one goal for the EU project. Although many of our national political leaders may have chosen to downplay the impact of the six main treaties on our independence, the euro-elite has often been remarkably candid about its intentions for our future.

The preamble to the Treaty of Rome stated that the signatory states were 'determined to lay the foundations of an ever closer union of the peoples of Europe', making it quite clear over half a century ago that a superstate was the only item on the menu.[5] Moreover, various members of the euro-elite have not been coy about their ambitions. In 1992 the German chancellor Helmut Kohl told us what was coming: 'The European Union Treaty . . . within a few years will lead to the creation of what the founding fathers of modern Europe dreamed of after the war, the United States of Europe.'[6] In 1993 Commission president Jacques Delors explained: 'We're not just here to make a single market, but a political union.' In 1996 German president Roman Herzog declared: 'The day of the nation state is over.' In 1999 Romano Prodi, who took over as Commission president from Jacques Santer, gave an excellent description of how the EU had developed over the years: 'The single market was the theme of the eighties; the single currency was the theme of the nineties; we must now face the difficult task of moving towards a single economy, a single political unity.' And he went on to explain where he was headed: 'For the first time since the fall of the Roman Empire, we have the opportunity to unite Europe.'[7]

The introduction of the euro gave the elite an excellent opportunity to explain where they were taking us. The head of the Bundesbank, Hans Tietmeyer, said:

A European currency will lead to member nations transferring their sovereignty over financial and wage policy as well as monetary affairs. It is an illusion to think that states can hold on to their autonomy.[8]

The first president of the European Central Bank (ECB) backed up this view:

The process of monetary union goes hand in hand, must go hand in hand, with political integration and ultimately political union. EMU [European Monetary Union] is, and always was meant to be, a stepping stone on the way to a united Europe.[9]

And the second head of the ECB, Jean-Claude Trichet, was also explicit about the EU's powers:

The Council of Ministers will have far more power over the budgets of member states than the federal government in the United States has over the budget of Texas.[10]

Perhaps one of the most forthright of those who proclaimed that a superstate had been created was EU Commission president Romano Prodi:

But what is the Commission? We are here to take binding decisions as an executive power. If you don't like the term government for this, what other term do you suggest?[11]

Then, just in case we hadn't quite got the message, he explained it again about a month later:

Here in Brussels, a true European government has been born. I have governmental powers, I have executive powers for which there is no other name in the world, whether you like it or not, than government.[12]

Although members of the euro-elite have often been forthright about wanting to create a superstate, many of them have also understood that the citizens of Europe were not ready to give up their national independence to the europhile dream of a centrally-controlled single European nation. They therefore planned that we would have to be led gradually into their brave new world. Jean Monnet, one of the key founders of the EU, laid out the tactics for moving Europe from a collection of nation states to one single superstate:

> Europe's nations should be guided towards the superstate without their people understanding what is happening. This can be accomplished by successive steps, each disguised as having an economic purpose, but which will eventually and irreversibly lead to federation.[13]

The prime minister of Luxembourg expressed similar sentiments in 2004 about how the electorate had to be led unwittingly into the eurocrats' single-state paradise:

> We decide on something, leave it lying around and wait and see what happens. If no one kicks up a fuss, because most people don't know what has been decided, we continue step by step until there is no turning back.[14]

And a memo written by a senior British civil servant in 1971, but released only 30 years later, reportedly gave an unambiguous insight into the attitudes of our leaders:

> Of course this is the end of British democracy as we have known it, but if it is properly handled the people won't know what's happened until the end of the century. With any luck, old boy, by then I'll be dead.[15]

Meanwhile, some outsiders looked on with puzzlement as the

European countries willingly subjected themselves to ever-increasing undemocratic, centralised control. The former Soviet president Mikhail Gorbachev was reported as remarking: 'The most puzzling development in politics during the last decade is the apparent determination of western European leaders to re-create the Soviet Union in western Europe.'[16]

THE DEATH OF DEMOCRACY

In the early days of the European project our leaders were not totally averse to allowing a few of their citizens the chance to vote on their treaties because the votes generally went the way our leaders wished. With the 1986 Single European Act, for example, two out of the 12 members were permitted a vote, and in both countries, Ireland and Denmark, the results were in favour of the Act.

By the time of the Maastricht Treaty in 1992, however, citizens were beginning to get a little more twitchy about what was being done in their name. Three of the 12 countries voted. The Irish approved the treaty and the Danes rejected it. In France, despite a massive PR campaign by the EU, the French government and most of the French media, the treaty was approved by just 51.05 per cent of the voters. But it was widely suspected that the offer to the inhabitants of French overseas territories of heavily subsidised flights to France to vote was what tipped the balance of the vote in favour of a 'yes'. The Maastricht Treaty specified that all 12 countries had to ratify it for it to be implemented. Given this clause, the Danish rejection clearly ought to have caused a problem, but the other 11 countries decided to breach the terms of their own treaty and went ahead with ratifying it anyway. Meanwhile, the Danes were given two opt-outs, on the euro and on defence, and told to vote again in 1993. This time they got the answer right, and the treaty was ratified by all 12 countries.

Because the Amsterdam Treaty did not make any constitutional changes, there were no referenda. Instead, the treaty was approved by all the member governments. When it came to the Treaty of Nice in 2001 only the Irish were given the chance to vote. Unfortunately, they chose the wrong box on the ballot paper and rejected the treaty. But the euro-elite just ignored the election result and gave the Irish another chance to vote in 2002 to see if they could get it right second time round. Fortunately they did, and the treaty passed into law.

Some Brussels insiders are even beginning to talk openly about what they call a 'post-democratic age'. They believe the world is now so complex that it is no longer appropriate to allow ordinary citizens to have a say in how they are governed. So, according to our rulers, it is better to leave important decisions to the bureaucratic, technocratic elite – the new rulers of the Empire of Good Intentions.

DOING JUSTICE AN INJUSTICE

At this point in the story the European Court of Justice (ECJ) deserves a special mention. When most of us think of 'justice' we probably imagine it has something to do with murderers, thieves, people traffickers or other criminals being caught and punished. Or perhaps we think of low-paid workers in the Third World being given acceptable wages. Or it may be that we imagine French and German energy companies being prevented from forming cartels to rip off European consumers. In short, we tend to believe that justice is meant to be connected with 'right' winning over 'wrong'.

So the ECJ's name is somewhat misleading. The ECJ is not there to decide on matters of right against wrong. Its job is to resolve any conflicts about the interpretation of European law, and its judgements always take supremacy over national laws. Moreover, it has the right to impose unlimited fines on any countries it believes are breaking EU law, and there is no right of appeal against its judgements. But perhaps most importantly, it must deliver all its judgements within the context of the Treaty of Rome's intention that all European states are committed to 'an ever closer union'. So anything a country does will be judged by the ECJ not in terms of whether it is morally right or wrong, not even if it is legally right or wrong and not on whether it helps or harms EU citizens. Instead, countries' actions have tended to be assessed based on whether they help or hinder the move to a single EU superstate – the 'ever closer union' mentioned in the preamble to the Treaty of Rome. The ECJ has repeatedly made it clear that its role is a political one of enabling 'the community interests enshrined in the Treaty of Rome to prevail over the inertia and resistance of member states'.[17]

In 2008 Ireland and Denmark were given a stark reminder of how much of their independence they had surrendered to the EU. Both countries had introduced new immigration laws to try to control the number of arranged marriages. But these laws were declared to be in breach of EU law by the ECJ, which meant that both countries would have to repeal their own laws and, possibly, pay compensation to anyone who could claim that their human rights had been breached by these supposedly 'illegal' national laws. In the same year Ireland fell foul of the ECJ when it tried to clamp down on foreign workers claiming social security benefits for months after leaving the country. The ECJ ruled that EU freedom of movement laws entitled foreign workers to Irish benefits even when they had returned home. In Germany a new law designed to help older workers find jobs was judged by the ECJ as discriminatory, even though the EU directive, which the German law supposedly broke, had not been implemented at the time of the law. As a basis for making its judgement in the absence of any actual EU law to support its opinion, the ECJ found a vague justification for its judgement by claiming that the new German law broke 'the constitutional traditions common to the member states'. Again in Germany, the ECJ banned cigarette advertisements in local German newspapers on the dubious basis that these local German newspapers could distort the workings of the EU internal market as they might be sold in other EU countries where tobacco advertising was banned.

In Belgium the ECJ found that a French student had been discriminated against when he was denied Belgian welfare benefits even though Article 1 of the EU Students Directive specifically states that a student may study abroad solely if 'he and his family have sufficient resources to avoid becoming a burden on the social assistance system of the host member state during their period of residence'. In this case, the ECJ just blatantly ignored EU law because it put the political principle of 'ever closer union' above the EU laws that were in place. So, rather than judging the case against existing EU law, which is what any normal court should do, the ECJ made its decision based on how the law might look if the EU was one single country ruled by the EU Commission. By doing this, the ECJ set a worrying precedent that even the EU's own laws no longer had any legal basis if they were found to be detracting from the creation of one single superstate governed from Brussels.

The EU Commission has been particularly effective in using the ECJ to reduce member countries' sovereignty in order to further the cause of greater integration. In 2008 several countries objected to the Commission's demand that all telecoms operators should keep customers' phone and internet data for a fixed period of time in order to assist the fight against terrorism and crime. However, an ECJ advocate general curiously ruled that the Commission's requirement was primarily aimed at ensuring the functioning of the single market and was not a matter of security. He thus dismissed the member countries' action, 'taking the view that the directive was correctly based on the EC treaty' enabling the single market.[18]

When Britain opted out of the EU Working Time Directive that sets a maximum working week of 48 hours Brussels used the ECJ to force the UK to institute the 48-hour maximum anyway. The Commission claimed, without any statistical proof, that the previously agreed UK opt-out was a danger to health and safety. This has had a major impact, particularly in Britain's health services. For example, before the imposition of the directive, British junior hospital doctors could be on duty for over 60 hours a week. Often they would be able to get a few hours' sleep during their long shifts. However, under the new rules, even if a doctor managed to sleep for eight hours during a night shift, it was now considered that the doctor had worked for the eight hours, and this limited the number of hours left for the doctor to work during that week. Some estimates have concluded that when qualifying today, many British surgeons have less than half the work experience of doctors who were trained before the introduction of the Working Time Directive.

Governments of EU countries have also been quick to use the ECJ to further their own economic ends. When Britain implemented the Merchant Shipping Act to try to prevent the massive, unpoliced Spanish fishing fleet from buying British fishing quotas and destroying Britain's limited remaining fish stocks, the ECJ ruled that the UK's law was illegal, that Britain should give the Spanish fishing armada free access to its territorial waters because these were considered a 'common resource' and that Britain should pay around €150 million in compensation to the Spanish fishermen it had tried to keep out. When Ireland tried to maintain a low rate of corporation tax in order to encourage investment in the country, other member states with high rates of taxation to support their bloated public sectors were able to use the threat of action in the ECJ to force Ireland to raise its tax rates by claiming that Ireland was in breach of EU competition laws. But Ireland's tax rates are still low compared to the high-tax countries like France and Germany. It is likely that after the Lisbon Treaty has been pushed through, the ECJ will again be used to force Ireland to raise its corporation tax, this time to around 30 per cent, on the somewhat arguable basis that low taxes constitute 'unfair competition'.

France, however, which always claims to be supporting greater European solidarity and cooperation, has repeatedly been condemned by the ECJ for things like banning British beef, protecting its energy market against suppliers from other EU countries and giving generous tax breaks, state aid and other help to major French companies. But the French have been particularly successful at lobbying the Commission to have ECJ decisions overridden in their favour.

The ECJ has dealt with over 10,000 cases. In its judgements it tends to interpret EU law in its widest possible understanding as to whether the case furthers the cause of European integration or not. It is thus a political court, continually extending the power of the central EU institutions over countries and individuals, rather than a real court of justice that exists to protect ordinary citizens against criminal activity or authorities abusing their power.

By late 2008 the ECJ's judgements had become so untenable that one of Germany's most distinguished legal experts, Roman Herzog, the former German president and former president of the Federal Constitutional Court of Germany, wrote that the ECJ 'blithely ignores' national law, pulls judgements 'out of a hat', acts 'as legislator', 'systematically ignores fundamental principles of the Western interpretation of law' and 'invents legal principles serving as grounds for later judgements'.[19] He accused the ECJ of 'arrogance' and of giving 'increasingly astonishing justifications . . . for depriving member states of their very own fundamental competences and interfering heavily in their legal systems'. He went on to argue that the ECJ was no longer fit for purpose because it made judgements based on the political principle of 'ever closer union' rather than on actual EU and member states' laws:

> The conclusion one comes to is clear: The ECJ is not suitable as a subsidiarity controller in the last instance and a protector of the member states' interests. This is not

surprising as, first of all, according to Articles 1 and 5 of the EU Treaty, the ECJ is obliged to participate in the 'process of creating an ever closer union'.[20]

Journalists seldom write about the ECJ. Probably it is seen as being too boring for the average reader, but the political importance of the ECJ is consistently underestimated by outsiders. The ECJ probably has more power to force through European integration than even the Commission, and internally some EU officials call the ECJ 'the silent integrator'. A former Commission spokesman admitted that the Commission sometimes leaves the wording on more controversial new laws deliberately vague in order to get them accepted by the European parliament.[21] The Commission knows that once such laws are passed the ECJ will tighten up the wording, and always in the interests of greater harmonisation and further European integration. By then it's too late for the parliament to object.

Chapter 5

THE CONSTITUTION CON

POWER TO THE PEOPLE?

The ink on the Treaty of Nice (signed on 26 February 2001) had hardly had time to dry before the EU elite had their next attack of euro-inspiration. In December 2001 they met in the town of Laeken near Brussels and issued the Laeken Declaration. This established the Convention on the Future of Europe under the chairmanship of former French president, Valéry Giscard d'Estaing. The Convention quickly gathered up many enthusiastic and well-rewarded members, almost exclusively from the ranks of the euro-elite, and within a year their numbers had grown to 105 delegates and over 100 official substitutes, observers, experts and other no doubt useful contributors. The aim of this well-staffed Convention was to come up with proposals to make the EU 'more democratic, more transparent and more efficient'.[1] The Laeken Declaration also clearly stated that 'within the Union, the European institutions must be brought closer to its citizens'; that European citizens wanted 'institutions to be less unwieldy and rigid and, above all, more efficient and open'; and that we did not want 'a European superstate or European institutions inveigling their way into every nook and cranny of life'. In particular, the Convention was tasked with clearly defining the powers of the EU and the powers of the member states 'in a way which does not lead to a creeping expansion of the competence of the Union'. The solution that the Convention came up with was to write a constitution for the EU.

Though based on the Philadelphia Convention of 1787, which led to the US Constitution, this European Convention was very different. In 1787 the US Convention members were mainly elected democratically. However, the members of our Constitutional Convention were almost all chosen by the euro-elite, from the euro-elite and for the euro-elite. Moreover, the 55 participants in the Philadelphia Convention were rather less numerous than the hordes of eurocrats tasked with writing our constitution. One of the members of the 12-strong praesidium that oversaw the drafting of the constitution explained the worrying conflict of interests that arose when a constitution was written by a large, undemocratically chosen group of insiders, many of whom had very real career and financial interests in ensuring that as much power as possible was taken from the member states and conferred on the EU:

> The Convention brought together a self-selected group of the European political elite, many of whom have their eyes on a career at European level, which is dependent on more and more integration. Not once in the 16 months I spent on the Convention did representatives question whether deeper integration is what the people of Europe want, whether it serves their best interests or whether it provides the best basis for a sustainable structure for an expanding Union.[2]

If you buy a chicken, you're likely to get an egg. Likewise, if you bring together a couple of hundred eurocrats with big salaries and even bigger expense accounts, many of whom are looking to create new job opportunities for themselves within a Greater Europe, then you're likely to get a centralised, bureaucratically run EU superstate, rather than more democracy, openness and freedom. And so it came to pass.

HERE, THERE AND EVERYWHERE

Perhaps the first noticeable feature about the 2004 constitution for Europe is its length. The US Constitution of 1787 was a mere 4,600 words; the European constitution managed to stretch to over 160,000 words. This suggests that it was a little more comprehensive and far-reaching than its American predecessor. Moreover, given that the EU constitution is around 40 times longer than the US version, it is likely that EU countries' freedom to act independently will be somewhat more circumscribed than that of the states of the USA.

The constitution is marginally more readable than most EU treaties. However, anyone except an ardent europhiliac who tries to work their way through it might be unpleasantly surprised. The preamble, always an important part of any EU legislation, makes it pretty clear that the purpose of the constitution is to found a single EU superstate rather than a loose federation of countries that have agreed to trade with each other and harmonise a few rules and regulations:

> Convinced that, while remaining proud of their own national identities and history, the peoples of Europe are determined to transcend their former divisions and, united ever more closely, to forge a common destiny.

The first article of the constitution confirms the writers' belief that the vast majority of Europeans passionately support the new superstate:

> Reflecting the will of the citizens and states of Europe to build a common future, this constitution establishes the European Union, on which member states confer competences to obtain objectives they have in common.

Furthermore, Article 5 warns us that countries signing up to the constitution must subordinate their national independence and security to the higher purpose of creating the new union:

> The member states shall facilitate the achievement of the Union's tasks and refrain from any measure which could jeopardise the attainment of the Union's objectives.

The new constitution gave the EU all the main symbols of statehood, including a president, a foreign minister, a police service, a judiciary, military forces, a flag and a national anthem. It also gave the EU the competence to set out policies and produce regulations in an extraordinarily wide number of areas. The constitution confirmed that the EU had exclusive powers over all issues connected with the operation of a single market, including trade agreements, tariff levels, agriculture, industrial support, fisheries, competition policy, movement of capital and movement of people. Moreover, the constitution made it brutally clear that EU countries had forever forfeited the power to pass any of their own legislation of any kind in any of the areas where the EU had exclusive competence:

> When the constitution confers on the Union exclusive competence in a specific area, only the Union may legislate and adopt legally binding acts.

The constitution also gave the EU power over many other aspects of our lives, including tourism, culture, asylum, education, healthcare, industrial relations, workers' rights, environmental policy, social policy, humanitarian aid, youth sport, care of the elderly, human rights, consumer protection, food safety, energy, space exploration and some areas of taxation. The competence in energy could allow the EU, for example, to claim that Danish, Dutch and British offshore oil and gas reserves were a 'common resource' belonging to all EU members. The competence in asylum policy could, in the interests of what the constitution called 'solidarity' and 'burden-sharing', allow the EU to ship hundreds of thousands of illegal immigrants from countries with porous borders like eastern Europe, Italy and Spain up to northern Europe at the expense of the northern European countries. The competence in industrial relations could allow the EU to force all businesses to consult with workers before making any strategic decisions. And the competence in social policy could allow the EU to insist that all EU citizens had the right to claim social security benefits and social housing payments in any EU country they chose to visit, probably prompting a vast and unstoppable population migration of the disadvantaged, the feckless and the unemployed from the poorer to the richer countries and the bankrupting of many richer countries' social security and pensions budgets.

In many of these areas the constitution gave the EU what the eurocrats called 'shared competence' with member states. The words 'shared competence' would suggest to most normal people that the eurocrats and the member countries should work happily together as equal partners in these areas of shared competence. However, the constitution's definition of 'shared' was rather far from the normal everyday meaning:

> When the constitution confers on the Union a competence shared with member states in a specific area, the Union and the member states may legislate and adopt legally binding acts in that area. The member states shall exercise their competence to the extent that the Union has not exercised, or has decided to cease exercising, its competence.[3]

In plain language, in the areas of supposed 'shared competence' countries could manage their own affairs and pass their own laws only if the EU had specifically decided not to legislate in that area. Given the tendency of the EU to continually extend its authority wherever it can, the scope for countries to pass their own laws under shared competence would become ever more limited.

Perhaps the most worrying features of the constitution for anyone who actually believed that their country maintained any form of national independence were the powers passed to the EU to take over economic policy, employment policy, foreign policy and to increase its control over defence:

> The member states shall coordinate their economic and employment policies within arrangements as determined in Part III, which the Union shall have competence to provide . . .

> The Union shall have competence to define and implement a common foreign and security policy, including the progressive framing of a common defence policy.

Not only did the constitution remove the right of countries to have a foreign policy position, it also gave the EU the authority to present the EU's policies at the United Nations Security Council, thus preventing countries like Britain and France, both of which have a permanent seat on the Security Council, from expressing their own countries' policy positions independently:

> When the Union has defined a position on a subject which is on the United Nations Security Council agenda, those member states which sit on the Security Council shall request that the Union Minister for Foreign Affairs be asked to present the Union's position.

Linked to having a common foreign policy was the idea of an EU military force:

> Member states shall make civilian and military capabilities available to the Union for the implementation of the common security and defence policy.

This meant that in the future we might see Irish or Swedish or Danish or British soldiers dying to defend the business interests of Bulgarian politicians under the leadership of Italian officers being commanded by French generals. All in all, this was not exactly something likely to inspire many young soldiers to want to sacrifice their lives.

One of the most crucial aspects of the constitution was that it gave the EU a legal personality in international law. This meant that the EU could now sign international treaties on behalf of all member countries without those countries' parliaments having any chance to debate those treaties.

The final step to ensure that the almost unseemly rush towards the single superstate could not be derailed by any recalcitrant voters in any of the member countries was the constitution's legendary self-amending clause. This allowed the euro-elite to change the constitution to give themselves new powers at any time and in any of the areas of the EU's activities without ever again having to go through the hassle of proposing a new treaty:

> If action by the Union should prove necessary, within the framework of the policies defined in Part III, to attain one of the objectives set out in the constitution, and the consti-tution has not provided the necessary powers, the Council of Ministers, acting unanimously on a proposal from the European Commission and after obtaining the consent of the European parliament, shall adopt the appropriate measures.[4]

As for national parliaments, in the areas of exclusive EU competence they had lost the power to legislate at all, and in the areas of shared competence they could only tinker around, providing they first had permission from the EU. Moreover, national parliaments had no power to revise any existing EU legislation or regulations and had no power to block any new laws or regulations. The only freedom of action left to the elected governments so eagerly signing up to the constitution on our behalf was the power to make a recommendation to the EU Commission, providing at least one-third of the member states' parliaments agreed to back that recommendation. Yet even if a third of democratically elected parliaments made a recommendation to the EU Commission, the non-elected EU Commission was under no legal obligation to accept that recommendation – it could just ignore it. Thus the constitution would formally change the role of countries' elected parliaments from having some responsibility for the business of government to being largely toothless hot-air factories that were increasingly ignored by national civil servants and courts, which are all too busy implementing the ever-increasing tsunami of new laws and rules pouring out of Brussels.

The president of the EU Commission claimed that the constitution was aimed at improving democracy in the EU: 'The constitution reconnects Europe with both citizens and national parliaments.' He particularly stressed a new proposal that allowed citizens to suggest new legislation ideas to the Commission provided they could collect a million signatures across several member states:

> It gives citizens the right to invite the Commission to introduce proposals on appropriate issues, if they can gather one million signatures in a significant number of member states.[5]

But this was only included against the eurocrats' wishes after a major lobbying campaign by outside groups trying to protect our democratic freedoms. Moreover, in 2006 when a few conscientious MEPs did manage to collect over a million names asking for the EU to stop wasting billions by having the European parliament meet in Strasbourg for one week every month, the EU Commission just ignored this brief stirring of the democracy it claimed it was eager to promote.

The German minister for Europe was just one of the many members of the euro-elite who confirmed the arrival of the superstate that the Laeken Declaration had specifically stated should not be created: 'The EU constitution is the birth certificate of the United States of Europe.'[6] The Belgian prime minister made a similar claim: 'Those who are afraid do not appear to have grasped what is happening at the moment. We are creating a political union.'[7]

VOTERS BEGIN TO WISE UP

As several European countries prepared to vote on the 2004 Constitutional Treaty, the Belgian prime minister made clear the position of the euro-elite: 'If the answer is no, the vote will probably have to be done again, because it absolutely has to be yes.'[8] In Lithuania, Hungary, Slovenia and Italy the constitution was ratified by the countries' parliaments without asking the voters if they agreed with their leaders' massive surrender of their independence to the EU. The Spanish were the first to put the constitution to a referendum. As usual the Spanish, always eager recipients of EU cash, voted hugely in favour (76 per cent) of anything European, even though an opinion poll just before the vote found that 88 per cent of Spanish voters had no idea of the contents of the constitution. One leading Spanish politician explained: 'You don't need to read the European constitution to know that it is good.'[9]

The parliaments of Austria, Greece, Malta, Cyprus and Latvia approved the constitution without a referendum. About a month before the referendum in Luxembourg, the Luxembourg prime minister informed his country's voters: 'If it's a Yes, we will say "on we go", and if it's a No we will say "we continue".'[10] That made it pretty clear to even the dimmest of the voters just how much influence their vote would have on their government's intention to press ahead regardless. Sure enough, Luxembourg got its 'Yes' vote, though considering the vast amount of EU money that has gone to Luxembourg, the majority in favour of the constitution was surprisingly small at only 56.5 per cent.

In Belgium, Estonia, Slovakia, Germany and Finland the constitution was also ratified by the national parliaments. Bulgaria and Romania had to agree in advance to the constitution as part of their joining the EU, so there was no vote for them. Then came the 29 May 2005 French rejection and the 1 June 2005 Dutch 'No' vote. The prime minister of Luxembourg dismissed the results of the two referenda in typical euro-elite fashion:

> I really believe the French and Dutch did not vote no to the Constitutional Treaty. Unfortunately, the electorate did not realise that the Constitutional Treaty was specifically aimed at meeting their concerns and that's why we need to have a period of explanation for explaining this to citizens.[11]

The architect of the EU constitution, Valéry Giscard d'Estaing, was a bit more forthright in his dismissal of the voters' rejection of his constitution:

> The rejection of the constitution was a mistake which will have to be corrected. The constitution will have to be given a second chance . . . If the Irish and Danes can vote yes in the end, so the French can do too. It was a mistake to use the referendum process, but when you make a mistake you can correct it.[12]

And the Italian foreign minister mysteriously came to the conclusion that the 'No' votes were 'a request for more Europe not less'.

One fact that especially worried the euro-elite was that whereas only around 40 per cent of French and Dutch voters had bothered to turn out for the 2004 European parliamentary elections, around 70 per cent voted in the referenda on the constitution. This meant that our leaders could not claim that the referenda were unrepresentative. Nevertheless, following the French and Dutch rejections, all 25 EU leaders put their names to a joint declaration that claimed that 'the results do not call into question citizens' attachment to the constitution of Europe'. Moreover, the EU just went ahead anyway with taking the powers that were outlined in the rejected constitution. For example, the Commission proceeded with creating its own diplomatic service, the European External Action Service, even though it had no legal right to do so. The day after the French rejection of the constitution, the EU foreign policy representative gave a speech in which he said:

> Even if the constitution was rejected in France, I think that it is suitable to keep on working on the establishment of a European External Action Service. This service will definitely come into existence sooner or later.[13]

Some of the euro-elite were furious that the French and Dutch had disrupted their carefully laid plans. The vice-president of the European Commission, perhaps forgetting that the referenda were actually a democratic expression of popular opinion, said: 'We must not give in to blackmail.'[14] The architect of the constitution didn't seem too pleased either: 'People say "we cannot vote again". What is this joke? We have to vote again until the French see what the stakes are.'[15]

But there were some euroleaders who realised that they had probably overstepped the mark with the constitution and were more philosophical:

> Since we had to ask for confirmation from time to time, the recalcitrant peoples were told they had no choice, that it was for their own good, that all rejection or delay would be a sign of egotism, sovereignty, turning inward, hatred of others, xenophobia, even Le Penism or fascism. But it didn't work. The passengers unhooked the carriages.[16]

And others understood that there was no chance of forcing through their constitution in its current form:

> France was just ahead of all the other countries in voting No. It would happen in all member states if they have a referendum. There is a cleavage between people and governments . . . A referendum now would bring Europe into danger. There will be no treaty if we had a referendum in France, which would again be followed by a referendum in the UK.[17]

After the double rejection the euro-elite could see that with several even more eurosceptic countries about to vote, there was a serious risk of a string of 'No' votes that could irretrievably sink their beloved constitution. So our leaders decided that they would have to change their approach, and they generously offered to 'allow' the more eurosceptic countries, like Sweden, Denmark, Ireland, Poland and the UK, to postpone their referenda indefinitely, thus avoiding the risk of further humiliating 'No' votes. Then the euro-elite went back to Brussels, got out their treaty-writing software and set about transforming the constitution into the shiny new and supposedly different Lisbon Treaty, a bit like a bunch of washing powder marketers redesigning the box for the same old washing powder.

SAME DIFFERENCE

In 2007 the Lisbon Treaty was wheeled out for EU members to approve. The constitution had to be put to a referendum in ten countries because it made major changes to the constitutions of the member states. However, by calling the Lisbon Treaty just an 'amending treaty' and not a constitution, the EU needed to subject it to a referendum in only one country, Ireland, whose own constitution forced the government to allow electors a vote.

One study of the differences between the constitution and the new Lisbon Treaty found just ten changes in the original 250 proposals, meaning that the two documents were 96 per cent the same.[18] The main differences were that the structure of the constitution document had been shifted around while maintaining the same wording, and that the three main symbols of a superstate – the flag, national anthem and motto – had been taken out, although this hardly mattered as the flag and anthem already existed. The other noticeable change was that the title of EU foreign minister had been changed to 'High Representative for the Union for Foreign Affairs and Security Policy'. Yet the job description for this person remained exactly the same in the Lisbon Treaty as in the constitution. The politicians seemed to be queuing up to explain that this change in title was irrelevant: 'We were prepared to find a title other than foreign minister, but we are not prepared to change the substance of his role'; 'It's the same job – it's still going to be the same position'; 'If your name is Maria, you can call yourself Jane, but you will still do Maria's job . . . We have exactly what we wanted, the foreign minister will have the political clout necessary to do his job'; and 'As long as we more or less have a European prime minister and a European foreign minister then we can give them any title.'[19]

Although the Lisbon Treaty was presented as being less of a change to EU members' national independence than the constitution, the new treaty actually went further in reducing national independence than the rejected constitution. There are just six paragraphs in the preamble to the constitution, but 16 in the preamble to the Lisbon Treaty. The Lisbon Treaty preamble added things like 'ever closer union', 'advance European integration' and 'strengthen the convergence of their economies'. All these were clearly aimed at further creating a central superstate at the expense of the diminishing independence of member countries.

One might have thought that our leaders would at least

maintain an embarrassed silence while they tried to slip through their constitution-by-another-name before the electorate noticed what was going on. But reticence is not something the euro-elite seem particularly good at. Once more, we had an almost disorderly queue of our euroleaders keen to share their thoughts with us as they explained that the constitution and the Lisbon Treaty were very much one and the same. Here are just a few of many choice comments:

- 'The substance of the constitution is preserved. That is a fact.' German chancellor Angela Merkel[20]
- 'There's nothing from the original package that has been changed.' Astrid Thors, Finland's Europe minister[21]
- 'The substance of what was agreed in 2004 has been retained. What is gone is the term "constitution".' Dermot Ahern, Irish foreign minister[22]
- 'The good thing is . . . that all the symbolic elements are gone, and that which really matters – the core – is left.' Anders Fogh Rasmussen, Danish prime minister[23]

In this way our leaders were put in the quite extraordinary position of brazenly claiming to their electorates that there was absolutely no need for a series of referenda on the Lisbon Treaty, even though they all agreed that it was virtually identical to the rejected constitution that fundamentally shifted power from member states to the EU bureaucrats.

Not only did our leaders openly admit that the two documents were almost identical twins, but they also couldn't help what seems like boasting about how clever they had been in the way they would fool the electorate into accepting the Lisbon Treaty. The architect of the original constitution explained several times the euro-elite's ingenious new plan to get their treaty through without asking us voters:

In terms of content, the proposals remain largely unchanged, they are simply presented in a different way . . . The reason is that the new text could not look too much like the constitutional treaty.[24]

The difference between the original constitution and the present Lisbon Treaty is one of approach rather than content . . . the proposals in the original constitutional treaty are practically unchanged. They have simply been dispersed through old treaties in the form of amendments. Why this subtle change? Above all, to head off any threat of referenda by avoiding any form of constitutional vocabulary.[25]

His vice-chairman also gave the impression that the new treaty was more a sleight of hand than a real change to the rejected constitution: 'The good thing about not calling it a constitution is that no one can ask for a referendum on it.'[26] He also explained that while the constitution was intended to be reasonably clear and understandable, this had not been the intention with the Lisbon Treaty:

They decided that the document should be unreadable. If it is unreadable, it is not constitutional, that was the perception . . . Should you succeed in understanding it at first sight there might be some reason for a referendum because it would mean that there was something new.[27]

This goal of intentional unreadability was seemingly confirmed by the Belgian foreign minister:

The aim of the Constitutional Treaty was to be more readable; the aim of this treaty is to be unreadable . . . The constitution aimed to be clear, whereas this treaty had to be unclear. It is a success.[28]

Other politicians admitted that the whole exercise of transforming the constitution into the Lisbon Treaty was merely a way of avoiding any need for referenda. For example:

As for the changes now proposed to be made to the constitutional treaty, most are presentational changes that have no practical effect. They have simply been designed to enable certain heads of government to sell their people the idea of ratification by parliamentary action rather than by referendum.[29]

So by slightly reordering the rejected constitution, by making it impenetrable and by avoiding calling it a constitution, the euro-elite hoped to get it ratified and implemented without any further bothersome delays. 'Public opinion will be led to adopt, without knowing it, the proposals that we dare not present to them directly,' the constitution's architect explained and added: 'All the earlier proposals will be in the new text, but will be hidden and disguised in some way.'[30]

NOT SO GREAT BRITAIN

Eurosceptic Britain was perhaps the country where the politicians most entertainingly seemed to tie themselves up in ever more complicated knots as they tried to dance around the reality of the loss of their country's independence to Europe. When he first stood to become a Member of Parliament, Tony Blair had paraded his euroscepticism: 'We'll negotiate withdrawal from the EEC which has drained our natural resources and destroyed jobs.' However, in his 1997 election manifesto he stressed the need for Britain to be at the centre of Europe: 'Britain will be a leader in Europe.'

Shortly after being elected in 1997, the new prime minister stressed how he would let the people have their say on any further moves towards an integrated Europe: 'If there are any further steps to European integration, the people should have their say at a general election or in a referendum.' But in 2003, when the constitution was being finalised, Mr Blair seemed to have changed his mind somewhat: 'I see no case for having a referendum on the new EU constitution. We don't govern this country by referendum.'[31] Later that year, Mr Blair confirmed that there would be no referendum: 'There will not be a referendum. The reason is that the constitution does not fundamentally change the relationship between the UK and the EU.'[32]

However, by April of the following year Mr Blair was saying that there should be a referendum:

> There is no question of any constitutional treaty going through without the express consent of the British people . . . Regardless of how other members vote, we will have a referendum on the subject.[33]

In the run-up to the general election in 2005 Tony Blair's government was keen to avoid the constitution becoming a major issue in the election and didn't want to be tarred as too europhile by the Conservatives. So they repeated the prime minister's latest commitment to hold a referendum on the constitution in their election manifesto: 'The new Constitutional Treaty ensures the new Europe can work effectively . . . We will put it to the British people in a referendum.'

By 2007 Blair had gone and had handed over the thorny issue of whether to hold a referendum to his successor, Gordon Brown. Brown was adamant that his government would live up to any promises it made in its election manifesto: 'The manifesto is what we put to the public. We've got to honour that manifesto. That is an issue of trust for me with the electorate.'[34] Three months later, however, Brown seemed to have decided that there was clearly no need for a referendum as he brazenly claimed that the new Lisbon Treaty was nothing at all like the Constitutional Treaty and, according to him, made little or no difference to Britain's relationship with the EU:

> If we needed a referendum we would have one. But I think
> most people recognise that there is not a fundamental
> change taking place as a result of this amended treaty.[35]

The UK government then hastily pushed the Lisbon Treaty
through parliament, allowing just two weeks' debate in the
House of Commons, and ratified it in its entirety. Some cynics
wonder whether, faced with being pushed out of power by his
ambitious chancellor, Blair could have been looking to do a
backroom deal, seeking a new, important, remunerative job as
the new EU president. He could have achieved this by agreeing
to push through the treaty in Britain without a referendum in
return for German chancellor Angela Merkel and French
president Nicolas Sarkozy supporting his application to become
the first EU president. This would both give Blair a well-paid
new job and also conveniently make way for Gordon Brown to
make his long-coveted move into No. 10 Downing Street. All
this can only ever be speculation, however, and we will never
know why Blair and Brown both reneged on their unambiguous promises to hold a referendum on the treaty.

THE 'UNGRATEFUL' IRISH

The decision by almost all EU leaders to spare their voters the
trouble of having to vote on the Lisbon Treaty left only one tiny
micro-hurdle in the way of the full implementation of the
constitution-by-another-name – a referendum in the normally
europhile Republic of Ireland. Given that Ireland had benefited
by around €40 billion since joining the EU in 1973, it was
assumed that the referendum would be a pushover for the
euro-elite. Actually it didn't really matter which way the Irish
voted, because a few months before the referendum the
European parliament voted by a large majority of 449 to 129 to
reject Amendment 32 to a report on the Lisbon Treaty. That
amendment stated: 'The European parliament undertakes to

respect the outcome of the referendum in Ireland.'[36] So the decision had already been made, long before the Irish referendum, to ignore the result if it wasn't the one that the parliament wanted. Given this extraordinary vote in the EU parliament, one wonders why the Irish bothered to hold a referendum at all. Amazingly, our MEPs' contempt for voters' wishes wasn't reported by the main European press.

At first things looked pretty good for the euro-elite. An opinion poll in mid-May 2008 showed 35 per cent would vote 'Yes', 18 per cent 'No' and 47 per cent had not yet decided. However, a vigorous and unexpected campaign by opponents of the treaty started to turn the tables, and a poll in June suggested that opinion had swung in favour of a 'No' vote, with 30 per cent going to vote 'Yes', 35 per cent 'No' and 35 per cent undecided. The final result was that the 'No' vote won with 53.4 per cent.

As usual, the euro-elite was quick to dismiss this rejection of the constitution-by-another-name as being undemocratic, even though the Irish were the only country actually allowed to vote: 'It is not truly democratic that less than a million people can decide the fate of almost half a billion Europeans.'[37] Others seemed outraged that the Irish, having received so much cash from the EU, could be appearing to bite the hand that fed them: 'We think it is a real cheek that the country that has benefited most from the EU should do this. There is no other Europe than this treaty.'[38] French president Nicolas Sarkozy was quick to suggest the Irish should vote again: 'Les Irlandais devraient revoter.'[39]

Apparently breaking ranks, the Polish and Czech presidents both said the Lisbon Treaty was dead. However, after a bit of Franco-German arm-twisting, their position became less clear. At the time of writing, it looks very much as if 26 countries will push the treaty through their parliaments in order to leave the Irish isolated. So, as with other treaty rejections, the EU juggernaut just carries on regardless.

As for the EU flag, motto and anthem and the establishment of a 'Europe Day' on 9 May – all these symbols of a superstate had been removed from the constitution when it morphed into the Lisbon Treaty in order to avoid upsetting national sensibilities. In late 2008, however, the European parliament voted to adopt them anyway, thus furthering the creation of the single superstate in spite of the wishes of the superstate's often unwilling citizens.

As we move into 2009, the euro-elite seems undecided about what to do with the ungrateful Irish. Some seem to think that the Irish parliament should just ignore the referendum result and ratify the treaty anyway with, if absolutely necessary, a few cosmetic changes. However, others believe that Ireland should hold another referendum – they can't quite decide when this should be. There are those who would prefer that it was carried out before the June 2009 European elections so that the treaty could be done and dusted as soon as the new Commission takes office. But the majority seem to want to avoid any problems that could arise if the EU is seen to be bullying the Irish, as these might upset voters before the June 2009 EU elections. So it looks most likely that once the June elections are over, a new referendum will be held in Ireland towards the end of 2009. There are some in Brussels who want to punish Ireland by taking away the country's right to have a commissioner, cutting its farm subsidies, refusing economic assistance and even threatening to expel the country from the EU. 'We need to change minds by dramatising how serious the consequences another No vote will be for Ireland,' one official explained rather ominously, while another opined: 'The economy might be going into freefall and the Irish really did not help things. Sympathy for their difficulties is running out.'[40] One former commissioner insisted that the Irish government should resign. But others think that it's best to try to seduce the Irish back into the warm embrace of mother Europe by showing sympathetic understanding of Irish doubts and spending millions of

European taxpayers' money 'explaining' the whole issue again to the Irish so they make the correct choice next time.

The Irish vote may have been the only real expression of democracy during the whole process of ratification of the constitution-by-another-name. But the one thing that is sure is that the eurocrats will just dismiss the 2008 Irish 'No' vote as a last peevish act of ignorance from voters apparently unable to understand all the sacrifices our hard-working euroleaders are making for the benefit of their unappreciative citizens.

Chapter 6

FROM DEMOCRACY TO EUROCRACY

HOW DEMOCRACY (ALMOST) WORKS

A basic requirement for joining the EU is that member countries must be seen to have a democratic system of government. This is not to say that the democratic systems of the member states need to be anywhere near perfect. Far from it. Western democracy is a pretty blunt and clumsy instrument, and most European democracies are fairly flawed.

For example, since the collapse of communism the ideological differences between the main political parties in most European countries have rapidly decreased. This has led to a situation where politicians with their large salaries, liberal expenses and generous pensions have similar interests and are like members of an elite club, protected from and distant from the economic realities of the lives of their voters. Yet while different political parties have become closer and almost indistinguishable from each other, the gap between politicians and voters has widened.

Moreover, most national parliaments have fairly limited powers. In theory, they can pass or reject laws proposed by their governments. In reality, however, those governments have almost unlimited power because politicians from the ruling party will usually side with the government in order to further their own careers, and the occasional rebel can easily be bought off with the promise of promotion or other honours.

Furthermore, many governments manage to cling on to

power because massive corruption gives them financial resources that opposition parties cannot match. In Britain there have been suspicions that the government has been selling peerages in return for sizeable political donations, and major companies that get big public-sector contracts regularly make supposed 'loans' (which never have to be repaid) to the ruling party. In France companies getting public-sector contracts have been expected as a matter of course to funnel around 10 per cent of the contract value into the pockets of the main political parties. In Germany the ruling party was caught receiving hundreds of millions in bribes from major companies in return for favours. In Italy connections between the mafia and some politicians are so close that one former prime minister was sentenced to 27 years in jail for corruption and the alleged mafia murder of an investigative journalist, while many others have repeatedly been under investigation for corruption. And in countries like Bulgaria and Romania local investigative journalists have claimed that corruption is widespread among politicians. But in spite of these obvious weaknesses, most European democracies do manage to stumble along without social unrest, and governments do occasionally lose elections, so the semblance of a democratic process is maintained.

Clearly, all the EU member countries have slightly different political structures, and these reflect how democracy was introduced – by gradual development as in Britain, Denmark and Sweden, through revolution, as in France, by breaking free from dictatorship like the PIGS or after liberation from communism like the BEES. However, in spite of their differences, there are a number of features that are common to all democratic systems (see Figure 1). These include:

- Voters elect a political party (or parties) that will form the government.
- When people vote they know what each party's policies are.

- The elected government will be responsible for governing and passing laws.
- All laws have to be approved by the country's parliament.
- Laws are then implemented by civil servants.
- Parliament approves the country's budget.
- At the next election voters have the power to change the government.
- If a new government is elected it has the power to change laws passed by the previous administration.

Figure 1 Most countries have a fairly straightforward system of democracy

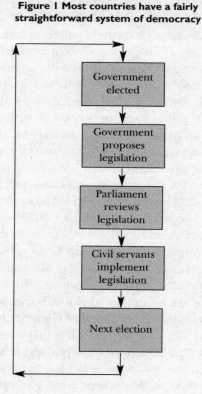

But that's not how they do things in Brussels.

Unfortunately, not one of these basic preconditions for democracy is present in the way that we are governed by the EU. In fact, the whole process of eurocracy is really quite different from what most people would call democracy. For a start, in democracy voters elect a political party (or parties in coalition governments) that will form the government. However, in eurocracy the political parties do not make up the EU government. Instead, the EU is governed by the European Commission, a group of unelected eurocrats appointed by member states. Other key differences include:

- In a democracy the elected government will be responsible for governing and passing laws. In eurocracy only the unelected EU Commission has the power to propose new legislation.
- In a democracy when people vote they know what each party's policies are. In eurocracy the European parliament has no power to propose any new laws, and so politicians standing for election cannot make any promises to the electorate about what they will do when in government, because they will never actually govern even if elected and they have no idea what laws the new Commission will propose.
- In a democracy all laws have to be approved by the country's parliament. In eurocracy the European parliament has some limited power to suggest some changes to just a few of the laws proposed by the European Commission.
- In a democracy laws introduced by the government are implemented by civil servants. In eurocracy all laws come from Brussels civil servants via the Commission. They are generally rubber-stamped with few amendments by the European parliament and most then pass straight to the member countries' civil servants for implementation,

completely by-passing national parliaments, which have almost no power to debate or change any of them. This means that EU laws are produced by unelected civil servants and not by elected politicians.

• In a democracy each country's parliament has the power to discuss and approve the country's budget. In eurocracy the European parliament has no power to debate or even look at almost half the EU's €134 billion or so budget.

The most important difference between democracy and eurocracy is probably that democracy is built on a kind of self-correcting, feedback loop. At each election voters have the power to change the government. Then, if a new government is elected, it can revise laws passed by the previous administration. But in eurocracy the voters can change just a very small number of the politicians in the European parliament, and this has virtually no effect on the make-up of the EU Commission, which actually governs the EU. Moreover in eurocracy almost every time a law is passed it becomes part of what is called the *acquis communautaire* (a body of laws with which all member states must comply), and it is virtually impossible to change it.

Most commentators on the EU have identified the absence of democracy in an institution that claims to promote democracy, and they call this the EU's 'democratic deficit'. Some have even said that if the EU applied to join itself, its rules requiring democratic processes would prevent it from joining.

HOW EUROCRACY WORKS

Eurocracy is so different from most people's views of parliamentary democracy that it is perhaps worth spending just a little time outlining how this unique, new political system actually works. Vastly simplifying what is a complex and rather impenetrable process, eurocracy could be described as follows (see Figure 2).

Figure 2 In eurocracy, voters have little influence on legislation

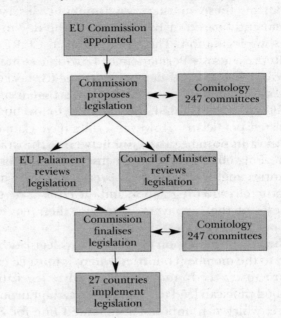

Only the European Commission is allowed to propose new legislation. The 27 members of the EU Commission are appointed by member countries, and they never have to face voters to explain what policies they intend to pursue, even though they are among the most powerful people in Europe. The European Commission, backed up by its 247 committees, proposes new legislation and regulations. Some of these then pass to two main bodies for approval – the Council of Ministers and the European parliament. These two bodies can propose amendments, although the Commission is only required to consider these amendments. It is not forced to adopt them.

The Council of Ministers can be viewed as two connected entities. There are regular meetings of EU member countries' ministers for areas like agriculture, trade, environment and so on to decide on the general direction of EU policy-making. Supporting these ministers is a group of civil servants who are permanently based in Brussels to do the day-to-day work of reviewing legislation. This group is called COREPER (Comité des Représentants Permanents). Europhiles often argue that this group brings some democracy to the EU because these civil servants are appointed by elected government ministers from the EU states and should, therefore, be following the direction of elected politicians. However, critics have claimed that these civil servants soon become assimilated into the welcoming arms of the euro-elite and tend to justify their existence by the quantities of legislation they produce, rather than actively working to restrict regulation and the costs of regulation in the interests of the taxpayers, who pay their enviable salaries, pensions and expenses.

When the Commission finalises its new legislation it is handed down to the member countries, where it must be implemented. Failure to correctly implement any EU legislation within a specified time can lead to a complaint to the European Court of Justice, which can impose an unlimited fine for each day that the new legislation remains unimplemented.

Critics of eurocracy have often expressed concerns about the poor quality of some of the people who reach positions of power. The unelected commissioners, for example, are not always appointed because of their exceptional political or administrative talents. Some are despatched to Brussels to get them out of national politics, either because they are an irritant to their national governments or because they have been involved in so many national scandals that they are unemployable at home. Others are political has-beens, sent to a lucrative sinecure in Brussels as a reward for years of unquestioning service to their political masters back home. The president of the European Commission, arguably the most powerful person in Europe, has never had to face the electorate to get the top job. Instead, EU presidents are chosen behind closed doors by a process of secretive and often undignified haggling by national leaders. The result is that the person appointed is often a compromise candidate – never a good sign if outstanding leadership is being sought. When assessing the Commission's handling of the 2008 financial crisis, a former German foreign minister made clear his opinion that the process of choosing a president may not always give the best candidate. He described the Commission as: 'Weak right now, with an even weaker president who, as a reward for his weakness, is about to get another five-year term in office.'[1]

One EU textbook reviewed the work of the last 11 EU Commission presidents and concluded that eight had been weak and only three strong. Some were also criticised for being 'lacklustre', 'long-winded', 'prone to blunders' and 'incomprehensible in any language'.[2] Another concern about EU presidents and commissioners is that several have gone on, or tried to go on, to leading political roles in their home countries. Raymond Barre became French prime minister and stood for the presidency, and Romano Prodi likewise became Italian premier after his time in the Commission. Critics have therefore wondered to what extent they were motivated to work in the best interests of Europe or whether they tended to use their EU presidency to boost their chances of being elected back home after their lucrative EU appointment was over.[3] Insiders say that one of the most entertaining periods in the EU occurred during the six months when Romano Prodi was president of the Commission and his Italian rival, Silvio Berlusconi, was the rotating head of the Council of Ministers. The two men later went on to fight against each other in two Italian elections. However, they both seemed to use much of their time in the EU to practise tripping each other up, rather than attending to EU business. This was a highly unproductive use of EU time and money, but hilarious for the rest of the euro-elite as they observed the squabbling and other antics of these individuals.

A POLITICAL JOKE?

Theoretically the European parliament is the main representative of democracy in the EU because it is the only part of the
EU that is actually elected by ordinary voters. Yet although the
EEC started with the Treaty of Rome in 1957, it wasn't until
1979, over 20 years later, that the first European parliament was
elected. By this time the EU bureaucrats had managed to
produce much of their 100,000 pages of regulations and laws
without any proper scrutiny by elected politicians. So rather
than being a form of elected government, the European
parliament is more like an assembly that has been clumsily stuck
on as something of an afterthought to a massive, already
functioning legislative machine in order to give the impression
of democratic legitimacy. This has meant that the bureaucracy
has maintained most of its power and that the parliament's
authority, although gradually increasing, is limited. The
European parliament cannot, for example, propose legislation –
that is the exclusive right of the Commission assisted by its many
committees. The parliament can only make proposals to amend
legislation, but even here the parliament is excluded from areas
like trade with non-EU countries, foreign affairs and defence.
However, the fact that the parliament is excluded from any
discussion of trade policy and any influence over it did not
prevent 30 MEPs deciding that they needed to go on a luxury,
taxpayer-funded trip to Hong Kong in order to 'monitor progress' in the Doha trade talks.

Moreover, the parliament has only limited power to examine
the EU's budget. The budget is split into what are called
'compulsory' and 'non-compulsory' expenditure. The European
parliament has the authority to look at the 'non-compulsory'
part of EU expenditure only. In order to protect payments to
their farmers, the French managed to get all agricultural
payments classed as 'compulsory' expenditure, and all spending
connected with international treaties is also considered as

'compulsory'. This means that almost half the EU's budget manages to escape the possibly prying eyes of the only elected politicians in the EU.

The parliament also has the right to be consulted on appointments to the Commission and to veto the nomination of the Commission president, and, in extreme circumstances, it can theoretically force the Commission to resign. However, the parliament has been largely ineffective in using these powers. Internal squabbling among the political groupings meant that the parliament wasn't even able to force the discredited Santer Commission to quit in 1999. It was only after a critical independent report released its findings that the Santer Commission eventually resigned. Moreover, the parliament cannot censure individual commissioners. Thus the incompetent, venal and self-serving can hide behind their colleagues and so escape any well-deserved criticism or sanctions.

In spite of all these limits to its power, the parliament appears to feel that it is doing a vitally important job: 'As the only elected institution of the European Union, parliament takes very seriously its role as a guardian of liberties and democracy, both in Europe and throughout the world.'[4] The parliament claims that 'the MEPs' task is primarily to represent citizens at European level and pass on their views to EU leaders and the institutions of the Union'. Unfortunately, like most EU institutions, the parliament has hardly done much to endear itself to its electors. Even academic textbooks cannot help but admit that 'arguably still a minority [of MEPs] take their work seriously'.[5]

Most Europeans probably have little idea of who their MEPs are, what they actually do and whether they have even bothered to turn up to any of the parliamentary sessions at which there have been votes on key pieces of legislation. For some debates less than 10 per cent of MEPs actually attend parliament even though many times more than that will have turned up in the morning in order to sign on to get their €287 daily attendance allowance before going off to do other, more important things.

Moreover, most European voters have probably never heard of the political groupings in the European parliament, such as the European People's Party, the European Democrats, the Party of European Socialists and the Alliance of Liberals and Democrats for Europe. Nor do most voters know what each of these groups stands for, even though these groupings between them make up almost 80 per cent of the members of the parliament. At the 2004 EU elections only around 45 per cent of voters bothered voting, in spite of some countries having compulsory voting. In France 43 per cent of people voted, and in Holland it was just 39 per cent. So, many MEPs will probably have been elected by less than 20 per cent of their constituents, hardly making them representatives of the majority of their citizens.

THUMBS UP FOR THE PARLIAMENT

It is in the daily workings of the parliament that its dubious democratic credentials are most clearly demonstrated. The majority of the work involving discussing new laws produced by the Commission is done in meetings of the parliament's 20 standing committees. This is where debates are held and where you hear the nitty-gritty of what the European parliament actually does for a living. All MEPs have to be a member of at least one standing committee, but only a few MEPs ever actually bother to attend the committee meetings. Most of these meetings are highly technical and might be about the finer points of financing projects to carry goods by water along the canals of Europe or progress of the Lamfalussy plan, a much delayed piece of financial regulation. Every four weeks there is a plenary session in Strasbourg at which all the amendments to Commission laws proposed by the MEPs' committees are put to the vote. With 785 MEPs it's impossible to hold a proper debate in the main meeting chamber. When MEPs do want to air their views to all their colleagues, they have to apply in advance to parliamentary officials to get an agreed speaking spot, and they are usually restricted to one minute to present their opinions. So most contributions consist of reading short, pre-prepared statements, and there is little to no real discussion. This is deemed to have been carried out in the committees. When MEPs do get the chance to speak, it is usually to an almost empty chamber because most of their colleagues will have retired to the coffee lounges to relax before the next vote. Unlike the British parliament where the two main political parties face each other in adversarial style, the European parliament is organised on continental lines with seating arranged for the 785 MEPs in a semicircular amphitheatre called the Hemicircle. MEPs do not sit in national blocks, but in EU-wide political groups. Everyone faces into a focal point at the centre of what would be the circle where the chairman and other key personalities sit.

Voting at the plenary sessions tends to occur on Tuesdays, Wednesdays and Thursdays and starts at around midday. Normal speed is around two votes a minute. An amendment is proposed, MEPs register their votes by pushing a 'For' or 'Against' button, and the results are displayed on electronic boards placed high up in the chamber. Then the next amend-ent follows, there's a quick vote and so on. One amendment might be something to do with an international agreement on the importation of tropical hardwood; the next one on accidents at sea; then perhaps on a common approach to the use of the spectrum released by the digital switchover.

With so many widely varied and often highly technical subjects to vote on and with votes following each other at such speed, it can be easy for MEPs, who between them speak over 20 different languages, to become confused about exactly which amendment is being decided. However, help is at hand. All the MEPs have to do is watch the thumbs of the leaders of the party to which they belong. The party leaders sit in the front row, in the right-hand seat of the party block of seats. If the thumb turns up, you vote in favour. If the thumb points down, then you vote against. Even a child could follow. So if MEPs' minds are concentrated on golf, planning new furniture for their living rooms, working out how much profit they're making on their expenses, their next encounter with the lovely young ladies of Strasbourg or whatever, all they have to do is watch their leaders' thumbs in order to fulfil their well-rewarded democratic duties. The statute defining MEPs' rights and duties clearly states: 'Members shall vote on an individual basis. They shall not be bound by any instruction and shall not receive a binding mandate.'[6] A cynic might think that our parliamentarians obediently and unquestioningly following the directions of someone sticking their thumb either up or down hardly looks like voting 'on an individual basis'.

From time to time the voting is interrupted to allow a visiting dignitary – a senior religious leader or the head of a minor state, for example – to address the parliament. At least three-quarters of the MEPs immediately file out and head once again for the coffee lounges. They return to the chamber only when told that voting is about to resume. Unfortunately, many visiting speakers get carried away with all the fine and noble sentiments they wish to express to the mostly deserted chamber and over-run the time allocated for their pitch to the parliament. Moreover, having the votes at midday, just before lunch, puts pressure on MEPs who are starting to feel a bit peckish. Fortunately, the parliament has an accelerated voting procedure to ensure that MEPs don't miss their meals. Using this, MEPs can manage to reach the dizzying speed of at least three votes a minute. Everything is very well organised. The European parliamentary authorities appear proud of how efficiently their machine works: 'For the work to proceed smoothly there needs to be good organisation and administrative support. The machinery runs well, everyone knows their role and nothing is left to chance.'[7] Efficient the whole voting process may be, but it might not fully correspond with what most of us would call democracy.

Often on Thursday afternoons there's a session to discuss

human rights in some politically impoverished, undemocratic Third World country or other, and then MEPs pass a resolution or two condemning the country in question's government. But as most of our parliamentarians have already headed off home, this is probably not worth mentioning.

Chapter 7

GETTING CONTROL

WHAT DO OUR GOVERNMENTS ACTUALLY DO NOW?

The EU usually produces well over 2,000 new laws every year, and these cover almost every area of our lives. For example, in one 12-month period the EU passed 2,156 laws on subjects ranging from trivial matters – windscreen wipers for agricultural and forestry vehicles, milk deliveries, the marketing of headed cabbages, the characteristics of olive oil, the treatment of pregnant animals, the use of alien species in aquaculture, plane steps, the training of air-conditioning personnel and the storage of pig meat – to major issues such as taxation, immigration, political parties, environmental protection, terrorism and labour market regulations.

Everything to do with agriculture, fisheries and trade has long been under complete EU control (see Figure 1). The EU is close to establishing full control over areas like economic, environmental and energy policy and asylum and immigration. Moreover, judgements made by EU courts have supremacy over member states' laws so that countries' national legal systems take greater direction from the EU than from their own governments (see Chapter 4, The Takeover). The next series of targets for an EU takeover include policing, defence, human rights, transport, the media (including the internet) and foreign policy. In fact, the EU has expanded its power so successfully that there are actually very few things that can still be decided by national parliaments or local councils. The only areas that are still mainly under member countries' jurisdiction are health, tax, education, sport and social policies, but even here Brussels is beginning to issue directives and regulations that limit the scope of national authorities to pursue their own plans.

Figure I The EU is constantly increasing its control over our lives

1. In full control	2. Almost done	3. Half-way there	4. Last to go

Agriculture
Fisheries
Trade
	Asylum/
	  immigration
	Economic
	  policy
	Energy
	Environment
	Legal/courts
		Defence
		Employment
		Foreign policy
		Human rights
		Media/Internet
		Policing
		Transport
			Education
			Family policy
			Health
			Research &
			development
			Sport
			Tax
			Tourism

There are over 100,000 pages of EU regulations and directives, plus probably several million more pages of recommendations, proposals, white papers, green papers, communications and framework decisions. All of these greatly expand the EU's powers, and all correspondingly reduce member states' freedom to make their own policies and laws. Given that there's too much material to cover, here we'll just focus on some of the main new developments in the last 18 months or so. This will give a feeling of the extent to which the EU is trying to control every aspect of our lives. It will also show how, in its obsessive attempts to seize power from national governments, the Commission is finding ever more dubious justifications to take control of policy areas that are well outside its legal areas of action (its competences) and way beyond its managerial capabilities.

IN FULL CONTROL – NO GOING BACK

When it comes to agriculture, fisheries and trade with non-EU countries, EU member states have completely surrendered their rights to make their own decisions. Each year the EU produces a flood of new regulations in these areas, all of which have to be implemented in member countries. Failure by a member to implement any of these regulations can lead to almost unlimited fines for the country in question. Moreover, a breach of any of these regulations by EU citizens will usually be considered a criminal offence by the courts.

Even when member countries see EU policies in these areas that are wasteful, absurd or morally wrong there is absolutely nothing they can do but obey commands from Brussels. For example, we now know that around €36 billion of the EU's €43 billion agriculture budget goes into the pockets of the wealthiest farmers, major landowners, large agri-businesses and fraudsters (see Chapter 12, The Most Stupid Policy in Human History?). None of these recipients actually needs this money, although they are all certainly very glad to get it. If we had any national politicians with courage and integrity they would surely want to take action against this obscene waste and mismanagement. However, national governments have completely given away their ability to change any aspects of agricultural policy, even though they all know that our money is being hijacked by powerful self-interest groups, which have cleverly diverted agricultural support away from its original purpose in order to enrich themselves.

A similar situation exists with fisheries. While northern European countries tend actively to police the activities of their own fishing fleets, the PIGS (Portugal, Italy, Greece and Spain) and France take up to twice their allotted quotas without their ever-somnolent fisheries inspection departments apparently noticing (see Chapter 13, Destroying the Environment). Now that the PIGS have practically turned the Mediterranean into a

European version of the Dead Sea, the PIGS and France need new fishing grounds to plunder and destroy. Given their collective power in EU decision-making, the PIGS have been granted free rein to empty much of the sea around Britain. Moreover, many millions of euros of our money have been thrust into the coffers of African kleptocrats to allow the PIGS to decimate fish stocks around the African coast, impoverishing thousands of already poor African fishermen in the process. All the member states' governments know that what is going on is both a perversion of the original intentions of the EU's fishing policy and morally, environmentally and economically wrong. Yet none could do anything to stop this, even if they wanted to, because although individual countries can negotiate their annual fishing catches, they are virtually powerless when it comes to deciding how fisheries policies are implemented.

ALMOST DONE – SOON UNDER CONTROL

Saving the world

In environmental protection and energy management the Commission has massively extended its control. There is no specific part of the Treaty of Rome that authorises the Commission to take over the areas of environment and energy, and for the first few decades of the EU the Commission's actions here were fairly limited. However, the prominence given by politicians to the threat of global warming has allowed the Commission to make a huge power-grab. Under the most recent climate change agreements the EU has effectively taken control of Europe's environmental policy. The EU now dictates how much of member states' energy must come from renewable sources, how much CO_2 each country's major industries can produce and how much biofuel each country should use. For countries like France, which has a large nuclear industry and the possibility to sell their expertise to other countries, the EU targets will result in an almost unimaginable gold rush. For poorer countries such as Poland, which rely heavily on coal for power, the targets could be an economic disaster. At the time of writing, some countries are trying to resist French pressure to get a deal signed. If an agreement is reached it will open the door to a flood of new EU environmental legislation, which member states will have to implement, regardless of the economic consequences.

The Commission seems particularly worried about the potential for water shortages and drought as a consequence of climate change. Our leaders appear to think that we, its citizens, waste too much water. The Greek EU environment commissioner explained: '44 per cent of water is wasted in the Mediterranean and 40 per cent in the rest of Europe'.[1] We are so profligate with water because, among other things, we apparently don't pay enough for it: 'Inadequate water pricing, inconsistent land use planning and bad water allocation automatically lead to overuse.' Naturally, the Commission is planning to do something about this: 'Applying efficient pricing policies, making water-saving a priority and improving efficiency in all sectors are already essential elements of the EU's approach.'[2] The commissioner has said that he wants to 'move the EU towards a water-efficient and water-saving economy'. Under a strengthening of the EU's Water Framework Directive we can all soon expect to pay considerably more for our water:

> Economic instruments and the user pays principle should be applied across all sectors, including households, transport, energy, agriculture and tourism. This will provide strong incentives to reduce water consumption and increase efficiency of use.[3]

This probably makes a lot of sense for drought-stricken southern Europe, where the commissioner comes from, but in rain-drenched, regularly flooded northern European countries, paying even more for something that's falling out of the skies in excessive quantities may seem somewhat counter-intuitive. While we probably all agree that we should waste less water, some people might think that it is not appropriate for the EU to try to apply the same rules to all countries regardless of climate. Moreover, it would not be unreasonable to question whether it really is the job of Commission bureaucrats to dictate how much water we should use and how much we should pay for it.

Another Commission idea to save the world from climate change is to force car manufacturers to comply with new CO_2 emissions targets by imposing a penalty on any manufacturer that fails to meet Commission targets. To put pressure on manufacturers, the Commission plans that this penalty 'should increase over time'. Rather than having individual countries collect this premium, the Commission suggests: 'manufacturers' compliance with the targets under this regulation should be assessed at the Community level'. The Commission justifiably argues that giving it control would help stop countries cheating to protect their auto industries, but it also intends to keep any money raised for itself: 'The amount of the excess emissions premium should be considered as revenue for the budget of the European Union.'[4] Most of us would be sympathetic to the policy of building cleaner cars, but we might be less enthusiastic about the way the Commission wants to turn environmental legislation into a way of increasing its own bureaucratic budget.

Managing the borders

As with environmental and energy policy, the Commission has no explicit remit from the Treaty of Rome to manage EU asylum policy. This was gradually added in later treaties. In order to extend its authority, therefore, it had to find a reason why asylum and immigration should be managed by the Commission rather than by member countries. So the Commission claimed that creating a Common European Asylum System (CEAS) should be under Commission control on the slightly questionable grounds that a CEAS would be based 'on the common values shared by all member states'.[5] This assertion of 'common values' is a useful catch-all the Commission tends to use when it can find nothing in any of the treaties to justify its interference in an area that is outside its agreed competences.

The EU has already passed at least ten pieces of legislation to introduce a uniform way of managing asylum-seekers. According to the EU, this is aimed at 'increasing efficiency, protection, solidarity and facilitating integration'. In practice, it means that the EU, rather than individual governments, will decide the criteria for people being granted asylum and the processes for granting asylum. The EU will also have the power to amend these criteria as it sees fit.

The EU Commission will also be introducing a new Blue Card system for economic migrants who wish to move to the EU. After they get their Blue Cards they will probably be free to work in any EU country of their choice. This will be a wonderful present for Bulgarian and Romanian people-smugglers. From now on all they will need to do is bribe officials in their own countries to hand out blue cards to immigrants with enough money, and those immigrants can then legally go anywhere in Europe. In late 2008 the Commission managed to get European leaders to agree to a 'European pact on immigration and asylum', which by 2012 will effectively remove individual countries' power to dictate their own policies. Given that some parts of Europe, such as the Netherlands and England, already have quite high population density, this loss of control over how many people can settle in their countries is not very reassuring to citizens already worried about the environmental and social problems resulting from overcrowding.

Running the economy

At the time of writing 16 of the EU's 27 members use the euro. This means that their overall economic policies concerning matters such as budget deficits, interest rates and borrowing levels are decided by the EU. Naturally, when smaller countries break EU economic targets they are forced to take action. However, when Germany and France break the rules, the rules are relaxed, changed or just ignored. Over the next few years nine more countries have committed to join the eurozone, making their national economic policy-making rather redundant. That just leaves Denmark which will probably also vote to join, and Britain which is likely to retain its own currency.

While he held the post of EU president in late 2008, French president Sarkozy proposed a further economic power-grab by suggesting that the EU should set up its own 'sovereign wealth fund' with our money. This was intended to be part of a 'united European response' to the global economic downturn and was aimed at buying stakes in European companies while their shares were at a low price in order to prevent non-European money taking over our companies. In a speech to the European parliament, Sarkozy said: 'I don't want European citizens to wake up in several months time and find that European companies belong to non-European capital, which bought at the share price's lowest point'. However, suspecting that this was yet another French attempt to channel European taxpayers' billions into failing French companies, the idea was thankfully shot to pieces by other European leaders. On this occasion Sarkozy's attempted power-grab was too blatant to be accepted. But the Lisbon Treaty requires that: 'The member states shall coordinate their economic policies within the Union'. So using the Lisbon Treaty as a justification, the Commission will soon find many good reasons why a 'common European response' to economic issues is better than individual countries acting alone – and a 'common European response' always means more power to often unqualified bureaucrats in Brussels to dictate one-size-fits-all economic policies for 27 countries, most at very different stages in their development and most with quite different economic structures.

HALFWAY THERE – PLANS TO TAKE OVER

Here comes the euro-army

The EU has already gone a long way towards building its own military planning and operational capabilities. Under the European Common Security and Defence Policy (CSDP) the EU has conducted around 20 missions since 2003, the largest being the deployment of 7,000 peace-keeping troops to Bosnia. In 2005 the EU established its own military planning unit, the European Union Military Staff (EUMS), which is separate from NATO. The list of EUMS's roles and tasks covers over three pages, and it has all the functions of a full military management structure – intelligence-gathering, planning, operations, logistics, training and so on.

Also in 2005 France, Italy, the Netherlands, Portugal and Spain established a European gendarmerie force that could deploy over 2,000 military policemen to any international crisis. The Lisbon Treaty further advanced the creation of an EU military force by greatly extending the areas covered by the CSDP to include an armaments clause under which 'the member states shall undertake progressively to improve their military capabilities'; a huge extension of the range of operations that could be carried out by a European military; a 'permanent structured cooperation' clause, which provides a legal basis for joint EU battle groups under EU command; and a commitment to mutual defence whereby: 'if a member state is a victim of armed aggression on its territory, the other member states shall have towards it an obligation of aid and assistance by all means in their power'. There are six so-called non-aligned EU countries (Austria, Cyprus, Finland, Ireland, Malta and Sweden). When the Lisbon Treaty is eventually fully ratified these countries will find that their neutrality is considerably reduced.

One of the clearest and least commendable reasons for the move towards militarisation in the EU is the obsession of

the French and their ever-obedient supporters, the PIGS, to try
to set up a rival military power to the US and to have the EU
usurp the role of NATO.

Europhiles will no doubt view greater EU military integration
as a benefit because it further reduces the independence of
member countries and makes another European military
conflict impossible. But sceptics might be tempted to look at
some of the EU's recent military adventures and worry that the
EU will just create a uniformed bureaucracy rather than an
effective fighting force. In Afghanistan, while US, Canadian,
Danish and British forces bear the brunt of the fighting, the
rules of engagement imposed by the French and German
governments prevent their forces providing effective support
to their allies. The Germans, for example, don't allow their
planes and helicopters to fly when it is starting to get dark, even
when British troops fighting the Taliban desperately need their
support. In addition, a report published in 2008 by the
Bundeswehr found that German troops in Afghanistan were
too unfit to fight. The parliamentary commissioner for the
German armed forces explained, 'Plainly put, the soldiers are
too fat, exercise too little and take little care of their diet.'[6] The
quality of French soldiering was put in question in an incident
in France in 2008 when French paratroopers shot 17 of their
own citizens, 15 of them innocent civilians, including five
children, while demonstrating a hostage liberation exercise,
because they had mistakenly loaded live rounds rather than
blanks.

Euro-police and euro-justice

One sensitive area where the Commission has expanded its
powers is in policing and criminal justice. We now have Europol
(the European Police Office), which is meant to facilitate
cooperation in order to combat serious international crime. In
2000 the European Police College (CEPOL) was established to

train senior police officers, and at least 2,500 officers have now attended its courses. Then in 2002 we were given Eurojust, which should coordinate actions between member countries' prosecution services. At first we were told that these bodies would deal only with matters like terrorism, drugs trafficking and other 'serious crime with a cross-border dimension'.[7] But since then the Commission has been trying to expand the power and scope of its policing and prosecution powers. It has decided to add offences such as xenophobia, employing illegal immigrants and breaching intellectual property rights to the list of offences for which the Commission could recommend punishments and request arrests and prosecutions.

In 2004 the Commission introduced a European Arrest Warrant (EAW), making it easier to speed up extradition for serious crimes. The Commission has also given its own officials powers to access information from police data bases throughout the EU and is pressuring police forces to share information. A report from a Commission working group describes the chilling extent of proposed EU surveillance of its citizens as the EU makes increased use of what the Commission group called the 'tsunami of data' available to law enforcement agencies:

> Every object the individual uses, every transaction they make and almost everywhere they go will create a detailed digital record. This will generate a wealth of information for public security organisations, and create huge opportunities for more effective and productive public security efforts.[8]

The Commission made a breathtaking but little-reported power-grab in 2005 when it used a ruling from the European Court of Justice on an environmental case to claim that in the future the Commission could create a criminal offence for any breach of any EU regulation by any EU citizen in any EU country:

> The basis on which the Community legislature may provide for measures of criminal law is the necessity to ensure that Community rules and regulations are complied with.[9]

This gave the Commission extraordinary new powers and made EU citizens potential criminals if they breached any of the tens of thousands of pages of EU regulations. Often the punishments for breaking EU regulations are greater than those for what most of us would consider 'real crimes' like theft and assault. To enforce this power-grab the Commission is also pushing to strengthen Eurojust by turning it from a coordinating body to a fully functioning European prosecution service with authority over individual countries' prosecution services. This would then give Eurojust the power to prosecute alleged criminals itself or to instruct national prosecution services to take action, considerably reducing the independence of each country's judiciary.

The latest – and possibly most worrying – move from the Commission is to strengthen the EAW, allowing people to be extradited following trials *in absentia*. A possible scenario could be as follows. A German, Dutch or British family decide to buy a flat in a development in a ski resort in Bulgaria and pay a deposit to secure the flat. Just before completion, the developer asks for a full payment. The father of the family goes to Bulgaria to check that everything is as promised but finds that the building is far from finished, the workmanship is shoddy, water pipes are leaking, ski lifts that had been planned have not been built and so on. He refuses to pay and asks for the family's deposit back, but the developer demands the rest of the money. A stalemate is reached. Six months later the police arrive and arrest the father to extradite him to Bulgaria. He discovers that he has been accused of rape and sentenced to 15 years in prison. He also finds out that his lawyer (whom he did not know existed) has appealed and had the sentence reduced to ten years, but that the prosecutor appealed and the sentence was put back to 15 years. He then finds out that as he has used up his right of appeal, he is now being extradited to serve the sentence for his heinous crime.

This may seem far-fetched, but it is based on a real case. In 2004 a British man gave some money to a beggar in Romania. Soon after he was arrested for alleged sexual assault. After three months of delays, during which the supposed victim never appeared to give evidence, the British man was released without trial and expelled from the country. About three years later, after Romania had joined the EU, the man found out that he had been tried *in absentia* and sentenced to seven years imprisonment, but that the sentence was reduced to four years on appeal but reinstated to seven years at a final hearing. He had known nothing about this, because the papers from Romania had been sent to the wrong address (if they were ever sent at all), even though the courts had his correct address. Moreover, he had, of course, never met the lawyer who had apparently been 'defending' him and running his 'appeal'. Eventually he was extradited on an EAW back to Romania. Fortunately for him, a charity called Fair Trials International took up his case and he was eventually freed. In 2007 a report by Transparency International, a group that monitors levels of corruption across the world, noted that in Romania's justice system: 'Corruption and lack of transparency in relations between court users and court personnel are also systemic.'

Similar cases of corrupt police and judiciaries are also common in Greece, Portugal, Italy, Latvia and several other EU countries. It's easy for bureaucrats in Brussels to pass ever more laws and regulations governing our lives without bothering about the practical implications, but it's ordinary EU citizens who have to pay the price when things go wrong – as they inevitably will.

Other bits and pieces

When it was introducing proposals to extend its control over road safety and transport, the Commission actually admitted that it did not have the legal competence to act: 'The proposal does not fall under the exclusive competence of the Community.'[10] However, by claiming that Commission action will be more effective than action by individual countries, the Commission allows itself to interfere in any area it wishes: 'Community actions will better achieve the objectives of the proposal.' Completely ignoring the fact that most road-users in any EU country will come from that country rather than other EU members, the Commission maintains that 'the trans-European road network needs common and high safety standards throughout the European Union'. So, over the next few years we will see the Commission introducing a whole series of actions and standards that will take responsibility for traffic safety management away from individual countries.

Moreover, the Commission has found that 'throughout Europe, increased traffic in town and city centres has resulted in chronic congestion with the many adverse consequences this entails in terms of delays and pollution'.[11] The Commission has calculated that €100 billion are lost every year due to congestion and has decided that it needs to intervene. Again, it has no legal right to meddle with an area that should be left to city councils, so, as usual, the Commission uses the familiar excuse that 'local authorities cannot face all these issues on their own; there is a need for cooperation and coordination at European level' in order to take responsibility for dealing with the problem away from local councils and even away from national governments. The Commission has proposed 25 areas where it believes it could become involved, including the introduction of congestion charges, increased parking fees, planning restrictions, tougher traffic management and putting into place 'an appropriate EU legal framework' to force European cities to provide 'European urban mobility that lives up to people's expectations'.[12]

When it comes to railways the Commission is planning a similar power-grab. The Commission is worried that too much freight is being transported by road rather than by the more environmentally friendly railways, so it is proposing that it should assume the authority for creating 'a rail network giving priority to freight'. As it yet again doesn't have the legal basis to legislate on this issue, the Commission is using the excuse of helping the environment to give it the power to act. Agreeing to the Commission's proposals would give Commission bureaucrats, rather than individual countries, the task of deciding the overall strategy for Europe's railways. The Commission claims that 'allowing the players in the sector and the member states to act without any new Community input' would be 'inadequate', and it has therefore decided that the Commission should launch 'a specific programme leading to a European freight-dedicated network'. This would allow the Commission to decide the overall shape of Europe's rail network, which tracks should be prioritised for freight rather than passengers and where countries should build new capacity to remove bottlenecks. Implementing the Commission's proposals would thus severely restrict individual countries' freedom to decide their own railway transport policies.

The Commission has also been interested in increasing its influence in media and electronic communications. For example, from 2009 an EU directive compels all internet service providers (ISPs) to store records of all internet usage by everyone in Europe for at least two years. One of the Commission's latest ideas is to create a new regulator for electronic communications, the European Electronic Communications Market Authority. This would give the Commission the power to regulate radio, internet and mobile phones. As the legal basis for this new EU regulator, the Commission claims that it would 'improve the functioning of the internal market in electronic communications'. The new regulator would influence matters such as network and information security, the allocation of frequencies, numbering systems, standards, competition, price controls and even measures taken 'to better meet the needs of disabled or elderly citizens'.[13]

LAST TO GO – PICKING OFF THE SURVIVORS

Unhealthy control?

In many of the areas where the Commission has so far not fully extended its authority, it openly admits that member states have responsibility. But all too often it goes on to give its reasons why the Commission should become involved in what member countries do. In health, for example, the Commission confirms that 'member states have the main responsibility for health policy and provision of healthcare to European citizens'.[14] However, by claiming that citizens' health is important to areas where the Commission has authority – the effective functioning of the internal market, consumer protection and environmental policy – the Commission maintains without any evidence that 'work on health at Community level adds value to member states' actions'. So it now plans to define a Statement on Fundamental Health Values to which all member countries' health services must adhere. The Commission will also start gathering information on the health of EU citizens by setting up a 'system of European community health indicators with common mechanisms for collection of comparable data at all levels'.[15] Using this statement of values and the measurements of our health, the Commission proposes to start legislating in areas such as reducing inequalities in health; the promotion of health literacy programmes for different age groups; measures 'to promote the health of older people and the workforce and actions on children's and young people's health'; developing guidelines on cancer screening; developing organ donation and transplantation; and establishing a 'Community framework for safe, high quality and efficient health services'. All these actions may be laudable. They may even encourage some countries to make real improvements in the healthcare they provide. However, they mean that within a few years our health services will be controlled more by Commission dictate than by our countries' elected national governments. It is not obvious that most countries' citizens anticipated being cared for by a Commission-run health service when they originally voted to join the EU.

The eurotaxman is coming

We can see the same picture emerging in taxation. The EU accepts that taxation is an area that should be left to the individual member states: 'Taxation is central to national sovereignty, for without revenue governments cannot conduct policy.'[16] However, the Commission also thinks that 'as European integration progresses . . . the complex interactions between tax systems need to be analysed and perhaps managed'.[17] So the Commission sees a need for what it calls 'tax coordination' in order to avoid 'tax competition between member states', and it appears worried that this has not been moving fast enough: 'Progress on the harmonisation and coordination of taxation has been fairly slow.' Strangely, when explaining why it needs to get involved in running the internal market, the Commission extols the benefits of competition for its citizens: 'Consumers now enjoy lower prices and a diversified choice of services as utilities like telecoms, electricity and gas have been forced to compete for customers.'[18]

Tax competition can actually be good for EU citizens, as it exposes those countries with high taxes and expensive, inefficient public services to competition from countries that can run their affairs more effectively. However, now that it wants to get control of taxation, the Commission has decided that competition is bad and so wants to make sure that 'some member states' tax policies do not have an undesirable impact on others'. So, taxation has subtly moved from being an area under the control of individual countries to a subject that should be dictated by the Commission because it believes that: 'Differences in national tax law remain a serious obstacle to the completion of the single market.'[19]

In the next few years, under the guise of ensuring the effective functioning of the single market, we can expect further Commission interference in our taxation rates and systems: 'The EU is also introducing new tax policy instruments which will enable it in the coming years to cope with new challenges.'[20]

Educating the new eurocitizens

A similar situation is developing in education. When planning its takeover, once again the Commission stresses that member countries have authority over education policies: 'Member states are responsible for the organisation and content of education and training systems.'[21] However, because the Commission claims that education is important for the competitiveness of the European Union, it proposes working closely with 'member states to help them develop and modernise their education and training policies'. The Commission already has several educational programmes, including the Education and Training 2010 Work Programme and the Lifelong Learning Programme, which cost us well over €1 billion a year. Moreover, it has also developed 'the European framework of key competences, a reference tool on the key competences that all people require for a successful life in a knowledge society'. It plans to use this framework to help member states in 'redefining school curricula'. In this way, the Commission is trying to create an important role for itself in such areas as helping 'schools equip young people with the competences and motivation to make learning a lifelong activity'; supporting schools 'to promote equity, to respond to cultural diversity and to reduce early school leaving'; and 'to prepare young people to be responsible citizens, in line with fundamental values such as peace and tolerance of diversity'. Again, the Commission's aims may be well-intentioned and may even give beneficial results in some countries, but allowing EU bureaucrats to micromanage our education systems is a clear surrender of our national freedom to the control of a single European superstate. Moreover, a one-size-fits-all European framework of key competences may keep hundreds of highly paid Brussels bureaucrats busy, but it might not be the best way of addressing the different challenges faced by the education systems of 27 countries.

Creating happy families

When it comes to our private lives the Commission asserts that it believes in its citizens' freedom to decide how they wish to live: 'The choices which men and women make in combining the professional, private and family aspects are primarily personal.'[22] As usual, however, the Commission manages to find good reasons for involving itself in areas that it has just said are outside its authority: 'At European level, successful recon-ciliation of work and private life is particularly relevant to a number of key policy objectives.' These 'key policy objectives' supposedly include improving the productivity of the EU's labour market and promoting gender equality. So the Commission has decided to develop a 'legislative framework' to help us all achieve 'a better work–life balance' by providing 'stronger support for reconciling professional, family and private life'.[23]

First, as it often seems to do, the Commission plans to set up a way of measuring citizens' work–life balance so that it can make comparisons between different countries: 'A common Europe-wide basis for obtaining timely comparable and perti-nent statistics on reconciliation between work and private and family life.'[24] This will help the Commission to actively regulate areas such as the provision of childcare facilities, entitlement to leave, flexible working-time arrangements, maternity and paternity leave (even for the self-employed), and 'gender mainstreaming in employment, social inclusion and social protection'. The aim of all this activity is for the Commission to help us all live happier lives:

> The improvement and modernisation of the European regulatory framework which should be achieved by the proposals accompanying this communication and the negotiations launched by the social partners will enable women to achieve greater economic independence and encourage men to play a greater role in family life.[25]

We all probably believe that society would be better off if people managed to have happier family lives. However, there may be those who doubt that Brussels bureaucrats should be allowed to probe into, measure and regulate how we manage our relationships and marriages.

GOING TOO FAR?

The Commission is preparing similar legislative forays into areas such as tourism, sport and scientific research. In tourism, for example, the Commission has already planned 'better monitoring and reporting of the sustainability of tourism, activities that further sustainable tourism consumption patterns by European citizens and promoting sustainability in the tourism value chain and destinations'.[26] Although the Commission is not proposing any immediate regulation in this area, should it not be satisfied that individual countries are doing enough to encourage 'sustainable tourism' it has stated that it intends to legislate to ensure that we visit the places it wishes, at the times it considers best and in the manner it considers appropriate.

In sport the Commission sees an important role for itself in supporting the 'societal and economic aspects of sport, such as public health, education, social inclusion, volunteering, external relations and the financing of sport'.[27] As part of this, it will as usual start measuring what we are up to – the Commission will 'develop a European statistical method for measuring the economic impact of sport'.[28] This measurement will then give the

Commission an excuse to become involved in things like introducing 'the award of a European label to schools actively supporting physical activities'; promoting 'the use of sport as a tool of the EU's development policy'; and improving 'opportunities for supporting social inclusion and integration through sport activities by mobilising EU programmes and funds'.[29]

In scientific research the Commission wants to build the European Research Area (ERA) in order to improve the competitiveness of European industry in a globalised world. The ERA is intended to be 'a cornerstone for a European knowledge society'.[30] The Commission proposes to launch a series of actions aimed at ensuring 'effective European-level coordination of national and regional research activities, programmes and policies'. Basically, it will try to give itself overall responsibility for organising much of European scientific research. Once you also throw in further planned Commission land-grabs over employment law, social security policy, foreign aid and trade union representation on company boards, some people might wonder what exactly our elected national governments are going to be left controlling.

Chapter 8

A MONSTER THAT REGULATES EVERYTHING?

Regulation in itself does not need to be a problem. As the EU Commission explains, there are good reasons for regulating:

> Regulation serves many purposes – to protect health by ensuring food safety, to protect the environment by setting air and water quality standards, to set rules for companies competing in the marketplace to create a level playing field. Regulation is a necessary and accepted aspect of modern society.[1]

Most people would probably agree with these sentiments. After all, few of us would want to return to the days when people were being poisoned by adulterated, less than virgin Spanish olive oil or Austrian white wine with a generous portion of added anti-freeze; when others were killed by exploding Italian chemical plants; when the Rhine was just a torrent of poisonous effluent; when many 'vintage' French wines got their fine taste more from chemicals than from grapes; and when British beaches were awash with raw sewage. Moreover, at a time when Chinese children in their tens of thousands are being injured and killed by poisonous chemicals added to milk and other foods while the authorities try to keep the scandal under wraps, it is clear that it is safer and healthier to live in a properly regulated, rather than an unregulated, society.

However, the most frequent and well-worn criticism of the EU is that it goes too far and seems obsessed with over-regulating our lives. The eurocrats naturally reject this criticism: 'Although Brussels may be caricatured as being the source of burdensome regulation and red tape, the reality is different.'[2] In fact, not only does the Commission deny excessive regulation, it actually claims to have reduced the amount of regulation that we have to live with: 'Legislating at European level has reduced much red tape.' However, by 2005 EU regulation had become so flagrantly excessive that even one of the incoming commissioners admitted that Europeans see the EU as 'a bureaucratic monster that regulates everything'.[3]

Since its inception the EU has made around 103,000 new decisions, laws and regulations – about ten for every single working day for the last 50 years. In its first 35 years the EU was smaller and less inclined to produce stuff, so it was only knocking out a thoroughly modest five new laws a day. It may be interesting to note that as the number of eurocrats has more than doubled in the last 15 years – from fewer than 20,000 to over 44,500 – the number of laws produced by Brussels has also more than doubled. Enthusiastically propelled by its tens of thousands of new employees, the Brussels administration machine seems to have really shifted up a gear and is now comfortably running at about 12 new laws each working day. This might lead ordinary European citizens to the rather obvious but depressing conclusion that the more people our EU leaders employ to produce new laws, the more new laws we are going to get as the bureaucrats look around for useful new things to regulate in order to justify their substantial salaries, expenses and other benefits. So the extraordinary quantity of new regulation pouring out of Brussels may actually be a function of the increasing number of new people working on the regulation production lines rather than arising from any real need for that regulation.

A PROFUSION OF EMPTY PROMISES

Confusingly for us EU-twitchers, over the many years that the EU has denied that it over-regulates, it has also consistently pledged to deal with the problem of its own over-regulation. But EU promises to cut red tape and improve regulation have a long and not very honourable history (see Figure 1). As far back as March 1985 the EU committed to set up a watchdog group within the Commission to prevent too many regulations that were a burden on business. Ten years and about 15,600 regulations later, the EU made another of its supposed assaults on its own over-regulation. When the ill-fated Santer Commission took over in 1994, its slogan was 'Doing less but doing it better'. Santer's initiative was duly reported by the admiring press with headlines like 'Onslaught begins on EU regulation',[4] yet the promise seemed to backfire rather spectacularly. In the five years before Santer's arrival the EU was producing only about 1,400 regulations and directives a year. Under Santer's 'less but better' philosophy the number of new laws adopted more than doubled, reaching its highest point ever at 2,860 a year.[5]

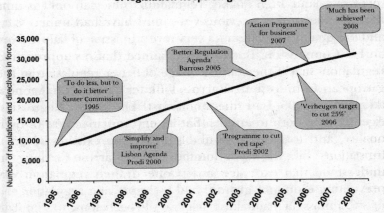

Figure I In spite of promises of better regulation, the mountain of legislation keeps on growing

Next up was the Prodi Commission. At the 2000 Lisbon Council this Commission showed its concern for its citizens' welfare when it promised to simplify and improve regulation to make the EU 'the most competitive economy in the world by 2010'. Yet for the next two years the number of new EU laws being produced for our benefit remained at an historic high of 2,780 a year. The Prodi Commission seemed to have another near fatal attack of good intentions two years later in 2002 when it launched its 'Better Regulation' exercise. This was described as 'a far-reaching programme to simplify and generally improve the regulatory environment'.[6] EU companies and citizens were informed that the Commission would 'cut red tape, improve the quality of regulation and design better laws for consumers and business alike'. However, this latest attempt at bureaucracy-bashing seemed to have only a limited effect on the eager efforts of the Brussels bureaucracy factory, which continued to churn out around 2,400 new laws each year.

A new blitzkrieg on the ever-growing EU bureaucratic burden appeared to be on the way when the Barroso Commission moved into its lavish, newly refurbished EU offices. Barroso's lot promised a 'paradigm shift' in the Commission's approach to lawmaking and pledged that from now on we would only get 'necessary' and 'high quality' regulation.[7] One can only assume that this meant that previously we must have had unnecessary and low quality regulation – a very rare admission of failure from an EU Commission. Barroso also claimed that his approach to regulation 'marks the coming of age of better regulation in the European Commission'. Barroso's Better Regulation Agenda, adopted in 2005, had fine ambitions: 'The Better Regulation Agenda aims both to ensure that all new initiatives are of high quality, and to modernise and simplify the existing stock of legislation.'[8] Like the Prodi Commission, the Barroso Commission understood that excessive and poorly drafted regulation was preventing economic growth, and by improving regulation the new Commission maintained that it would be 'helping to stimulate entrepreneurship and innovation, to realise the full potential of the single market, and thereby promote growth and job creation'. So, ten years after the newspaper headlines like 'Onslaught begins on EU regulation', which had greeted the failed Santer Commission's 'doing less but doing it better', we once again had journalists announcing things like 'EU starts war on red tape' and 'EU announces shift in approach to lawmaking'.[9]

The Barroso Commission set a goal of scrapping or simplifying 54 laws in the year 2005–6. When it took office there may have been as many as 25,000 EU laws in force (see note 5). Compared to this total, the Barroso target of just 54 – equivalent to 0.2 per cent of EU regulation – could appear quite modest and likely to have a limited effect on the ever-increasing regulatory mountain. Nevertheless, over a year after the start of Barroso's courageous campaign against excessive bureaucracy, he had to admit that progress had been 'slower than expected' as just 15 of the 54 targeted laws had been dealt with. Seemingly undaunted, the Commission moved ahead with its Simplification Rolling Programme, which planned to deal with 164 measures in the period 2005–9. Each year the Commission listed in its work plan the laws and regulations it intended to remove or, at least, simplify. However, on closer inspection this effort also looked less than dramatic. In its 2008 work plan, for example, the Commission listed no fewer than 30 pending proposals that it was intending to withdraw.[10] Of these, 26 had become obsolete before they were even adopted, and in the other four the schemes covered by the intended regulation 'effectively expired at the end of 2006', so the regulation that Barroso's Commission had targeted for the scrap heap would have been irrelevant anyway.

BUSILY ACHIEVING NOTHING

An important new front in the supposed war against red tape seemed to be opened up in November 2006 by the commissioner for enterprise and industry, the German Günter Verheugen. His department had apparently calculated that the administrative cost to European businesses of both EU and national regulation was around €600 billion a year. This was just the cost of providing information, not of compliance to the regulations. In general, the costs of compliance would be several times the administrative costs.

Verheugen announced an ambitious target: to reduce the amount of regulation faced by businesses by 25 per cent by 2012. According to the Commission this would boost EU output by €150 billion a year. Verheugen explained his plan: 'The objective is to get rid of red tape to make investment and business activity easier in Europe.'[11] Verheugen also reportedly claimed that this new war on regulation would reduce the *acquis communautaire* (the entire quantity of EU law) from 80,000 pages to 50,000 pages and that it was 'an important project to bridge the gap with the European public'.[12]

The plan soon hit opposition. The president of the European parliament questioned whether the Commission had the authority to withdraw legislation that had already gone through the parliament. Then in February 2007 member states' industry ministers refused to accept binding targets for the reduction of bureaucracy. Those countries that had the most business-friendly regulatory environments (the Netherlands, Britain, Sweden and Denmark) backed obligatory targets, but many other countries, especially the PIGS and France, opposed EU targets and argued that it would be better if 'member states are invited to set their own ambitious national targets', which is probably diplomat-speak for doing nothing. However, the countries did agree to 'carry out analyses of their national legislation by 2008, particularly in the 13 areas highlighted by the Commission as crucial for business', which is definitely diplomat-speak for doing nothing.

All was not lost, however, and at a meeting a month later EU heads of state confirmed that they supported the idea of a 25 per cent reduction of EU regulation on business. But they still insisted on their countries' freedom to 'set their own targets of comparable ambition'.

Adding a bit of icing on the deregulation cake, in September 2007 Barroso appointed a High Level Group of Independent Stakeholders on Administrative Burdens, which was headed by the former Bavarian prime minister Edmund Stoiber and was aimed at cutting red tape across the EU. Barroso claimed that this new group would be 'a flagship project for the Commission', and commissioner Verheugen said that 'the group will play a crucial role in identifying the unnecessary admin-istrative burdens we need to remove'.[13] The group was appointed for three years and consisted of 15 honorary members. However, it had only three to four full-time staff and would meet only about twice a year. This might appear some-what insubstantial compared to the almost 100,000 people working full- and part-time to produce new regulations.

The group's first efforts unfortunately didn't seem all that promising. On the plus side, it identified that billions could be saved by European businesses if the EU reduced their reporting requirements. Stoiber explained: 'Currently there are 344 different reporting obligations for European companies. The total cost for all the companies to provide this information is around €20 billion.'[14] He went on: 'The high-level group has put forward a proposal that €7.3 billion could be saved if these obligations were reduced.'

The proposals were presented to the relevant commissioner in May 2008, but by the end of September nothing much seemed to have happened: 'We presented these proposals already in May to commissioner McCreevy,' Stoiber reported in September 2008, 'and he said a decision will be taken in the near future, but actually we haven't heard anything more from him since'.[15]

In addition to waiting to hear from commissioner McCreevy, the high-level group also launched an online EU competition asking us citizens for 'the best idea for red tape reduction'. The three entrants with the best idea would be invited to attend the European Enterprise Awards on 13 May 2009 in Prague where the competition winner would be announced. There was no commitment that the chosen idea would be acted upon.

By the start of 2008 the Barroso Commission had managed to increase the overall number of EU laws by about 4,700 in fewer than three years. This meant that under Barroso the *acquis* had actually risen by almost 20 per cent rather than starting its planned 25 per cent reduction. Nevertheless, the Commission published a report extolling the success of its Better Regulation initiative. As the number of EU laws increased by the day, the Commission claimed: 'This work on simplifying EU legislation has reached cruising speed.'[16] Worryingly, the report went on to reassure us that 'the Commission will maintain this momentum'. The Commission's Better Regulation report concluded that 'much has been achieved in developing better regulation in the EU' and claimed that the review 'shows that the EU is delivering on its commitment to regulate well'.

So, by the start of 2009 – after over four years of Barroso's and Verheugen's five-year term in office – we had more EU regulation than ever before, in spite of the Commission's claims of success in reducing regulation. Perhaps, given sufficient time and goodwill, the Barroso and Verheugen plans could have produced some results, but in 2008 the supposed brave bureaucracy-bashers were still working on their plan to deliver firm proposals for reducing administrative burdens to the European parliament and council of ministers by spring 2009. Yet a new Commission would take office shortly after the June 2009 European elections, and a new Commission would mean new commissioners with new priorities and different interests. So it would not be unrealistic to expect Barroso's Better Regulation initiative with its Simplification Rolling Programme and its Action Programme to Reduce Administrative Burdens on Business to crash ignominiously into the murky mud of EU inaction in much the same way as its many hapless predecessors.

RHETORIC AND REALITY

An entertaining illustration of the difference between words and action came at a Brussels discussion meeting in late 2008 featuring representatives for the EU's 23 million small and medium-sized enterprises (SMEs) and a Commission deputy director general. The success of SMEs is critical to the EU's economy – they provide about 75 per cent of private-sector jobs – and eight years after the Lisbon Agenda to promote growth and jobs the Commission finally came up with a proposal, the European Small Business Act (SBA), which was designed to make life easier for Europe's SMEs and encourage them to expand and take on more staff.

The Commission functionary made a speech to explain why the SBA was 'very concrete' and 'a great leap forward'. However, although it was called an 'Act', the SBA was only a set of proposals and was not legally binding on member states, which could ignore it if they wished. Repeatedly, several of the businesspeople asked the deputy director general if the SBA could be made mandatory legislation because they wanted action and not just words from the Commission and their own governments. But repeatedly the Commission functionary refused and said that it was sufficient that the Commission would be monitoring how well countries implemented the SBA.

Speaking afterwards to the SME representatives, it was clear that they were quite pessimistic about this latest Commission idea to help business. 'It's just a mish-mash of diluted policies,' one said. Another claimed she spent far too much time supplying 'idiot statistics' and complained that the Commission was 'not reducing red tape – they are adding to it all the time'. A third explained that the same promises had been made by the Commission for at least the last 20 years, but nothing ever happened. There didn't seem to be anyone at the meeting, except the Commission deputy director general, who thought any progress at all had been made with the Commission's latest effort at red tape reduction for SMEs. Then all the businesspeople and journalists who attended the meeting went off to drown their sorrows with seemingly unlimited quantities of champagne.

IT'S NOT OUR FAULT

There are two main ways in which the Commission makes laws for us: directives and regulations. Directives lay out the general features of a law to be implemented and mandate when it should be implemented, but allow individual countries discretion over how they will adapt that law for their own particular circumstances. Regulations have to be passed into each country's laws exactly as they are written by the EU and allow no local adaptation at all. Whenever it is criticised for excessive bureaucracy, the Commission tends to claim that it makes extensive use of directives and that if there is too much regulation it must be the fault of individual countries doing what is called 'gold plating':

> The EU often pursues its objectives by adopting 'directives' setting out broad principles and objectives and leaving implementation to be defined by the member states. Member states can then choose how to meet the goals of the directive, adapting to their own institutional and administrative cultures. It is often at this stage that embellishments and refinements, not prescribed by EU law, are introduced. These can go well beyond the requirements set out in EU law, resulting in extra costs and burdens. This is sometimes referred to as gold plating.[17]

At first sight this could seem like a fairly plausible argument – the only weakness is that it is completely contradicted by the facts.

About 20 years ago the EU seems to have been reasonably happy to use directives, which allowed member countries some discretion in how they applied EU laws, and almost 20 per cent of all EU laws in force were based on directives, with the remaining 80 per cent or so deriving from regulations. However, the EU seems to have lost patience with us and now prefers to make almost all new laws by regulation, with very few directives. Over the last ten years the Commission has introduced around 2,340 regulations a year compared to just 103 directives a year. So about 96 per cent of all new laws passed during the last decade are actually regulations, giving the lie to the Commission claim that it 'often' uses directives. This meant that by the start of 2009 only about 6 per cent of the total body of current EU law was now based on the more flexible directives, with a massive 94 per cent coming from completely inflexible regulations (see Figure 2).

Figure 2 While claiming to use directives, the EU is increasingly using regulations to make new laws

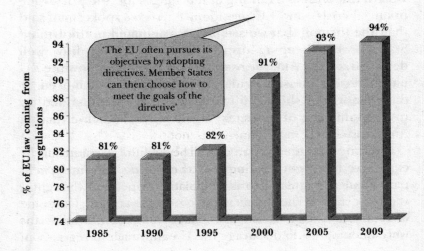

REGULATING THE MOLEHILL WHILE MISSING THE MOUNTAIN

At the start of September 2008, as US banks seemed to be falling like ninepins and the Fed rushed around like a headless chicken, Commission mandarins and EU politicians sneered in self-satisfaction at how the unregulated US financial system had spun out of control, and they assured their citizens that thanks to decades of careful EU regulation such a disaster could never happen here. But just a couple of weeks after the US meltdown, a colourful selection of the largest European banks went crashing into an enormous financial hole of their own making, and our rulers copied their US counterparts with their version of the headless chicken routine.

While the European banking crisis grew, our leaders were quick to appear on TV to blame 'cowboy capitalism' for all the world's problems. France's president, Nicolas Sarkozy, attacked the 'excesses of Wall Street' and said that the land of free enterprise gave too much room for financial speculation.[18] Germany's chancellor, Angela Merkel, blamed the US's 'irresponsible' granting of mortgages for 'the worldwide financial crisis', and EU president Barroso's spokesman said that 'the turmoil that we are facing originated in the United States'.[19] But heaping opprobrium, no matter how well deserved, on the Americans didn't really explain how the EU had been ceaselessly regulating everything that moved or didn't move for the last 50 years and yet we still ended up in the same sea of monetary *merde* as the much-criticised Americans.

It has now become clear, with the benefit of extraordinarily expensive hindsight, that none of the world's extremely well-paid financial regulators, in the US or Europe, ever thought it was important to check that any of our banks actually had some of the money they were so eager to lend. So while EU politicians were queuing up to disparage the US approach to regulation, it is not clear that regulators in the EU countries were any less incompetent than the Americans.

Although financial regulation failed in a similar way on both sides of the Atlantic, if we look at other areas of regulation there are indications that the US and the EU have radically different, almost opposite, approaches. The US tends to regulate for what it doesn't want to happen. So it will try to prevent unpleasant things like nuclear power stations blowing up, car manufacturers producing death-traps that explode when involved in accidents and people being debilitated by dodgy medicine. However, the US trusts its citizens to choose what kinds of fruit and vegetables they want to buy, its parents to judge whether children's playground equipment is safe for their children and its farmers to decide for themselves if they want to drive their tractors on their own fields when those fields are slightly waterlogged. One of the main reasons why US companies will try to produce safe products and operate reasonably responsibly, and why American farmers don't send their workers into dangerous situations, in spite of limited regulation, is because they know that the slightest mistake will be ruthlessly exploited by America's army of civil litigation lawyers, all out to find a company or individual stupid or careless enough to make them fantastically rich. So the US system works through lighter regulation being balanced by the constant fear of being sued.

The EU by contrast seems to regulate for both what it wants to prevent and also what it wants to happen. This means it will regulate for all the nasty things that US regulators have to deal with – dangerous products, harmful medicines, environmental pollution and so on – but it goes much further. Usually because of its belief that you cannot have a well-functioning single market without almost everything being harmonised, the EU appears to be constantly trying to define exactly how things should be done. But at times this can seem like an obsession that unduly interferes with how we live our lives. EU directives on how large a typeface should be used on 'No Smoking' signs in public places, how much rooting material pigs should have to avoid boredom and when farmers can drive their tractors on their fields might seem the kind of thing that would better be left to EU citizens' common sense. And, of course, eurocrats believed we were not capable of deciding what kind of cucumbers, bananas, kiwi fruits or oranges we should be buying, and so they decided to specify the 'marketing standards' for these and many other foodstuffs. These standards mandated lengths, curvatures and overall sizes of most fruit and vegetables and even the maximum weights of bunches of fruit such as grapes.

In late 2008, as food prices soared and as the EU moved into recession, the Commission magnanimously announced that to prevent up to one-third of the food that was produced being wasted, it was relaxing some of the rules governing the size and shape of fruit and vegetables that could be sold. The Commission seemed proud of its proposal. A spokesman proclaimed: 'Rules governing the size and shape of fruit and vegetables will be consigned to history.'[20] One of the main people behind the decision, the agricultural commissioner, appeared to have realised what all the EU's citizens have known for the last half century: 'We simply don't need to regulate this sort of thing at EU level. It makes no sense to throw perfectly good products away, just because they are the "wrong" shape.'[21]

However, as is usual with supposedly bold EU decisions on reducing regulation, the truth was rather less dramatic than the eurocrats' excited PR might lead us to believe. It was true that the rules on size and shape were being relaxed for 26 products, but these tended to be for items sold in smaller quantities, and they only made up about 30 per cent of the volume of fruit and vegetables used in the EU. Owing to resistance from some countries, especially France, tough shape and size regulations would remain in place for the ten types of fruit and vegetables that accounted for about 70 per cent of EU consumption. So while things like walnuts in their shells, chicory, watermelons, cucumbers and Brussels sprouts could now be sold in a greater range of shapes and sizes, many popular products, like apples, citrus fruit, lettuces and tomatoes, would still be heavily regulated. As for the curvature of bananas, so often the subject of derision for EU regulations, that wouldn't change. Like most fruit grown outside the EU, bananas fall under different legislation and would not be affected by the supposed loosening of the rules.

The Commission spokesman may well have been taking himself seriously when he told us that 'this is a happy day indeed for the curvy cucumber and the knobbly carrot' and explained that the decision would get rid of about 100 pages of EU legislation. But to most European citizens the whole affair just underlined how the Commission's obsession with over-regulation had driven it into a blind alley from which it seemed unable to emerge.

It is probably this self-imposed need to regulate what should occur, rather than what should not happen, that means that the mountain of EU rules and regulations will continue to grow, in spite of EU Commission assurances of their commitment to less and better regulation. Moreover, with more than 44,500 EU staff assisted by at least 50,000 experts, whose only justification in life is to find something new that definitely needs regulation for the benefit of the citizens of Europe, it's hardly likely that the EU's repeated promises of less and better regulation will ever be fulfilled.

Chapter 9

MAKING THE NEWS

EU'RE SO POPULAR

Leafing through the EU budgets it's quite difficult to find out exactly how much of our money the EU uses to convince us that the EU is good for us, but there are strong indications that it's quite a lot. The annual budget of the DG (Directorate General) Communication is around €200 million which seems to include €85 million a year spent on communication actions 'providing full and comprehensive information on the EU and involving people in a permanent dialogue'.[1] But many other DGs are also throwing our money at propaganda efforts to help build the new Europe. It appears that the DG Education and Culture gives grants of €960 million a year to almost 500 organisations, universities and schools, including €23 million for the Citizens for Europe programme, which 'gives citizens the opportunity to interact and participate in constructing an ever closer Europe', and another €126 million for Youth in Action, which 'fosters the idea of belonging to the European Union'.[2]

The DG Information and Media has a budget of €1.4 billion and hands out grants of €1.24 billion to almost 800 media organisations, of which €86 million co-finances media projects with a 'European dimension'. The publications office also gives out grants of about €26 million a year to help us learn more about our common European destiny. So the total amount of our money used to make us more euro-friendly is probably comfortably above €2 billion a year and may well be an awful lot more.

But whatever the real amount is, it is clearly an extremely good investment for the eurocrats. Or at least that's what the EU's figures would have us believe. Every year the EU conducts a series of Eurobarometer market research surveys across all EU and pre-accession countries to find out what we citizens think about life in general and the EU in particular because: 'Measuring public opinion is central to listening to what Europeans think about, and what they expect from the EU.'[3] The latest survey must have brought tears of joy to the euro-elite's eyes. According to Eurobarometer, a majority of citizens absolutely love almost everything to do with the EU. For example, 48 per cent of people have a positive opinion of the EU compared with only 15 per cent who have a negative opinion; 52 per cent think membership of the EU is 'a good thing' compared to a mere 14 per cent who believe it is 'a bad thing'; and 54 per cent are convinced that their country has benefited from being in the EU, while only 15 per cent think their country has not benefited.

We EU citizens are apparently so impressed with the EU, that many of us appear to prefer the EU's government to our own. An impressive 50 per cent of us trust the EU, yet only 32 per cent trust our national governments, and 42 per cent of us believe 'things are going in the right direction' in the EU, while just 32 per cent say 'things are going in the right direction' in our own countries. Because we apparently believe the EU is so great, many of us would prefer that the EU, rather than our national governments, took responsibility for dealing with problems like fighting terrorism (81 per cent of us want the EU to take this over), protecting the environment (71 per cent), scientific and technological research (70 per cent), defence and foreign affairs (64 per cent), energy (61 per cent), immigration (58 per cent) and fighting crime (58 per cent). There are some areas like pensions, education and health that we feel should remain under national governments' control, but all in all the

Eurobarometer surveys give the impression that a significant proportion of the EU's population would much rather that country boundaries and governments disappeared and were replaced by a single EU superstate. This is certainly exactly what the eurocrats want to hear and we can expect the market research companies that provide the Eurobarometer surveys to keep their lucrative contracts for many more years if they carry on producing these kinds of europhiliac results.

So can we trust what the Eurobarometer surveys are telling us? Some critics of Eurobarometer's results have been so impolite as to suggest that the questions are asked in such a way that they bias the answers given. For example, in a question about how the EU helps deal with the effects of globalisation, the survey could have asked something fairly neutral like 'Do you think the EU helps you benefit from globalisation?' Instead, those surveyed were given two extremely complimentary statements about the EU and globalisation – 'The EU enables European citizens to better benefit from the positive effects of globalisation' and 'The EU helps protect us from the negative effects of globalisation'. Respondents were asked if they agreed or disagreed with the pro-EU statements. Anyone who has worked with market research knows that this approach virtually guarantees a majority of positive responses (see Figure 1).

Figure 1 Using positive statements about the EU to get pro-EU answers

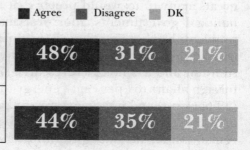

There is also another problem with the Eurobarometer survey: a general lack of knowledge about the EU and its main institutions among those surveyed. One of the surveys conducted by Eurobarometer looked at people's attitudes towards the European parliament. So few people had any knowledge or opinions at all about the EU, that Eurobarometer were forced to conclude: 'The European Union's active image is therefore insufficiently clear to enable us to draw any real conclusions.'[4] This seldom mentioned result could seem to contradict the extraordinarily positive attitudes to the EU that the main Eurobarometer survey regularly manages to find.

WORRIED ABOUT WARMING?

The EU is particularly keen to portray itself as responding to the concerns of EU citizens by championing the fight against the threat of global warming. It has constantly claimed that 'most Europeans are very concerned by climate change' and that 'the overwhelming majority of European Union citizens are concerned about climate change'.[5] It helps to have some handy Eurobarometer figures to back up your claims when you make statements like these, but sometimes it seems as if Eurobarometer has to work quite hard to get the answers required by its EU masters. In the general survey about attitudes to the EU, citizens were asked to identify the two most important issues facing their country. Rising prices, unemployment, crime, healthcare, pensions, immigration, taxation, housing, education and terrorism all figured as significant worries for EU citizens, but unfortunately for the euro-elite the environment came in at number 12 on the list of 14 concerns shown to those being surveyed, with only around 5 per cent of people choosing it.

That's obviously not the answer that our rulers needed. So they tried again and commissioned a special Eurobarometer survey to look at our attitudes to global warming. The first question consisted of interviewees being shown a card with eight issues on it, and they were then asked to choose which one is 'the most serious problem currently facing the world as a whole'. Helpfully, global warming was at the top of the list and even more helpfully it had a '1' against it (see Figure 2).

Figure 2 The Eurobarometer questionnaire helpfully puts global warming at the top of the list and gives it the number '1'

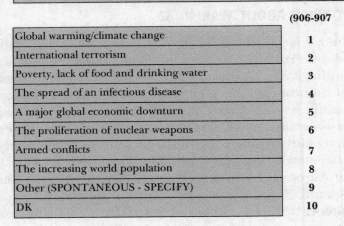

| QE1a1 | In your opinion, which of the following do you consider to be the most serious problem currently facing the world as a whole? |

(SHOW CARD – ONE ANSWER ONLY)

(906-907

Global warming/climate change	1
International terrorism	2
Poverty, lack of food and drinking water	3
The spread of an infectious disease	4
A major global economic downturn	5
The proliferation of nuclear weapons	6
Armed conflicts	7
The increasing world population	8
Other (SPONTANEOUS - SPECIFY)	9
DK	10

Yet in spite of this enormously suggestive way of posing the question, the majority of EU citizens asked were so stupid that we still gave the 'wrong' answer when we chose 'poverty, lack of food and drinking water' as the major concern facing the world (see Figure 3).

When the EU issued its press release to communicate the results of this survey, it could have written: 'Poverty and hunger are top of the list of EU citizens' concerns'. It could even have announced: 'Poverty and hunger – more important than global

Figure 3 Global warming came only second on the list of our concerns

Q. In your opinion, which of the following do you consider to be the most
serious problem currently facing the world as a whole?

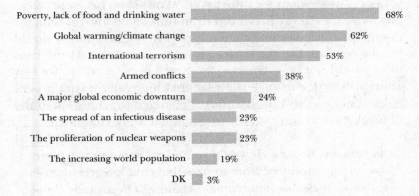

Poverty, lack of food and drinking water	68%
Global warming/climate change	62%
International terrorism	53%
Armed conflicts	38%
A major global economic downturn	24%
The spread of an infectious disease	23%
The proliferation of nuclear weapons	23%
The increasing world population	19%
DK	3%

warming.' But it didn't. In fact, the EU never even mentioned
our concerns about poverty and instead chose to highlight the
issue of global warming with its press release headline:
'Eurobarometer: Europeans support greater EU action on
energy and climate change'. This convenient result allowed the
EU energy commissioner to assert: 'This survey clearly shows
that EU citizens expect the EU to shape a common European
response to face energy and climate change challenges.' His
colleague, the environment commissioner, also chipped in with:
'Climate change is happening. EU citizens expect EU leadership
on this issue. The EU must use this political momentum in order
to put Europe and the World on the path to a more energy-
secure and low-carbon future.'[6] The two men made no mention
of the real number one issue – poverty and hunger. Naturally all
the journalists, not having actually looked at the survey results
closely, dutifully reported the EU's politically motivated spin.

Although the EU press release claimed that we EU citizens
were desperately worried about global warming and that most of
us wanted the EU to tackle the issue, it omitted to mention that

we weren't sufficiently worried about global warming to want to do much about it ourselves. In other Eurobarometer surveys a majority of us (54 per cent) said 'no' (compared to 40 per cent who said 'yes') when we were asked 'Would you be prepared to pay more for energy produced from renewable sources than for energy produced from other sources? If yes, how much would you be prepared to pay?' Moreover, an impressive 81 per cent of us would not be willing to pay over 5 per cent more for our energy in order to save the planet. This really wasn't a very helpful statistic, so Eurobarometer changed the question in the 2008 global warming survey to the much more suggestive:

> Personally, how much would you be prepared to pay more for energy produced from sources that emit less greenhouse gases in order to fight climate change? On average, how much, in per cent, would you be ready to pay more?

This is rather like the question, 'If you saw a man starving to death would you give them £10 or £20 or £30 or nothing?' Not many people are likely to answer 'nothing'. Sure enough, the changed questions made it possible for our leaders to get the answer they were looking for: the majority of us were now apparently willing to pay more for clean energy. Whereas previously 54 per cent of us would not be willing to fork out more for clean energy, now this had fallen to only 30 per cent (see Figure 4).

A cynic might suggest that the large number of 'Don't knows' in the second survey were really people who were too embarrassed to say they weren't prepared to pay any more, in which case the number of us unwilling to pay more for clean energy hadn't really changed. But the key issue here is that while we may all agree that we ought to be acting to prevent global warming, in a supposedly democratic society it is less than honest for the eurocrats to keep twisting survey questions and fudging survey results in order to justify their self-serving power-grab over environmental policies.

Figure 4 Changing the question can help get the 'right' answer

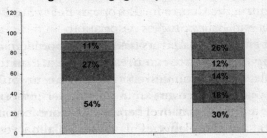

First survey – Would you be prepared to pay more for energy produced from renewable sources? If yes, how much would you be prepared to pay?

Second survey – Personally, how much would you be prepared to pay more for energy produced from sources that emit less greenhouse gases in order to fight climate change? on average, how much, in per cent would you be ready to pay more?

A LITTLE HELP FOR MY FRIENDS

Each year the EU distributes about 24,000 grants worth over €9 billion to various organisations and individuals both within the EU and across the world. Some of these organisations are genuinely apolitical and humanitarian. For example, according to the latest figures, Oxfam got €40 million in one year, the Red Cross €23 million and Médecins sans Frontières €3.7 million. Many environmental organisations such as Friends of the Earth, the World Conservation Union, the International Network for Sustainable Energy and Naturfreunde Internationale also receive a constant flow of EU money. But a large number, probably the vast majority, of these grants go to organisations and individuals that seem to support the single Europe ideal. Over €77 million goes to over 100 organisations such as Fondation Génération Europe (€3.5 million) and the European Youth Forum (€2.2 million), which are aimed at promoting the European Union to young people. Many women's groups, including Lobby Européen des Femmes (€0.8 million) and Women in Europe for a Common Future (€0.3 million), get our financial support. Large numbers of generally pro-EU think-tanks also share in this feeding frenzy. These include the European Policy Centre, the Centre for European Policy Study and the Trans European Policy Studies Association.

A huge number of grants go to universities and other academic institutions that support the European dream. Some are quite sizeable – for example, one Belgian university received over €10 million in just one year, another got €5.8 million and others received €4.8 million and €3.1 million. There are EU educational programmes aimed at people of all ages. Their stated aim is 'to strengthen the European dimension of education at all levels', and they range from the Comenius Programme, which targets children in primary and secondary schools, to the Gruntvig Programme, which is directed at people in adult education.

One of the largest of these EU educational undertakings is the Erasmus programme for students in higher education. Erasmus encourages educational exchanges across Europe and reaches over 200,000 EU citizens each year. More than 2,000 universities participate, and around 175,000 lucky students and 29,000 university lecturers receive grants of our money. Happy recipients have explained how Erasmus has helped Europeanise them. An Austrian participant said: 'People sometimes accuse the EU of being too distant from the citizens, but personally I experienced the European spirit every day. I think that the Erasmus programme leads to a stronger pan-European "we" feeling.' A British student seemed to agree: 'After studying international law in Utrecht in the Netherlands, I learned what it is to feel European. Indeed, I now truly think of myself as a European and proudly so.'[7]

The EU also influences academic thought strongly in its favour through the Jean Monnet Programme, which 'stimulates excellence in teaching, research and reflection on European integration in higher education institutions throughout the world'.[8] There are 798 Jean Monnet professorial chairs and a network of 1,500 professors all producing a vast amount of academic research into European integration issues. Moreover, they teach an impressive 250,000 students each year about the integration of Europe. To get your hands on some Jean Monnet money, it helps to proclaim that you are a believer in the dream of European integration.

For anyone who believes in freedom of thought and speech, perhaps the most worrying aspect of EU largesse with our money is the large amount that goes to supposedly independent media organisations. In Britain the BBC, which was once respected across the world for its editorial independence, was reported to have borrowed almost £141 million in three low-interest loans from the European Investment Bank and received EU grants of £1.4 million. The BBC claimed that even though it had its snout deep in the eurotrough, this had absolutely no influence on its reporting of EU affairs: 'There were no editorial obligations whatsoever attached to the three EIB loans.' [9] However, organisations tend not to bite the hand that feeds them, and some people might be tempted to link the BBC's receipt of EU money with its many years of lack of enthusiasm for any hard investigative reporting of EU waste and corruption.

The BBC is not alone in gorging itself on EU cash. In France Radio France (€5.8 million) and TV5 take money from the EU. In Denmark all the main newspapers receive EU grants. In fact, in most EU countries the main TV, radio and press are getting EU money to make and broadcast pro-Europe programmes. In Austria the main TV station received €836,000 for a programme called *Was Sie schon immer über die Europäische Union wissen wollen* (Everything you Want to Know about the European Union). German TV came up with *Go Europe* (€585,500), and German radio with *Gebrauchsanweisung Europa* (Instructions for Using Europe) costing us a mere €153,299. In Denmark TV2 received €204,000 for a programme called *Daily life in the EU*. In France €601,645 went on the TV programme *The EU, what's in it for me?* and another €504,297 for *L'Europe Proche de Chez Vous*. Italian TV gave us *Eurodreams Make it Happen* (€275,400 of taxpayers' money) and *In Europa: la Forze dell'Unione* (€95,872).

Greek TV produced *Getting to Know Europe* (€599,636), while the country's radio contributed *The Dream of Europe* (€114,055).

LISTENING TO YOU OR TALKING AT YOU?

Since 1957 the EU has worked intensively to convince us of the benefits of being a member, but it is generally believed that there has been a significant increase in communications activity during the last 25 years. In 1984 a European council meeting agreed to set up a committee to investigate ways of improving the EU's image. The committee, chaired by Italian MEP Pietro Adonnino, produced two reports outlining, among other things, strategies for promoting the 'European idea'. These proposals included a Europe-wide 'audio-visual area' with a 'truly European' multilingual TV channel; the formation of European sports teams; the transmission of more information and public awareness campaigns; school exchange programmes and voluntary work camps for young people; and the introduction of a stronger 'European dimension' in education. However, the committee went further, claiming that to transform the EC into a 'People's Europe' also required a new set of symbols for communicating the principles and values upon which the Community is based. As the committee noted:

> Symbols play a key role in consciousness-raising but there is also a need to make the European citizen aware of the different elements that go to make up his European identity, of our cultural unity with all its diversity of expression, and of the historical ties which link the nations of Europe.[10]

To this end, the committee set out various 'symbolic measures' for enhancing the Community's profile. Foremost among these was the creation of a new EC emblem and flag, which was hoist for the first time outside the Commission headquarters in Brussels at a formal ceremony on 29 May 1986.

According to the EU, the flag: 'is the symbol not only of the European Union, but also of Europe's unity and identity in a wider sense. The circle of gold stars represents solidarity and harmony between the peoples of Europe.'[11]

By the way, in case you've ever wondered why there are 12 stars on the European flag, many less than the number of member states, the explanation is as follows: 'The number of stars has nothing to do with the number of member states. There are 12 stars because the number 12 is traditionally the symbol of perfection, completeness and unity.'[12]

After the setback of June 1992 (when the Danish voted in a referendum to reject the treaty on European Union), Commission president Delors set up a 'committee of experts' chaired by a former EU commissioner, the Belgian Willy de Clercq, to examine ways to improve the Commission's communications policy. Their report, which was published in March 1993, proposed that a European identity must be 'engrained in people's minds' as a 'good product' using marketing techniques, and 'women and youth' should become 'priority target groups' (because the report's writers believed they were more amenable to persuasion). It pointed out that EU treaties were too technical for ordinary people to understand and so:

> The Commission should be clearly positioned as the guarantor of the well-being and quality of life of the citizen of Europe . . . It must be presented with a human face: sympathetic, warm and caring.[13]

It also suggested that 'newscasters and reporters' be targeted 'so that they subsequently become enthusiastic supporters of the cause'. Among its other recommendations were the creation of a centralised Office of Communications; a 'European library and museum'; a European 'Order of Merit', which should be above national honours; and 'personalised certificates awarded to all newly born babies attesting their birth as citizens of the

European Union'. The initiative was intended to improve public relations, but when it was unveiled at a press conference in Brussels on 31 March 1993 it provoked an angry backlash and mass walk-out by journalists, many of whom accused the Commission of behaving like a military dictatorship.

The part of the EU most directly charged with involving us in the EU is the DG Communication. In 2008 the DG celebrated the 50th anniversary of the European parliament with the catchy line '50 years of listening to you'. Its strategy is called 'Communicating Europe in Partnership', and its mission statement is: 'To help the European Commission communicate with the public and inform it of its activities and policies with the aim of increasing citizens' knowledge of and participation in European affairs.' Its objectives are all about dealing with 'the concerns of the citizens', working 'in partnership' and developing 'a European public sphere to promote discussions in Europe'.

The DG Communication seems to believe it can listen to our concerns and gain our trust by bombarding us with 'good news' stories about the EU. In the latest full year of activity it planned to have 60,276 video clips broadcast, 276,412 photos disseminated, 1,200 journalists trained in EU matters (costing us over €1 million), 500,000 people directly involved in communications about the benefits of being part of the EU and around 10 million documents about the EU printed. It set up a website with the less than original name of EUtube and has occasionally encouraged online referenda on important issues. The EU runs the EuRadio network (costing us €5.8 million a year), a TV information channel in Arabic (only €5.5 million a year) and Euronews (budget €5.25 million a year).

In 2008 it set up a new internet–based TV channel, EuroparlTV, which will cost us at least €9 million a year. According to the EU, EuroparlTV 'was launched at a glitzy ceremony in parliament by the assembly's president Hans-Gert Pöttering', and it aims to help bridge the gap 'between EU institutions and citizens'. EuroparlTV will offer a well-paid career to 15 full-time journalists, and its boss claims that it will be editorially objective: 'I am perfectly happy that the content and material will be objective and neutral.' However, were you to check out the latest 'news' you'd probably find endless interviews with MEPs and supposedly 'ordinary' EU citizens enthusiastically talking about the benefits of things like the EU's virtually uncontrolled immigration, its bold actions against climate change, its progress in giving EU citizens ever more rights (with no attached responsibilities), the stunning successes of the Common Agricultural Policy and the EU's defence of citizens' social benefits.

Since 1996 we have had a satellite TV channel, EbS, providing 'broadcast-quality, up-to-the-minute and free-of-charge audiovisual coverage of EU news to media professionals'. In 2009 another channel, EbS+, will be added 'so that the general public may use the service to follow important EU events, such as open debates of the council, presentations of the Commission's proposals or plenary sessions of the European parliament'.[14]

It is not clear if many EU citizens actually tune in to the various EU TV and radio broadcasts, so perhaps the most powerful way the DG Communication can influence what we watch, read and listen to is through the vast range of grants offered to all forms of the media and cultural life. These grants are given only to support activities that 'strengthen the feeling among citizens that they belong to the EU and believe in its activities'.[15] So if you were thinking about doing a balanced documentary or even a book about the EU's successes and failures, you probably need not apply for EU financial support.

REPORTERS WITHOUT REAL REPORTING

The EU is obsessed with projecting a positive image of itself. This means that it produces a constant torrent of 'good news' stories and aggressively polices its staff to prevent any unpleasant or embarrassing information leaking out. So we have to rely on journalists who are working at the EU to see through the EU's media manipulation in order to tell us what is really going on within the EU institutions. Unfortunately, it is not obvious that we are well served by the Brussels press corps.

There are around a thousand accredited journalists covering the EU. Most days, at around midday, the EU Commission holds a press conference at the impressive modern press centre in the Berlaymont building. Depending on the main topic of the day, between 100 and 200 journalists usually attend. Theoretically, this is the opportunity for journalists to ask tough questions of the commissioners who increasingly rule our lives. However, if you ever attend one of these press conferences expecting harsh and incisive interrogation of our rulers, you will be sorely disappointed. Most press conferences consist of a commissioner or their sidekick reading out a platitudinous prepared statement about some subject or other, and then this is followed by a few usually abjectly servile and self-serving questions from journalists apparently eager to create a good impression with the Commission. There are some honourable exceptions, but a large number of EU correspondents seem to be depressingly keen not to be seen to rock the EU boat.

There are several reasons why many journalists at the EU are severely constrained in what they report and tend not to expose the truth about what is really happening in the EU institutions. First, many work for media organisations that are recipients of EU funds and grants and so discourage their correspondents from filing any negative stories about the EU. 'Bad news' stories are particularly unwelcome in the periods leading up to EU elections because they are believed to make us less inclined to vote. Moreover, many journalists are also taking EU money. An insider estimated that at the same time as they are paid by the TV, radio and press organisations that employ them, around half of these journalists are also getting paid by the EU. A journalist can earn at least €3,000 for a couple of hours' work chairing one of the hundreds of meetings organised by EU politicians and lobbyists. For a whole-day conference a journalist can pocket up to €15,000. Then there are thousands of reports that need to be written every year, and for these the EU uses the services of EU-friendly journalists. All this means that many journalists earn more from EU work than they do from their main employers.

Second, journalism is a precarious and not always remunerative career. Getting a place in the EU bureaucracy, on the other hand, guarantees you a job for life, a good salary, an excellent pension, places for your children at special EU schools and a huge range of generous allowances. So it is not surprising that some journalists switch sides, often to become EU spokespeople. Then one of their jobs is to protect the EU against any investigative press attention. Of the 33 main spokespeople currently at the Commission, at least 17 are former journalists. The list of their pre-EU employers reads like a *Who's Who?* of leading media organisations and includes major newspapers, like the *Financial Times*, the *Sunday Times*, the *International Herald Tribune* and *El Mundo*, and there are several TV and radio broadcasters – ITN, Sky News, Hungarian TV and Polish National Radio. Journalists from most of the main press agencies have also joined the EU – Bloomberg, Reuters, Associated Press, ANSA (the main Italian news agency), ANP (a Dutch press agency) and Agence Europe. In addition, correspondents from a huge range of other national newspapers across the whole EU have decided to replace the rigours of an often peripatetic journalistic life with the comfort and security of a Brussels office. It seems likely that the EU would generally tend to offer jobs to journalists who enthusiastically espoused the cause of ever closer union. Thus, with so many journalists crossing over from being poachers to becoming gamekeepers, a sceptic might be tempted to wonder how objective their reporting of EU affairs was while they were journalists if they were at the same time angling for the offer of a nice, safe, well-paid job at the EU. Moreover, to help keep journalists on side, in 2008 the European parliament gave prizes of €5,000 to four journalists who have 'made an outstanding contribution to clarifying major issues at European level or have promoted a better understanding of the institutions or policy of the European Union'.[16]

On the few occasions when journalists do dare to ask searching questions, they are usually fended off by the spokespeople (half of them former journalists) with dismissive answers such as 'there is no logic to your question' and 'I am not in a position to give any further clarification'.[17] This defensive stance makes the asking of any real questions a fairly pointless exercise, and even the few genuinely investigative journalists eventually give up. As one investigative journalist said: 'If you want to find out what's happening in the EU, you don't go to the press conferences.'

Then there are two more subtle reasons why journalists tend to shy away from criticising the EU's activities. One is that the longer you spend in Brussels and the more you mix with people from the EU inner circle, the more you start to feel that you are part of a small, enlightened group at the heart of the Empire of Good Intentions. Then it's easy to begin to believe that, although it's far from perfect, the EU is fundamentally good for the people of Europe and therefore it is better not to be too critical. Moreover, the strongest eurosceptics in EU countries tend to be extreme nationalists, and most journalists would feel morally uncomfortable about being associated with their views. So this also makes journalists wary of appearing too negative towards the way the EU is being run.

A typical example of the professional impotence of most of the EU correspondents was a press conference given by Commission president Barroso and the visiting chairperson of the African Union, Jean Ping, in late 2008. One of the subjects under discussion was what was called 'the Barroso billion'. EU Commission president Barroso had suggested that the EU contribute an extra billion to poorer farmers in Africa to help them grow more food to alleviate the effects of rising food prices on the poor. In his statement Barroso talked about our 'African friends' and about the EU's 'partnership with Africa' and about '925 million human beings suffering from hunger, mostly in Africa'. Moreover, as Zimbabwe sank ever deeper into chaos and South Africa started looking as if it intended going the same way, Barroso proclaimed: 'African leaders are putting all their efforts into supporting development and improving governance.'

But when it came to questions, not one journalist seemed interested in asking Barroso how he could claim that African leaders were supporting development when so many were quite obviously incompetent, venal and thoroughly unconcerned about the suffering of their own people. Nor did any journalist seek to question why, if he was so concerned about the welfare of African farmers, the EU was driving tens of thousands of these selfsame African farmers into destitution by dumping heavily subsidised EU agricultural products on to the African market at prices that were below those of local producers. Then, when Mr Ping gave his statement about the need to give yet more money to help agriculture in Africa, there wasn't a single journalist who asked why, if Mr Ping and his colleagues were so concerned about hunger in Africa, they and the rest of the African Union had stood idly by while Robert Mugabe of Zimbabwe, a member of the African Union, single-handedly and unnecessarily wrecked the most agriculturally productive country in the whole of the continent. Nor did anybody ask why up to 80 per cent of all foreign aid given to Africa ends up in the pockets and offshore bank accounts of the political elite of the African Union that was now so keen to get even more EU money.

Unfortunately, this sham of a press conference is the rule rather than the exception, and a similar scene is played out almost every single day at around midday in the EU press centre.

PART 3

WASTE AND DESTRUCTION

Chapter 10

THE CRADLE OF CORRUPTION?

IS EVERYBODY AT IT?

For as long as most people can remember the EU has been synonymous with extremely dubious management of our money. As we have seen (Chapter 1, Who Wants to be a Millionaire?), becoming an MEP is almost like being given a licence to fill your pockets at the taxpayers' expense. Claiming attendance allowances for meetings that MEPs don't attend, taking cash to pay employees who don't exist, making huge profits from over-generous travel allowances, dishonestly filling up your pension fund with taxpayers' money – all these appear to be accepted and even encouraged practices at the thoroughly discredited European parliament.

Unfortunately, it may not just be the politicians who are indulging in a feeding frenzy with our money. If the investigative press are to be believed, channelling European taxpayers' cash into the pockets of acquaintances, friends, family, business associates and local criminals also seems to be a bit of a hobby for some of the eurocrats who are charged with spending our money wisely. Over the years there have been numerous reports of bribes paid to EU officials by companies to gain contracts for supplying services such as cleaning EU offices, building maintenance, security guards, printing, economic statistics and even running a kindergarten. However, as the investigations into these cases often seem to peter out without anybody being charged with anything, for legal reasons we are prevented from going into detail about who has been accused of what.

PROTECTING THE GUILTY?

The organisation responsible for investigating fraud and corruption in the EU is called OLAF (Office Européen de Lutte Anti-Fraude). OLAF was founded in 1999 after the resignation of the Santer Commission, and it replaced the previous investigative body, UCLAF, which was discredited by its failure to deal with the widespread financial mismanagement and corruption identified by the report that led to the Santer Commission's departure. However, as so often happens when a public sector body is shown to have utterly failed, many UCLAF staff were just moved over to OLAF, the heading on the stationery and signs on the doors were changed, but then things seem to have carried on much as before.

OLAF is notified of about 12,000 possible cases of fraud a year, and it claims that it adopts a 'zero tolerance' approach to fraud: 'OLAF operates a policy of "zero tolerance" towards corruption or fraud in the EU institutions, launching an investigation even if the source of allegations is questionable or the amounts of money involved are very small.'[1] But at the same time OLAF also says that each year it investigates only around 200 of the reported cases – that is, about 1.7 per cent. In other words, if you've been careless enough to get caught filling your pockets or your friends' pockets with EU taxpayers' money, there's already a 98.3 per cent chance that OLAF won't bother to investigate you. This makes the theft of EU funds a remarkably risk-free pastime. So OLAF's claimed diligence with protecting our money doesn't quite match up to its own reports, where it admits that over 98 per cent of cases reported to it are not investigated at all.

OLAF employs over 450 staff and costs us around €72.6 million a year. Most of OLAF's cases concern fraud with EU funds perpetrated in the member states rather than in Brussels. However, at the start of 2008 OLAF had 84 cases of suspected fraud in the EU Commission ongoing. In spite of its questionably serious efforts, over at least the last seven years not one EU official has been jailed or even convicted for the fraudulent use of EU funds.[2] In one of the few accurate statements it has ever made, OLAF itself admits: 'The number of proven cases so far is very low.'[3]

One difficulty facing OLAF is that it can investigate suspected fraud, but has no powers to prosecute. Instead, it has to pass on its information to the police in the country where the suspected fraud took place. Often this is in Belgium, because most of the EU institutions are in Brussels. In reality, few cases are ever investigated, and on the rare occasions that the Belgian police do carry out a half-hearted effort, Belgian prosecutors conveniently deem even the most blatant cases as being without any merit.

There is another slight difficulty that OLAF seldom mentions when it claims that it is always hard on the heels of miscreants. This is that EU law has given EU officials immunity from prosecution both while they work in the EU and then for the rest of their lives for any acts committed during the course of their duties. So even if the hapless OLAF actually managed to put together a reasonable case against an EU employee, the lucky employee could not be prosecuted anyway, no matter how guilty they are:

> In the territory of each member state and whatever their nationality, officials and other servants of the Communities shall . . . be immune from legal proceedings in respect of acts performed by them in their official capacity, including their words spoken or written. They shall continue to enjoy this immunity after they have ceased to hold office.[4]

This means that EU staff, including even those on short-term contracts, can theoretically steal, defraud and lie to their hearts' content with almost no fear of criminal proceedings. In a speech in 2008 Siim Kallas claimed that it was a myth that many EU officials were corrupt. As proof, he cited the fact that none had been successfully prosecuted for over seven years.[5] Perhaps he was forgetting that all EU employees have immunity from prosecution. It is possible for the EU Commission to remove this immunity in the case of a serious crime, but it's difficult to find any cases where it has actually done this. In most corruption or fraud cases errant officials keep their jobs and pensions, though sometimes they are moved out of harm's way to other EU departments. In the worst cases they are allowed to retire early while retaining their full pension and other EU benefits. A former Commission spokesman explained to us that the EU almost never fires anyone because they are afraid that if an official lost their income, they might be tempted to sell their stories to the press about what really goes on within the EU institutions. It is therefore in both the individual's and the administration's interest that any unpleasantness is settled quietly, discreetly, amicably and usually generously behind closed doors at European taxpayers' expense.

Perhaps the most entertaining case that OLAF has had to deal with concerns the decision of the French commissioner Edith Cresson to hire her live-in dentist and close personal friend as a highly paid EU adviser on HIV/AIDS, a subject in which he may not have been especially well qualified. It's an old story, but one that perfectly illustrates how the EU manages to say that it is acting against misuse of our money while actually doing the opposite. The dentist was paid €136,000 for two years' work, which culminated in 24 pages of notes that were found to be 'not even of minimum interest'.[6] A whole three years after Edith Cresson's resignation as a commissioner, a Belgian court ruled, as usual, that there were no grounds for criminal proceedings. Another two years later, five years after the events, the European Court of Justice surprisingly ruled that Edith Cresson did act 'in breach of her obligations as a European commissioner'. At the time it was thought that Mme Cresson might be deprived of part of her generous EU pension as punishment. However, in a judgement that probably made legal history for its pusillanimity, the Court declared: 'In light of the circumstances of the case, the Court holds that the finding of that breach constitutes, in itself, an appropriate penalty.'

There were two main issues with this outcome. First, one could wonder why it took five years to reach a decision. All the documents covering the dentist's work, qualifications, payments and the expensive 24-page report were readily available, so there was no need for an intensive, time-consuming, five-year 'investigation' – all the case's documentation could have easily been reviewed and a judgement delivered in five days rather than five years. The second interesting feature was the court's quite original view that a guilty verdict in itself was sufficient punishment. There are probably many ordinary people, found guilty by the courts but unlucky enough not to have a senior position in the EU, who are now languishing in jail and who would have wished the same non-punishment was meted out to them as was imposed on the fortunate and well-connected Mme Cresson.

PERSECUTING THE INNOCENT?

Although the EU seems to go to great lengths for long periods of time to avoid taking any action against corrupt employees or europoliticians, it can unfortunately sometimes appear that it is remarkably rapid and effective when it is acting against honest employees who have the temerity to expose any wrong-doing within EU institutions. A few years ago, we were presented with the spectacle of a string of whistleblowers revealing widespread alleged corruption throughout EU organisations. In almost every single case those responsible for the alleged corruption have gone unpunished, while those exposing possible corruption have been persecuted and hounded out of their jobs. But recently the stream of whistleblowers seems to have dried up. It might be worth briefly reviewing the various whistleblowers' stories before looking at why EU whistleblowers appear to have become extinct as a species.

Paul van Buitenen

Perhaps the first of the major whistleblowers was Paul van Buitenen. He exposed what appeared to be endemic abuse even at the highest levels of the European Commission, mostly through the use of fictitious or questionable contracts to outside consultants. One of the most famous cases was Edith Cresson and her dentist. The EU Commission denied van Buitenen's claims, and the socialist group in the EU parliament fought successfully to protect the Commission against calls for its resignation. However, van Buitenen's claims eventually led to an inquiry by a panel of experts that confirmed the accusations of financial mismanagement and widespread corruption and that stated that it was hard to find anyone in the EU Commission possessing 'even the slightest sense of responsibility'.

The report was so damaging that even the majority of MEPs who had tried to protect the Santer Commission were under pressure to act rather than continue to cover up the Commission's wrong-doing. However, sensing that they would be censured by the European parliament, the Santer Commission 'resigned' without submitting to a vote in the parliament. But the Commission was allowed to stay in office until the end of its appointed term, and several of the Santer commissioners managed to keep their jobs for another five lucrative years by joining the Prodi Commission that followed. One of the Santer commissioners who stayed in place was the British commissioner Neil Kinnock, who was charged with rooting out corruption and implementing improved financial management procedures.

Following his revelations, van Buitenen was suspended on half pay and eventually reinstated in a lower position in an EU agency in Luxembourg. In 2001, apparently feeling that nothing was changing, he sent Kinnock's office a 235-page dossier backed up by about 5,000 pages of documents alleging that many old fraud cases had been swept under the carpet and that many new ones were not being investigated. When questioned by journalists, a spokesman for Kinnock's office said: 'We are bending over backwards to investigate all these claims.'[7] Explaining why he sent the dossier, van Buitenen said:

> I saw the same people responsible for all these abuses still there in the Commission or even promoted. I read articles saying that Kinnock was pushing through all these reforms, when I knew it was not really happening. So I had to react.[8]

However in 2002, van Buitenen resigned. He returned to work in Holland where he was made a Knight of the Order of Orange-Nassau by Queen Beatrix. In 2004 he was elected as an MEP.

Dorte Schmidt-Brown

Next up for the 'whistleblower treatment' was a Danish EU employee Dorte Schmidt-Brown. She had worked at the EU's statistics agency Eurostat for about nine years and had been promoted to being responsible for collecting industrial statistics. Concerned by a number of dubious studies, she alerted her superiors to what she had found. She was transferred to another department, and after claiming that she was being victimised for speaking out she was sent on sick leave. When questioned about the case, a spokesman for Neil Kinnock's office said that these were 'internal staff matters' and that they had 'found no evidence for the allegations that Mrs Schmidt-Brown made'.[9] At the time one MEP on the European parliament's budgetary control committee said: 'Mr Kinnock has to decide whether the Commission is going to root out fraud and irregularities or just lift up the carpet and sweep them underneath.'[10]

A subsequent investigation into Eurostat revealed what the investigators called a 'vast enterprise of looting', in which senior employees had siphoned off millions of euros into companies owned by friends, family and others, often for work that was never done. Although Schmidt-Brown's concerns proved correct, the Eurostat directors were just moved into other jobs within the EU where they kept their salaries, benefits and pensions and even got a compensation payment for damage to their reputations from the way OLAF investigators had handled their case. Dorte Schmidt-Brown eventually lost her claim for compensation for the loss of her job and was ordered to pay her own costs.[11]

Robert Dougal Watt

A year later two more EU employees attracted the attention of the EU authorities. Robert Dougal Watt was a British accountant who worked in the European Court of Auditors, the body responsible for checking the EU's accounts to make sure that our EU money is spent lawfully. Watt complained to the European Ombudsman about what he suspected was corruption within the auditing body. First, he was downgraded; then he was sacked. In explaining why they fired him, the disciplinary board showed they didn't care whether Watt's concerns were justified or not: 'The veracity or otherwise of Mr Watt's accusations was not something which the board believed it was called upon to consider.'[12]

Understandably, Watt seemed concerned at how he had been treated and the effect that this would have on other would-be whistleblowers:

I would warn someone to think it through very carefully. It cost me my job in the first instance, my career as an accountant in the second and substantial financial costs associated with a great deal of personal upheaval and stress.[13]

Marta Andreasen

In the same year the name Marta Andreasen hit the headlines. She joined the EU in 2002 and was the first qualified accountant ever to hold the position of EU chief accounting officer. When asked to sign off the previous year's accounts she refused because she was unable to verify the accuracy of the accounts and she felt that the EU's accounting systems were like an 'open till waiting to be robbed'. She revealed her concerns and was quickly suspended on full pay and banned from all EU buildings and the EU email. A year after her revelations, the EU Court of Auditors concluded that it could only reliably trace less than 10 per cent of the EU's expenditure. Moreover, the EU's senior auditor described her as a 'focused and determined professional who was asking the right questions', wrote that her concerns were 'factually substantive and correct' and expressed his concern that her suspension 'would be a serious blow to reform, sending a signal that the old way of keeping things from happening still work'.[14] Moreover, the senior auditor also wrote of his worries about the way the Commission used its 'collective firepower' to 'trash' any individual who dared to challenge its corrupt and bullying culture:[15]

I would for no money have wanted to be in Ms Andreasen's shoes, recognising the unforgiving inclination of a bureaucracy once one is declared taboo by the powers that be, considering the collective firepower it can marshal to trash an individual singled out, if it so wishes, at taxpayers' expense. This is after all an organisation that can sanction people for not speaking well about the Commission.[16]

A year after her suspension, Marta Andreasen was voted Personality of the Year by the readers of *Accountancy Age* magazine. Andreasen was fired but then fought for three years to have her dismissal annulled.[17]

In November 2007 the EU's civil service tribunal rejected her appeal and upheld every single complaint against her. A spokesman for the Commission expressed its satisfaction at the verdict: 'The court has now rejected Mrs Andreasen's claims and upheld our decision to dismiss her for misconduct. The commission is entitled to respect, trust and loyalty from its officials.'[18] For the EU Commission, supposed loyalty to the ruling euro-elite is much more important than preventing the possible theft of billions of euros of our money.

Just a few days after this ruling, the Court of Auditors refused to sign off the EU's accounts for the thirteenth year running because the auditors did not have confidence that the accounts gave a reliable picture of whether the EU's money had been spent legally or not.

Robert McCoy

One more year and one more scandal. Robert McCoy had worked at the EU for more than 30 years and had risen to the post of Internal Auditor at the Committee of the Regions (CoR). The CoR's members are usually politicians from Europe's regions, and they are supposed to advise EU institutions on the impact of EU legislation. At the time the CoR consisted of 222 members and cost us about €47 million a year. It has since expanded to 350 members to take account of the EU's enlargement and increased its budget to closer to €70 million a year. Its members meet in Brussels about six times a year. No EU institution is obliged to follow the Committee's advice and there is little evidence that any ever has, and some critics have suggested that the CoR should be scrapped for being useless and a waste of money. One Commission spokesman admitted that the CoR was just an expensive travel agency offering taxpayer-funded freebie trips for its members to make them pro-EU and that anyone within the Commission would laugh at you if you said that the CoR supported any particular piece of legislation.

McCoy was concerned about what seemed to be the systematic abuse of travel expenses by CoR members. This included claiming allowances for meetings that didn't take place, for car journeys already paid by members' towns and councils and for train and air travel that similarly had already been reimbursed. McCoy asked the committee's secretary general to pass on the suspicious expenses claims to OLAF for investigation. This request was refused. Then McCoy discovered possible fraud on two printing contracts. Again, his request to his superiors to call in OLAF was turned down. McCoy was threatened with disciplinary action for asking inappropriate questions and warned that his bosses wanted to avoid any scandal. McCoy then went public with his concerns. OLAF and the Court of Auditors were eventually called in to investigate. The president of the EU Court of Auditors wrote to the president of the Committee of the Regions to reassure him that McCoy's allegations were found to be unsubstantiated. However, the abuses were so blatant and widespread that even the hopeless OLAF investigators concluded in an interim report: 'The investigation revealed systematic and flagrant incompetence within the Committee of the Regions to respect the essential rules of tendering procedures and financial management.'[19]

Even though OLAF's investigation apparently found that McCoy's allegations were correct, he was hounded, insulted and bullied until he left on sick leave. As for the committee members who had allegedly been stealing our money, no action was taken against them. They kept their positions and their generously subsidised junkets to Brussels. The CoR subsequently said it had improved its administrative procedures to cut down on expenses fraud. Yet over three years later, while auditing the EU's accounts, the Court of Auditors found that the CoR was still reimbursing travel expenses on the basis of hand-written travel agency invoices and that due to the addition of supposed 'administration costs' the amounts being charged were 'on average 83 per cent higher than the price charged by the airline for the ticket used'.[20] The auditors concluded: 'In the Court's opinion, the results of this investigation do not demonstrate that the amounts paid for administrative costs were justified.'[21] The audit also found that attendance registers for CoR meetings were unreliable, so many members of the CoR were getting attendance allowances to which they may not have been entitled. Naturally, neither the Commission nor OLAF took any further action.

Responding to a newspaper claim that 'Mr Kinnock has failed in his mission' of reform in the European Commission, commissioner Neil Kinnock, who was responsible for bringing in new administrative controls to stop fraud and protect whistleblowers, wrote: 'More objective assessors would recognise that – frustratingly but realistically – reform is a process, not an event, and that profound systemic changes can rarely have immediate effects.' He also confirmed that: 'Officials who exercise their statutory duty to report any suspected wrong-doing can do so with full protection for their reputations and careers.'[22]

Hans-Martin Tillack

Revealing EU corruption is not only bad for the health of whistleblowers, it sometimes doesn't do journalists too much good either. Hans-Martin Tillack was a German journalist for *Stern* magazine who got a bit of a reputation for writing about fraud in the EU, in particular the Eurostat scandal. On the orders of OLAF his home and office were raided by six Belgian policemen, and material including his computer, his archives and his personal papers confiscated. He was held for about ten hours without access to a lawyer and was told by one of the policemen that he was lucky he wasn't in Burma or central Africa where 'journalists get the real treatment'.[23]

The accusation against him was that he had bribed an EU official to get hold of EU documents about fraud in EU institutions. In 2007, three years after the police raid, Tillack was awarded costs and damages against the Belgian police by the European Court of Human Rights. In 2008, four years after the event, the Belgian police returned his files to him. For years OLAF had denied that it had been behind the police's decision to investigate Tillack, but in 2008 it admitted that the evidence it had given to the European Courts about the case 'was not factually correct'. However, an OLAF spokesman also claimed: 'But we do not think there is any indication the Court was misled.'[24]

WHERE ARE THE WHISTLEBLOWERS NOW?

A striking feature of the above stories is that they are all a bit old. They all happened in a brief and lively period between 1998 and 2003. So either the EU has managed to clean up its act and completely stamp out corruption or else something has happened to discourage whistleblowers from speaking out. The answer to the conundrum about why there are no more whistleblowers can probably be found in the events of 2004. As part of the EU's administrative reforms, a new set of regulations was introduced defining how whistleblowers should report their suspicions of corruption or other forms of financial mismanagement. The new article 22a of the staff regulations demanded that any whistleblowers must first inform their immediate superiors of any concerns:

> Any official who, in the course of or in connection with the performance of his duties, becomes aware of facts which give rise to a presumption of the existence of possible illegal activity, including fraud or corruption, detrimental to the

interests of the Communities, or of conduct relating to the discharge of professional duties which may constitute a serious failure to comply with the obligations of officials of the Communities, shall without delay inform either his immediate superior or his director-general.

The regulation then went on to say: 'or, if he considers it useful, the secretary-general, or the persons in equivalent positions, or the European anti-fraud office [OLAF] direct.' A key feature of most whistleblowers' stories is that they only went public with their concerns after their own department bosses and OLAF failed to act and because their hierarchical superiors and OLAF investigators often seemed more interested in covering up, rather than uncovering, the truth. It was this inaction that caused most whistleblowers to go to MEPs or the press with their concerns. Moreover, the EU authorities made some attempt to look as if they were doing something only when MEPs or the media started asking questions. Therefore to implement new staff regulations directing employees to confide in their own bosses or in other members of the tightly knit EU inner circle might not have been the most effective way of ensuring that criminal activity would be exposed. What this new regulation did mean, however, was that any whistleblower who now dared to go around their immediate superior or OLAF to reveal corruption to an MEP or someone outside EU institutions would have automatically broken the new staff regulation and therefore could be disciplined, whether their allegations were justified or not.

Introducing the new 'whistleblowers' charter', Neil Kinnock said: 'I have long held the view that conscientious and responsible whistle-blowing in public and private sector organisations is necessary and justified.'[25] But when questioned about these changes in 2007, Paul van Buitenen, then an MEP, seemed none too impressed: 'I would say: things have got even worse. There is now a regulation which supposedly protects so-called whistleblowers, which makes officials believe they can uncover scandals. But in reality if one does this they are destroyed. So the regulation does not work.'[26] Anyway, however honourable the original intentions, the new regulation seems to have had just one result: apart from one small blip, there weren't any more whistleblowers prepared to risk their careers to expose corruption within the EU.

The one exception occurred when a British employee who had worked for 16 years at an EU agency responsible for providing financial aid to companies in poorer Third World countries reported his concerns about possible corruption within the agency. According to one MEP's press release, OLAF investigated the allegations and confirmed that misconduct had taken place. The main official involved denied the allegations, blaming them on a 'disgruntled British employee', and was allowed to retire in order to pursue a political career back in his home country. The whistleblower was unfortunately not treated quite so gently. In 2008 he was removed from his job as head of information technology and put on a temporary six-month contract after being denied a permanent job. One MEP claimed that the employee had been the victim of a witch-hunt for having the courage to speak out.

Even the plodding OLAF seemed to become aware of the sudden dearth of whistleblowers after the new regulation was introduced. In its 2006 annual report it stated: 'No OLAF investigations were launched as the result of information received direct from a whistleblower.'[27] One of the jokes circulating in Brussels at the time of this new regulation was that during the reforms of the EU's administration, the EU had managed to sack many more whistleblowers than fraudsters.

FACTS, FIGURES AND FICTION

The body that is responsible for ensuring that the EU's €134 billion budget is spent properly and legally is called the Court of

Auditors. This is not actually a court, but rather a group of auditors who are based in Luxembourg and who review the EU budget and financial reports each year. Their only job is to ensure the 'regularity and legality' of EU spending. They do not assess if our cash has been used effectively and achieved value for money. At the end of 2007, for the thirteenth year running, the Court of Auditors refused to give the EU budget a clean bill of health. It concluded: 'Errors of legality and regularity still persist in the majority of EU expenditure due to weaknesses in internal control systems both at the Commission and in member states.' Each year, the Commission claims that the fault lies with the member countries, which dispense around 80 per cent of EU money. However, this excuse is rejected by the Court of Auditors: 'Regardless of the method of implementation applied, the Commission bears the ultimate responsibility for the legality and regularity of the transactions underlying the accounts of the European Communities (Article 274 of the Treaty).'

At the end of 2007 the president of the European Court of Auditors presented the Court's decision to reject the EU accounts yet again: 'Allow me to conclude by saying that . . . the Court once again provides an adverse opinion on the legality and regularity of transactions over the majority of the budget.'[28]

Curiously, the EU issued a press release claiming: 'The Court of Auditors has given last year, as it did in previous years, a clean bill of health on the EU accounts.'[29] Yet, seemingly contradicting the EU's own press release, Siim Kallas, vice-president of the Commission and, as Neil Kinnock's successor, the commissioner responsible for administrative affairs, audit and anti-fraud, admitted that things were far from perfect with almost 60 per cent of the EU budget being open to errors and fraud: 'In total, the Court now gives its green light to over 40 per cent of total payments, compared to roughly one-third last year and only 6 per cent two years ago.'[30]

All this meant that in 2004 only a ludicrously small 6 per cent of the EU budget could be reliably accounted for; by 2005 this had reached about 30 per cent, and by 2006 just over 40 per cent.

Every year the European Commission says it is improving its financial control. In the 2006 accounts the Commission had set a goal of meeting 41 objectives and claimed it had achieved 14 of them. However, the Court of Auditors found that only one of the 41 objectives had been completed, a success rate of just over 2 per cent.

Those who are supposed to represent us, the taxpayers, seem surprisingly relaxed about the fact that billions of our money are at risk of being siphoned off by eurocrats, crooks and other dubious characters. Despite the Court of Auditors failing to pass the EU accounts for 14 years in a row, each year MEPs in the European parliament approve ('grant discharge to' in eurospeak) the EU's budget and never even think about holding the Commission to account for its shockingly inadequate financial management. The former head of the European parliament budget committee explained his understanding of the situation: 'The auditors have concluded every year since 1994 that the accounts are reliable.'[31]

Cynics have suggested that expenses fraud is so rife among MEPs that they approve the budget because they don't want to rock the luxurious boat they are in with the eurocrats all cruising comfortably along on a sea of our money. Moreover, the member states' own audit bodies also seem to accept this sorry state of affairs. For example, in Britain the head of the National Audit Office till 2008 seemed to be rather unconcerned by the EU's appalling financial control when he claimed that a rise in the value of irregularities was 'partially due to improved reporting by some member states'.[32] He also stated that the failure of the Court of Auditors to give a positive Statement of Assurance to the EU accounts 'does not indicate that the European Union expenditure is subject to an excessive level of fraud'. Yet on specific budget items that they studied, the auditors found error levels of between 10 and 40 per cent in different areas of EU spending, and the president of the Court of Auditors confirmed that: 'Reasons for the errors in the underlying transactions include neglect, poor knowledge of the often complex rules and presumed attempts to defraud the EU budget.'[33]

At the time of Marta Andreasen's dismissal for daring to criticise the EU's accounts, the head of the EU's Internal Audit Service wrote about the 'chronically sordid state' of EU accounting and then said in an interview: 'The word chronic is I think an understatement rather than an overstatement – we're now in the tenth year that the European Court of Auditors will not be able to express a normal clean opinion on the accounts.'[34] In a memo to the British House of Lords he also claimed that efforts to improve the EU's accounts had 'been frustrated by a very effective but unaccountable coalition of the unwilling' and that eurocrats had a tendency to put their own careers before doing what was right: 'Career patterns driven by staff and management awareness that surfing the waves is a more secure route towards one's next career move than causing them.'[35] Following his critical statements, he was reported to have been warned: 'We have ways of breaking people like you.' Soon after, he took sick leave and then resigned from the EU.

At the end of 2008 when reporting on its audit of the EU's 2007 accounts, for the fourteenth year in a row the Court of Auditors again refused to sign off the EU's accounts, saying 'for most spending areas the Court cannot provide a clean opinion' and 'the opinion on the underlying transactions remains broadly similar to that of last year'.[36] Yet one commissioner claimed that the auditors' report showed 'an improvement on last year', and another stated: 'The European Commission welcomes the findings of today's report by the European Court of Auditors on the 2007 expenditure: they show that we are moving in the right direction.'[37]

The auditors did give a clean bill of health to the money directly spent on EU administration but noted that: 'Payments made to final beneficiaries, such as farmers and project promoters running EU-funded projects, have a too high level of error.' Just on cohesion funds (€42 billon) the auditors found that 'at least' €4.6 billion 'should not have been paid out'. This was around the same level as the previous year. The auditors found an unacceptable level of 'risk of illegality and irregularity' in payments for agriculture and natural resources; cohesion; research, energy and transport; external aid, development and enlargement; education and citizenship – basically all areas of EU spending except for the central administration.[38]

As usual, the EU claimed that its accounts were clean and that the problems with errors and possible fraud occurred mainly in the 80 per cent of the budget spent by the member states:

> In fact, as much as 80 per cent of the EU budget is spent by national or regional governments in the member states. These governments are responsible for selecting beneficiaries and are first in line for ensuring that the money is spent correctly.[39]

For at least 14 years we've had exactly the same excuses from the EU Commission at audit time. The EU wants as much of our money as it can get, is forever thinking of new schemes for spending our money and would even like to introduce special EU taxes in order to get control of and increase its own budget. But when the auditors come calling, eurocrats throw up their hands, protest their innocence and claim they are not responsible for how the vast majority of our money is spent. For the next 20 to 30 years or longer, we will probably have to go through this same sorry farce once a year – eurocrats grabbing ever more of our money to squander on their badly thought out, poorly-managed and inadequately-policed schemes and then denying any responsibility for making sure that this money is used properly. This begs the question: why should we funnel around €134 billion a year through the hands of the EU bureaucrats if they admit that they are completely incapable of guaranteeing that the money is not being stolen?

Even the auditors, who usually diplomatically shy away from any controversial criticisms, seem to admit that the entire way money is allocated and paid by the EU does not and cannot work. At the end of 2008 the auditors concluded that there are 'millions of payments' made to beneficiaries 'who deliberately, negligently or inadvertently make claims for reimbursement of expenditure that is ineligible because it does not meet the regulatory conditions, or is not properly documented or incorrectly calculated' and that 'the nature of primary level controls means that poor performance at this level cannot be compensated for by secondary level controls'.[40] The auditors' solution is to make 'greater use of lump sum or flat-rate payments instead of reimbursement of "real costs"'.[41] Flat-rate payments are precisely the way that MEPs' allowances have been paid, which has been open to massive abuse for decades and is gradually being phased out. Yet here the auditors are suggesting that in future our money should be disbursed with even less control than today and with little relation to the 'real costs'. Maybe the proper solution would be to call it a day on the current hopeless system, massively reduce the EU budget (and the number of eurocrats), let countries keep most of their money and allow them to decide how it is spent. This would hugely cut the costs of administration and greatly improve control, because countries would be accountable for spending their own taxpayers' money rather than siphoning off billions from a seemingly inexhaustible ocean of money provided by those member states like Germany, Britain, Sweden and the Netherlands that were stupid enough to allow themselves to become net contributors to EU funds.

Chapter 11

MAKING CRIME PAY

THE JOYS OF CRIMINOGENICITY

Criminologists have a word, 'criminogenic', which is often used to describe the EU. Criminogenic describes something that encourages people to commit crime. Farmers can hugely increase their income by a slight exaggeration or even seeing double when they count their cows or measure their fields; businessmen can earn millions by driving empty lorries across borders into and then out of EU member countries; lawyers can become multi-millionaires overnight by spotting gaps in the latest flood of poorly drafted EU legislation. In fact, anyone who can find their way around the EU's tens of thousands of rules and regulations can usually become extremely rich at European taxpayers' expense.

Estimates of the level of fraud and other forms of cheating with EU funds vary widely depending on people's attitudes to the EU. Each year when the Court of Auditors gives the thumbs down to the EU's accounts, there are a frenzied couple of weeks during which the eurosceptics and europhiles play the Euromyths game and engage in an energetic slanging match. The europhobes claim that the fact that over half of the EU's €134 billion budget cannot be reliably accounted for shows that fraud and corruption are widespread. The europhiliacs point to the fact that because only about €1.3 billion (1 per cent of the budget) of fraud is actually proved each year the EU exercises rigorous control over its finances.

Like any area of criminality, it is difficult to estimate reliably the actual levels of fraud because criminals tend to be somewhat reticent about broadcasting what they are up to. However, the europhiles' claims that because €1.3 billion of fraud is proved each year the level of fraud must be very low are palpable rubbish. It's a bit like saying that whenever the police don't solve a murder then the dead person isn't really dead. Investigations into the €2.5 billion a year given for five years to eastern European countries prior to their accession found fraud rates of close to 50 per cent, meaning that fraud was already about €1.25 billion a year on just 2 per cent of the EU budget. Therefore, if EU fraud really was just about €1.3 billion a year, as the EU's supporters usually claim, the other 98 per cent of EU funds would have to be completely fraud free, which they most definitely are not. Moreover, although EU apologists keep repeating the 1 per cent figure, on several occasions over the last few years Commission spokespeople have admitted that levels of fraud are probably around 5 per cent – almost €7 billion a year.

Independent studies of fraud levels in the EU have come up with an estimated figure of between 10 and 20 per cent of the EU budget – that is, around €13 billion to €26 billion a year.[1] Furthermore, these figures have been confirmed by research done by the European Commission.[2] That said, on almost every detailed study done – whether it was on the real number of animals owned by farmers, the actual amount of food being produced, the true number of olive trees grown, the contents of lorries entering and leaving the EU, the composition of products like butter, olive oil and meat or the use of development funds – invariably the level of misrepresentation and fraud is between 30 and 50 per cent. So it would not be unrealistic to put the theft of the money that we pay directly to the EU very comfortably in excess of 20 per cent of the EU budget – that is, over €26 billion a year. We should not be surprised by this figure. In Britain, for example, studies by the National Audit Office have consistently found the levels of fraud and error with social security benefits payments made by the British government are around 10.4 per cent a year.[3] Moreover, these are just the cases of fraud that were identified – obviously a lot of fraudsters are somewhat smarter than government officials, and sadly much of their genius will forever go undetected. The real figure for fraud with Britain's benefit payments is probably anywhere between 15 and 20 per cent. So the EU's supporters' repeated claims that only around 1 per cent of our EU cash gets stolen by fraudsters should be taken with a very large pinch of salt. A general rule of thumb for fraud levels with money handed out by governments and other agencies is that within individual countries 10 to 20 per cent will be siphoned off fraudulently; with policies directly controlled by international institutions like the EU and the UN, fraud will be at least 20 per cent to 30 per cent; and with Third World aid it is quite normal that anywhere between 50 per cent and 80 per cent will be skimmed off by corrupt officials, local politicians, the military and other influential figures.[4] Studies of health and educational programmes in Africa have found fraud levels of between 80 per cent and 99 per cent.[5] Moreover, the hyper-production of rules and regulations being churned out by inexperienced, desk-bound Brussels bureaucrats creates thousands of opportunities for the smart to become rich from exploiting the inevitable loopholes in EU legislation. For example, one entrepreneur found that the export subsidy for solid milk products was ten times higher than the subsidy for liquid milk products, so he froze all the yogurt he exported to get the higher subsidy. Similarly, when the EU introduced the concept of paying European farmers just to have land, irrespective of whether anything was grown, the number of supposed farmers in some countries increased massively – in one country the number went up from around 80,000 registered farmers to about 120,000 almost overnight, because almost anyone who claimed they had a bit of land could suddenly get EU subsidies, even if they had never farmed in their lives and would have been hard pressed to tell one end of a cow from the other. Later it was found that the lucky beneficiaries of our cash included organisations as diverse as railway companies (Britain), hundreds of horse-riding clubs (Germany, Denmark and Sweden) and golf clubs (Denmark), all of which were now claiming farming subsidies following the change in the rules. Moreover, many landowners were claiming subsidies for land they rented out to farmers, some of whom also managed to claim subsidies for exactly the same land. Just in Northern Ireland about 176,000 entitlements worth €13.8 million were paid out to landowners not actually doing any farming – we don't know on how many of these pieces of land subsidies were also paid to the people who farmed them.

Then, when the EU introduced special payments for land that was deemed to be of poor agricultural quality (LFAs or 'less-favoured areas' in eurospeak), the amount of land that was classified as being an LFA quickly and suspiciously increased by 56 per cent. Luxembourg, a country not generally associated with vast deserts or towering mountain ranges, suddenly found that 98 per cent of its land was 'of poor quality', Greece went for over 80 per cent and fertile Germany discovered that about half of its farms were on unproductive land.

TAKE WHAT YOU WANT

For any law enforcement to be effective there has to be a conflict of interests between the policed and those who police them. Crooks naturally tend to be motivated to fill their pockets with other people's money, and the police are paid to try to stop them. However, if it is in the interest of the police that criminals should get away with their crimes, there's not much incentive for rascals to be less rascally. Unfortunately for us taxpayers, the way EU money is paid out actually acts as an incentive to the authorities in each country to ignore, and sometimes even encourage, the mass theft of our money.

For a start, most countries view EU money as fair game, and the more they can grab for their citizens, the better it is for that country's economy. So there is little motivation within the country that benefits to make life difficult for those who decide to take a little bit more of our cash than they deserve. Furthermore, in most countries there is no policing of those who take our money. In France, Greece and many other member states it is farmers and farmers' unions who are responsible for inputting and checking the quality of the information provided by farmers to the EU to enable farmers' subsidies to be calculated. So they are all likely to be interested in maximising the amounts paid to their own farmers, even if this means a rather flexible inter-pretation of rules and a rather creative approach to the truth. This tendency to spray our money around in their own backyard is compounded by the way the EU hands out the money. Farmers and businessmen first claim their EU money from their own government, and then the government is reimbursed by the EU with our money. So if a government were to admit it had been defrauded of a few hundred million, it would not be reimbursed by the EU and in addition it would have to take legal action against the fraudsters to recover the money. So massive fraud is constantly overlooked to make sure that member states' governments get their cash back from EU coffers.

In spite of the obvious incentives for countries to turn a couple of blind eyes to fraud, misuse of our money is so widespread that even the wilfully blind cannot help but notice a few cases. In any year about 12,000 cases are reported to the rather hopeless OLAF, and in a few hundred of these OLAF does make some half-hearted efforts to find out what's going on. In 2006 OLAF's investigations led to the recovery of about €114 million. In 2007 this rose to a more impressive €204 million – around three times its own operating budget – but this represented only 16 per cent of the value of the investigated frauds. This means that with an investigation rate of about 1.7 per cent of reported fraud incidents (about 200 out of around

12,000) and a success rate of around 16 per cent, OLAF is getting hold of something like 0.27 per cent of the bad guys, which is not something that is likely to inspire fear and awe in the minds of those out to steal our money.

In addition, because OLAF can only investigate and has no powers to prosecute, it is up to the countries' legal authorities to bring wrong-doers to trial. Usually, even when they are handed clear evidence of gross theft of our money, member states' legal authorities don't bother taking any action against the perpetrators because they don't want the embarrassment of admitting that their own citizens have been pillaging EU taxpayers' money. Moreover, the average OLAF investigation takes two and a half years, and many take six to eight years. That gives even the least intellectually gifted fraudsters and their lawyers plenty of time to run rings around the lumbering, bureaucratic and largely ineffective OLAF. On the few occasions when legal action is taken it is often years after the event and only for a minor offence, which almost never leads to a custodial sentence. For example, in 2008 OLAF announced that a French court had acquitted two dairy managers 'on the charge of conspiracy to defraud' and instead given them only a few months suspended prison sentences each on a much lesser charge of 'selling products manufactured using adulterated butter'.[6] The suspected fraud valued at €23 million took place at the end of the 1990s. However, the two managers might still appeal, so the case could drag on even longer. Commissioner Kallas said: 'The judgement shows that fraud with the EU Budget will not go unpunished. This is a great success for OLAF.'[7] The director-general of OLAF was perhaps more modest when he explained that the case 'shows that OLAF's work cannot always be expected to bring results overnight'.[8]

Laughably, the people responsible for recovering EU money that is taken fraudulently by their citizens are the authorities in the member countries. Naturally, they have little desire to hand back lots of embezzled cash into EU coffers. At the end of 2007

Germany had failed to recover €592 million, Italy €434 million, Spain €249 million, Britain €178 million and little Slovakia, with a population of just over 5 million, still owed us €83 million. Overall, at least €1.7 billion was missing, although, as the EU so diplomatically admitted: 'The figures given in this table represent a theoretical maximum rather than the amounts that will actually be made available to the Communities' budget.'[9] Basically, we would never see most of this money again. Incidentally, this figure of €1.7 billion of identified wrong payments rather gives the lie to the eurocrats' constant claims that EU fraud is only worth at most €1.3 billion.

MONEY GROWS ON TREES (AND IN THE GROUND)

Those who have best shown the indomitable fighting spirit of the human race must surely be European farmers in the way they have plundered agricultural subsidies for the last half century. We now give our farmers €58 billion or so each year, paid out in agricultural subsidies and rural development. The latest report by the Court of Auditors showed that our farmers never seem to tire of using tried and tested methods of defrauding us. The most basic technique is to exaggerate the size of their fields – about 40 per cent of fields tested across the EU were much smaller than claimed by farmers. With farmers aware that checks are now being carried out using satellite technology, the size of fields in some countries has been mysteriously 'shrinking', thereby saving the taxpayer many millions. However, with about 9 million farmers claiming subsidies for over 80 million fields each year, it is impossible to police this effectively, and the farmers and farmers' unions know it.

Farmers also have a tendency to invent animals rather than going to the trouble of actually breeding them. In Slovenia about half of the cows for which we paid subsidies didn't exist; in Italy and Malta the proportion of 'ghost' animals was found to be well above 20 per cent; and in other countries millions of non-existent cows, pigs, goats and sheep are successfully chewing their way through vast quantities of our money.[10] In southern Italy €50 million was paid out over four years to farmers for selling surplus citrus fruit – neither the farmers nor the fruit ever existed. And for years, enterprising Greeks claimed huge subsidies for importing sugar cane from Croatia – this was only discovered when someone helpfully pointed out to EU officials in rainy old Brussels that although the Croatian climate is pleasantly sunny, it does not permit sugar cane to be grown there.[11]

Many food processors are also taking part in the farming feeding frenzy. For example, over a quarter (205 out of 787) of olive oil producers were found to have been cheating EU funds. About €2 billion a year is paid in subsidies to olive oil producers, and much of this is thought to be fraudulent – in Italy the business is believed to be controlled by the mafia. In one particularly productive period a single olive oil fraud cost the EU €113 million.

Dairies are also particularly skilful at skimming off EU taxpayers' money. In France just one dairy managed to defraud us of over €20 million, and an Irish dairy one of the authors knows of seemed to exist solely for the purpose of performing a Robin Hood role of relieving the EU of its cash and redistributing this into the welcoming hands of the ever cheerful local populace. In Italy we lost €3 million, which was paid out for around 900 tons of non-existent tobacco, part of which was supposedly 'exported' in order to get export subsidies and part of which was 'sold' repeatedly from producers to processors and back again in a continuous circle in order to claim EU subsidies each time the 'ghost tobacco' improbably changed hands. Agricultural fraud was found to be especially widespread among growers and food processors in Greece – it has been every year since the country's accession in 1981. Not surprisingly, Greece is the country that has most consistently and steadfastly refused to provide any information about the recipients of Common Agricultural Policy money.[12]

IMPORT–EXPORT SCAMS

The main area of agricultural fraud arises where farmers get subsidies for crops and animals that either don't exist or that are falsely classified as being of a quality or type that attracts a higher subsidy. However, another fertile source of money for farmers is by exporting, or at least claiming to export, their produce. In order to avoid building up huge grain mountains, wine lakes and other excess agricultural produce farmers are encouraged to export their excess production to countries outside the EU. Because EU prices are much higher than prices on the world market, EU produce is actually too expensive to be sold. However, by paying our farmers generous export subsidies, which are often greater than the price they can get selling the products in non-EU countries, the EU can dump our excess food outside the EU at more competitive prices.

Importing products into and exporting things out of the EU can be almost as lucrative a pastime as inventing animals and crops to cream off farming subsidies. Sometimes 'exported' food never even quite makes it across EU borders. Farmers have been found to have 'sold' their produce to merchants who forge export documents to claim generous EU subsidies and then sell the produce back to farmers or other merchants within the EU so that it can be sold for nice high EU prices. In one year, for example, 38,000 tons of beef were involved in just a single case; in another year it was thousands of tons of butter.

The enormous number of different import tariffs imposed by the EU to protect its own inefficient producers also creates an almost irresistible temptation for traders to be slightly creative when labelling goods in order to pay lower tariffs than they should. For example, by designating meat products as being lower quality than they actually are, importers can save millions because duties on higher quality meat can be eight times those on lower quality meat. Most of these frauds will never be discovered. One of the few cases that have been uncovered was known as the 'Romanian Affair'. Here the importers managed to save over €60 million by declaring high quality meat imported from Romania, before it joined the EU, as 'edible slaughterhouse by-products', mainly diaphragm muscle. Because the meat was ground up on arrival in Germany, there was no chance that investigators would have been able to discover the fraud. However, this fraud did come to light because someone calculated that the 10,870 tons of supposed diaphragm muscle that were imported would have required slaughtering every single cow in Romania, and possibly a few more.

Another common deceit is to change the country of origin to pay lower tariffs, which works particularly well with commodities like bananas, scampi, garlic and T-shirts. For example, by declaring that 18.5 million T-shirts had been produced in the holiday island nation of the Maldives, rather than in their real country of origin China, the importers both avoided paying import duties and avoided using up some of China's import quotas. Similarly, importers saved themselves about €20 million over four years by passing off 300 million Chinese cigarette lighters as coming from Malaysia and Indonesia. Moreover, one estimate by OLAF was that around 600,000 tons of Chinese clothing and footwear have entered the EU using false certificates of origin and misleading value declarations, losing us taxpayers around €200 million. Most spot-checks of trains and trucks entering the EU find fraud levels of close to 50 per cent through mislabelling, false certificates of origin and wrong quantities.

HELPING THE CORRUPT HELP THEMSELVES

The EU's €58 billion a year agricultural spending has long been the biggest pot of money available for the honest and not so honest to feed themselves and their families. But close behind come the €48 billion a year EU structural funds, also called 'cohesion funds'. This is money paid to countries before accession and to poorer regions long after accession to help them catch up with the richer parts of the EU. In the seven years from 2007 to 2013 about €308 billion of our money will be handed over, ostensibly to decrease disparities between the EU's poorer and richer regions. These structural funds have long been recognised as being especially subject to widespread fraud and corruption, and usually just a very few people in the poorer regions tend to rake off most of the cash, leaving the majority as miserable as they were before the funds mysteriously started to disappear. In the latest Court of Auditors study of a sample of structural funds projects 69 per cent of payments made were found to contain major errors. Many of these errors do not necessarily mean that fraud has taken place. Nevertheless, such a high error rate hardly inspires confidence that our tens of billions are being put to good, agreed, legal purposes.

Fraud with these funds can take many forms. On some projects there is simple old-fashioned overcharging; on others millions are lost because the work is not done at all. In the past countries like Italy and Greece were the EU champions at embezzling structural funds. In one case in Greece nine clothing manufacturers received €2.9 million to help them create jobs. So they just sacked their existing workers and then re-employed them in a new company with a new name. This arrangement seemed to suit everybody. The Greeks got our money to which they weren't entitled, and the EU could issue a few press releases boasting about how successful it was at job creation. There are many roads and bridges in both Italy and Greece that have not been built in spite of the supposed construction companies having long since pocketed our cash. About €5 million was given to a children's cancer centre in Italy, which still hadn't installed a single bed 16 years after receiving the money, and a hospital near Naples took a mere 35 years to be built. At the latest inspection it was found that the local mafia were using it as a weapons store.[13]

Moreover, fraudsters can operate their scams with impunity because many governments have been less than enthusiastic about encouraging investigations into the theft of EU money. In August 2008 the Italian government shut down the office of the Italian high commissioner against corruption, thereby ensuring that Italian fraudsters would have an easier life. In June 2008 Latvia's parliament voted to sack the head of the country's anti-corruption bureau for alleged mismanagement of the bureau's funds. And in Slovenia the government is trying to close that country's anti-corruption office. Meanwhile, in Austria in 2008 the anti-corruption agency was being investigated by the Austrian parliament following its over-zealous efforts to investigate allegedly corrupt politicians. Whatever the rights and wrongs of each case, taken together they do suggest that across Europe there has been a weakening of fraud investigators' powers.

As EU structural funds move towards the eastern European countries, levels of fraud and corruption are reaching heights that might even make the eyes of the Greeks and Italians water. The Czech Republic is scheduled to receive about €26.8 billion of our money over the 2007–13 budget period, in spite of the fact that in 2008 it was ordered to return €9.75 million allegedly embezzled by eight people, including at least two senior politicians. However, it is to Bulgaria and Romania that Italy and Greece seem to have passed the baton in the race to become the biggest embezzlers of our money.

Bulgaria and Romania both joined the EU on 1 January 2007. Before joining, as pre-accession states both countries had already received – and duly stolen – billions of euros. A Court of Auditors study found that over half of Bulgarian and Romanian projects reviewed 'are not operating as intended' (eurospeak for 'they've stolen our money'). There were excellent political reasons for encouraging these two countries to join the EU as soon as possible: membership would not only prevent them falling under Russia's influence but also improve their economies, thus avoiding the possibility of having two failed states on the EU's borders. One of the conditions for allowing both these countries to join the EU was that they would clean up their corruption and free their police and judicial systems from the control of organised crime. Unfortunately, not much progress seems to have been made in either country.

In Bulgaria there are about 20 high-profile professional killings each year. Football clubs are seen as an excellent way of laundering stolen EU money because it can be moved around by paying hugely excessive transfer fees. Three successive chairmen of just one football club were killed, presumably more because of their involvement in criminal activities than the footballing prowess of their players. Although many murders are carried out in broad daylight, there are seldom any witnesses and never any successful prosecutions. Moreover, in 2008 it was revealed that senior ministers had been holding meetings with one of the most powerful mafia bosses in the country. As a Bulgarian member of parliament and former counter-intelligence chief explained: 'Other countries have the mafia. In Bulgaria, the mafia has the country.'[14] An EU Commission report in 2007 concluded: 'Reform of the judiciary and law enforcement structures is necessary and long overdue. The fight against high-level corruption and organised crime is not producing results.'[15]

In 2008 a further EU report, described as the most scathing ever written about an EU state, reached similar conclusions: 'High-level corruption and organised crime exacerbate these problems of general administrative weakness in administrative and judicial capacity.'[16] Following this report, the EU withheld around €450 million from Bulgaria. The country's main response seems to have been to spend about €1 million hiring some PR consultants to lobby the Commission and produce 'objective' articles claiming that Bulgaria is being unfairly treated by the EU. No doubt, after a few more histrionics by the EU Commission and a few empty promises by the Bulgarians, our money will start to flow once more and the people who have been helping themselves to our cash will be able to treat every day as Christmas once again.

Romania is due to receive €17.3 billion in the 2007–13 budget period. Before the country's entry into the EU it appointed a tough and respected anti-fraud investigator as justice minister. However, once Romania was in the EU, despite protests from Brussels, she was sacked. Her replacement lasted less than a year before he was forced to resign after corruption allegations, which naturally he denied. By the end of 2008 there was uncertainty over the future of the country's latest head of anti-corruption. The leader of the Council of Europe's committee against corruption claimed that the investigator's 'only mistake was that he was non-partisan, impartial and objective and took his job seriously'.[17] Then an EU report indicated that rather than continuing the battle against corruption, the Romanian government actually seemed to be actively helping the corrupt to avoid prosecution. For example, in 2007, after EU accession, Romania amended its criminal code to require prosecutors to give advance warning to any senior politicians whose houses or offices they were going to raid. It also, usefully for corrupt politicians, required prosecutors to announce whose telephone calls were being monitored and to close any investigations more than six months old. In addition, large-scale banking fraud was decriminalised.[18] In Romania politicians have judicial immunity both while in office and after they have left office unless the national parliament votes to remove that immunity. In mid-2008 the parliament refused to allow corruption prosecutions against a former prime minister and a former transport minister.

At the end of 2007 an EU report clearly documented the weakening of law and order in this blighted country: 'Many of the measures that were presented, before accession, to be instrumental in the fight against corruption have been deliberately blunted by parliament or the government immediately after accession.'[19] The report then went on to describe the failure to prosecute a single person for corruption: 'All major pending trials concerning high-level corruption, started just before accession and only after many years of hesitation, have now been aborted and are, most probably, definitely abandoned for all practical purposes.'[20] The report concluded by saying that 'instead of progress in the fight against high-level corruption, Romania is regressing on all fronts', and it noted 'the intense resistance of practically the whole political class of Romania against the anti-corruption efforts'. However, when the final version of the EU's report was published in February 2008, its tone seemed to have softened somewhat so that it reached rather different – one might say almost the opposite – conclusions: 'In its first year . . . Romania has continued to make progress to remedy weaknesses that would otherwise prevent an effective application of EU laws, policies and programmes.' The final report did go on to admit: 'However, in key areas such as the fight against high-level corruption, convincing results have not yet been demonstrated.' So while the first draft suggested Romania was regressing, the second was styled to intimate that Romania was actually making progress. Based on this more positive final version of the report, the EU Commission has found no reason to withhold EU funds from the country.

Thus there has been a brief hiccup in the flow of our money into Bulgaria. But the river of cash pouring into its neighbour Romania will continue uninterrupted. Watching the evaporation of the money we sent to Romania, one of Germany's most influential newspapers commented: 'High-ranking politicians in Romania accused of corruption should not fear justice.'[21]

EU taxpayers watching their billions being channelled into the waiting arms of businessmen and politicians in these two viscerally corrupt countries would be more than justified in being concerned that their money will never benefit the poor for whom it is intended.

VAT'S HOW TO MAKE MONEY

Perhaps the largest and most lucrative fraud currently rife throughout the EU is what is called MTIC (Missing Trader Intercommunity Fraud), also known as 'carousel fraud'. This game has various different and increasingly complex forms, but fundamentally it involves someone setting up a company to import some goods into an EU country. They then sell the goods on to another company that exports the goods while reclaiming VAT. Meanwhile, the company that first imported the goods disappears without paying its VAT, hence the name 'missing trader fraud'. The goods then pass from company to company in country after country without any VAT ever being paid, but with VAT being reclaimed from the unsuspecting or even compliant tax authorities every time the goods change hands or cross a border. So the goods go round and round through different companies, which is why it has also been called 'carousel fraud'. The money being handed out to fraudsters doesn't actually come from the EU's €134 billion a year budget; it comes straight from the taxes we all pay to our national governments. But it means that billions of pounds and euros of our money are being given directly to criminals and so represents a massive loss of resources that could be used to improve public services, help the poor or lower taxes.

Experts' estimates of the scale of carousel fraud vary widely, but some tax specialists and criminologists are moving towards agreement that this VAT fraud costs us over €60 billion a year – €120 each a year for every man, woman and child in the EU.[22] However, recent EU documents now claim that carousel fraud actually costs us €100 billion a year.[23]

That the EU is apparently so forthcoming about the massive size of VAT fraud is interesting for us eurotwitchers because it reveals much about the eurocrats' flexible use of numbers to suit their own purposes. Whenever the EU estimates how much of its own budget is scammed off by fraud, it always selects as low a figure as it feels it can get away with while maintaining a straight face. This is because the EU wants us to believe its claim that our money is being used for 'good, agreed purposes' and is subject to 'proper management and control'.[24] However, the EU superstate is desperate to extend its own authority by establishing a fully-functioning European police force and by increasing the powers of its own prosecution service, Eurojust, by giving it power to prosecute criminals in any EU country. Any crimes committed in just one EU member state can be dealt with by that state's police without any need for the EU's intervention. So to justify expanding its power, EU authorities are always keen to talk up the threat of what they call 'cross-border crime' because they can claim that this can only be effectively combated by cross-border policing, namely an EU police force backed by EU prosecutors. So whenever there is a terrorist incident or a cross-border fraud like carousel fraud, the EU is usually keen to exaggerate the threat as much as possible as evidence for the need to give the EU yet further power over our lives.

But whether VAT fraud costs us €60 billion a year or the EU's figure of €100 billion a year, this is at least a billion pounds every week – a massive sum of money being haemorrhaged out of our taxes and being pushed by our tax authorities into the bank accounts of criminals. The most common items used for carousel fraud are small, high-value products like mobile phones and computer chips. To give just a few examples of the size of this problem, one recent single VAT fraud in France concerning mobile phones is estimated by the French police to have cost French taxpayers over €100 million.[25] French authorities have admitted that they may be losing around €19 billion a year on VAT fraud, much of it to carousel fraud. In Germany fraudsters pocketed around €162 million just from driving one truck of mobile phones back and forwards across the border between Germany and Switzerland for five years and reclaiming VAT every time the lorry left the EU.[26]

Germany estimates its VAT losses at around €17 billion a year. The finance minister for one German state explained: 'VAT fraud is the Achilles' heel of public finances, and with EU enlargement it is spiralling out of control.'[27]

In Britain Her Majesty's Revenue & Customs is trying to recover more than £10 billion from falsely reclaimed VAT, which is now thought to have ended up in Dubai. So widespread is carousel fraud in the UK that people as diverse as a law lecturer and a Labour MP's son were reported to have been successfully prosecuted for the offence. The law lecturer admitted cheating the government out of £51 million over ten years and was reported to have hidden some of his profits in waste bins full of cash.[28] The MP's son was convicted of laundering £845,000 accumulated from carousel frauds involving mobile phones and computer chips. Naturally, the MP said they would appeal the guilty verdict, as he claimed: 'I genuinely, sincerely and passionately believe that my son has done nothing wrong. Everything was legal and above board.'[29]

Given the extraordinary amounts of our money being hoovered up by carousel fraudsters, one might have thought that the eurocrats would have been keen to stop this brazen theft of our taxes. The Commission has been eager to talk up the magnitude and threat of cross-border VAT fraud in order to justify increasing its power over European policing and prosecution, but it has also been extraordinarily slow to take action against this kind of fraud even when it had the opportunity to do so. Some individual countries have tried to clamp down on carousel fraud, but with very limited success. Britain tried to implement a new method of repaying VAT (called 'reverse charging'), but was prevented by the Commission and allowed to apply the new tax regime to mobile phones and computer chips only. Most experts felt that this would just shift the fraud from these two products to other things, like iPods, MP3 players, digital cameras and even diamonds. One said: 'Professional criminals have been quick to notice the millions that can be made from VAT carousel frauds. While there has been a crackdown, I am sceptical it will halt this avalanche of huge frauds against the taxpayer.'[30] When asked about the introduction of 'reverse charge', the expert said: 'Many fraudsters are laughing all the way to their offshore tax haven. Fraud is set to keep on increasing as long as others see it as a safe route to making large amounts of money illegally, particularly in the case of VAT frauds.'[31]

When the Commission did finally get around to trying to do something, its attempts were blocked by some member countries, in particular Ireland. Ireland claims that it is only acting to protect its independence to choose its own tax rates. However, Irish fraudsters are known to have made billions from carousel fraud. In one year alone the number of computer chips supposedly shipped to Ireland was sufficient to have supplied the whole European and Asian computer industries. This might explain why Irish politicians have been reluctant to allow any EU legislation that could kill off this amazing source of golden eggs. And now that kleptocracies like Bulgaria and Romania, with incontinent borders and some corruptible customs officials and politicians, have been admitted into the EU, we can expect the Commission to keep on mysteriously dragging its feet in order to allow fraudsters with influence over the politicians to continue enriching themselves at our expense.

Meanwhile, those governments that are keen to reduce this Brobdignagian thieving have to ask for the EU's permission to act and are usually prevented from any effective enforcement by the EU superstate's top bureaucrats for reasons that are far from transparent and possibly even self-interested.

Chapter 12

THE MOST STUPID POLICY IN HUMAN HISTORY?

OPINIONS DIFFER

The initial intention of the Common Agricultural Policy (CAP) was to make Europe self-sufficient in food after the shortages caused by low agricultural productivity and by two major wars, and by the early 1970s the CAP had more than achieved its aims. Spurred on by massive amounts of taxpayers' money, EU farmers were producing far more food than EU citizens could eat or drink, as farmers grew whatever got the largest subsidies regardless of whether anybody actually wanted to buy their produce. So we were treated to the unedifying sight of food accumulating in butter and beef mountains at a time when about a billion people in the Third World didn't have enough to eat and around 9 million died each year because of hunger and malnutrition. The CAP managed to burden us with a 17.8 billion litre lake of extremely low quality wine – apparently enough to give four bottles to everyone in the world.[1] We also had to pay for much of this excess food to be stored, reprocessed and often destroyed. This hugely expensive over-production would have bankrupted the EU had Britain and Denmark not joined it in 1973. The large annual financial contribution generously made by these two countries' taxpayers gave Europe's farmers access to more much-needed cash to keep on growing more food to add to the already huge surpluses.

The EU claims that the CAP is a key part of sustaining the EU economy: 'The common agricultural policy is fundamental to the strength and competitiveness of EU farming and of the agri-food sector as a whole with its 19 million jobs.'[2] Among the CAP's benefits the EU lists 'spending the money where it is most needed', 'benefiting consumers by promoting quality, innovation and competition' and contributing to 'fairer world trade'. However, one UK diplomat seemed to have a different opinion when he called the CAP 'the most stupid, immoral state-subsidised policy in human history, communism aside'.[3] He accused it of paying farm subsidies that 'bloat rich French landowners and pump up food prices in Europe causing African poverty'. When these comments were made public, the British Foreign Office said they were meant as a joke, but the long-suffering EU citizens who pay at least €100 billion a year extra in taxes and higher food prices because of the CAP, and the millions of farmers in poorer countries who are impoverished by the CAP dumping taxpayer-subsidised food on world markets, might not appreciate the funny side of this absurdly wasteful and damaging policy.

If the CAP genuinely benefited poorer farmers, consumers and Third World countries we might not have grounds to resent the tens of billions of our taxes that get sprayed on the agricultural sector every year. However, there are clear indications that the way the CAP functions has fairly major negative consequences for at least three groups: many European farmers, all European consumers and, perhaps most seriously, hundreds of millions of the most impoverished people in the world's most deprived countries.

THE RICH SHALL INHERIT THE EARTH

Predictably, the biggest winners from the CAP are French farmers – hence the absolute refusal of French politicians to allow even the slightest tinkering with the system. Although less than 10 per cent of EU farmers are in France, the mysterious alchemy of the CAP ensures that these farmers get around 25 per cent of all CAP money. More than 130,000 French farmers, compared to nearer 40,000 in each of Spain, Germany and the UK, get over €20,000 a year, with about 3,000 French farmers receiving more than €100,000 each in subsidies. Although France and its farmers constantly complain and protest about how difficult it is to make a living from farming, the average earnings of farmers in France are around 60 per cent higher than the overall average earnings of all French workers.

When the BEES (the Baltic and eastern European states) started joining the EU it was thought that help to farmers in the rich countries would have to be channelled towards farmers in the new poorer member states, particularly to Poland, which has a huge farming sector. However, France and the PIGS (Portugal, Italy, Greece and Spain) managed to protect their farmers' share of our money by pressuring the EU Commission to agree to pay subsidies to farmers in the new member states at only a quarter of the rate received by the fortunate French and PIGS farmers. By 2013 payments to farmers in the BEES should reach the same level as those received by farmers in the richer countries unless over the next few years our Gallic and Mediterranean friends twist the Commission's arm yet again to get further concessions for France and the PIGS at the expense of farmers in the newer, less wealthy EU members.

The EU justifies the continuing existence of the CAP by claiming that it enables farmers to have a reasonable standard of living: 'Where necessary, the CAP supplements farm income to ensure that farmers make a decent living.'[4] However, when one looks at how CAP money is actually distributed it is far from obvious that our cash is going to the most deserving. About 85 per cent of the CAP's annual €58 billion goes to just 18 per cent of farms, and the richest 2 per cent of farmers and agricultural companies cream off over a quarter of the EU farm budget.

Governments have always been rather reticent about

revealing who actually gets all our CAP money, and many countries refuse to disclose this information at all. Others have fought for years to avoid letting us know who is taking our cash. One Scottish newspaper battled for two and a half years to get the names of the hundred farmers who received the largest CAP payments in Scotland. When the information was released, it showed that the country's largest farms had received an average of about £230,000 a year each over five years, while the average subsidy for all Scottish farmers was about £9,000 and over a hundred poorer farmers got less than £100 a year each over the same period. Similarly in Ireland, larger farms were being given about €250,000 a year each while the average Irish farmer was getting around €10,000 a year.

Many big businesses, which could hardly be classed as needing CAP subsidies to attain CAP's goal of making 'a decent living', receive seriously large amounts of the money we pay into the CAP, mainly from export subsidies. In Sweden and Denmark Arla Foods and Danisco are two of the largest beneficiaries. Arla has been given over €1 billion and Danisco over €500 million since 2000. In Germany, Holland and Belgium food company Campina has received almost €1 billion. In Britain, Austria, Denmark, Spain and Holland Swiss food giant Nestlé has also picked up hundreds of millions. One of Britain's largest CAP beneficiaries seems to be the sugar company Tate & Lyle, which is generously given over £100 million a year of our money from the CAP.

Other companies that don't look especially agricultural can also fill their pockets with CAP cash from export subsidies. When we eat the normally disgusting airline food on planes that are leaving the EU or stuff ourselves on cruise ships, the EU considers that the food we use is being exported. This has allowed cruise ships and airlines to take millions in CAP export subsidies. When questioned about this dubious use of our money, EU officials excuse their profligacy by saying that they are just following the rules. It never seems to occur to them that if the rules are stupid and are resulting in millions of euros of our money being given to the undeserving, then maybe the rules should be changed.

But perhaps some of the most surprising beneficiaries of EU CAP largesse have been French banks, which are based in some of the most fashionable and expensive areas of Paris, where the only cow, pig, chicken or duck you will see will be on your dinner plate. Four of France's six largest recipients are banks. The BNP, Crédit Mutuel, Crédit Agricole and Banque Populaire are all listed as having received over €100 million for their role in supporting France's agricultural community, mainly through offering loans to farmers.[5]

Many of Europe's elite seem to do very nicely each year out of the money that we taxpayers pour into the CAP. In 2007, after ten years of refusing to disclose the information, the Austrian government revealed that Hans Adam II, Crown Prince of Liechtenstein, with a fortune estimated at over €2 billion, was one of the country's largest individual recipients of CAP subsidies.[6] The prince, one of the world's richest heads of state, is neither an Austrian nor even an EU citizen, but he still receives millions of our money. One of the luckiest recipients in Germany was reported to be Baroness Karin von Ullmann, an aristocrat with assets valued at around €4.1 billion.[7] In Denmark one of the Queen's sons received €215,838 in just one year.[8] Albert, Prince of Monaco, reportedly pockets around €300,000 a year, several French politicians get over €100,000 each, and numerous EU politicians also receive similar amounts.[9]

The British royal family also seems to do nicely from the CAP: the Queen gets almost £400,000 a year, and her son, the Prince of Wales, receives over £500,000 a year.[10] The British aristocracy are similarly well supported by us taxpayers, with the Duke of Westminster (worth £5 billion) reportedly getting over £325,000 in just one year, the Duke of Marlborough (worth £1 billion) over £370,000, the Duke of Bedford £380,000, the Earl of Leicester £250,000 and the 4th Baron de Ramsey over

£200,000.[11] All this seems to give the familiar expression 'handing round the cap' a whole new meaning. In Scotland the largest recipients include several members of the aristocracy: the Earl of Roseberry, the Earl of Southesk, and Lord Morton.[12] In 2002 the EU Commission proposed imposing a ceiling of €300,000 on payments to any one landowner. Britain, a country where farms tend to be larger, led the opposition to this proposal after strong lobbying by the National Farmers' Union and the Country Land and Business Association. The rejection of the Commission's proposal guaranteed that Europe's wealthiest landowners and agri-businesses would continue to receive the biggest subsidies while the EU's poorer farmers would struggle to make a living. Anyway, even if such a ceiling were imposed, it would probably change absolutely nothing – the larger recipients could just split up their farms or activities among their families or different companies to bring them below the proposed €300,000 threshold and continue to receive just as much of our money as before.

The average CAP payment to EU farmers is probably less than £8,000 a year. So although we pay tens of billions a year to our farmers, every time someone suggests even slightly reducing farm subsidies, enraged poorer farmers invariably take to the streets. Many of them might well experience economic problems were their subsidies to be reduced. However, behind the protesting mobs of the genuinely needy, the rich landowners and large agri-businesses, who are taking most of our CAP money, are probably rubbing their hands in glee as the protesters make sure that the big-guns' massive payments remain intact.

One critic of the way the CAP works explained: 'Politically the policy survives on the myth that it is helping the small guy. But the more data we see, the more it becomes clear that wealthy landowners and large agri-businesses scoop up the lion's share.'[13] In fact, our money flows so generously to the already well-heeled across Europe that many businessmen and other speculators, with absolutely no connection to farming, are busily buying up land just for the subsidies that they can then bank every year. To qualify for payments, owners of land do not actually have to do anything that either looks like, sounds like or even smells like farming. One tax accountant, who owned a few acres and was thus eligible for CAP payments, criticised those cashing in on the EU's incontinence with our money: 'I would feel a bit of a fraud claiming this. It is for farmers, not for people like me. People are claiming money for really doing nothing on their land.'[14]

There are other ways in which the CAP actually harms the owners of smaller farms, precisely the group the policy should be helping. For example, because simply owning land can make the owner eligible for CAP subsidies, this increases the value of land. This pushes up both land prices and rents, preventing poorer farmers from expanding their farms to make them more economically viable.

The CAP has become such a goldmine for the already wealthy that even some French farmers are becoming frustrated with the way it favours the rich. One French farmers' leader said: 'In France there is no transparency about aid because they know that if details of how the money is distributed were published tomorrow nobody would continue to pay for it.'[15] The EU has promised that from April 2009 it will publish information about the recipients of CAP money, and it will be interesting to see if the release of this information, showing how the CAP makes the rich richer, causes journalistic outrage. Probably most of our supine, often EU-subsidised press, TV and radio reporters will feel that it is in their interests to avoid upsetting their Brussels paymasters and so the story of how we are being fleeced will hardly get any exposure (see Chapter 9, Making the News).

MILKING CONSUMERS

The EU maintains that another key aim of the CAP is 'supplying consumers with food at reasonable prices'.[16] However, in addition to the €58 billion that it gives directly to our farmers each year, the CAP also helps empty our pockets by saddling us with some of the highest food prices in the world. For the last half century the prices we have paid for items like sugar, butter and beef have been around twice what we would have paid had we been able to buy at world market prices rather than the much higher prices imposed by the CAP. For example, import duties on products like bananas, milk, rice and lamb of between 101 and 173 per cent have kept the prices of these commodities comfortably above twice the world market price.

Three different bodies have produced estimates of the real cost of the CAP to European taxpayers. The independent consumers' association, Which?, calculated that a family of four in Europe pays about £1,000 a year in higher food prices because of the way the CAP inflates the price of food. The World Bank put the cost of artificially high food prices in Europe at around $63 billion a year – in addition to the tens of billions spent on the CAP. And in a budget report the UK Treasury came up with similar figures to the World Bank. Moreover, the EU's high food prices unfortunately hurt poorer families most because they spend a greater proportion of their income on food than better-off households do.

One might have thought that the record high food prices and worldwide shortage of supply in 2008 might have forced the euro-elite to rethink pouring so much of our money into the CAP. After all, why should they hand out so many tens of billions of our cash to farmers at a time when the farmers were earning a lot more from selling their products than they had ever done before? Some countries did half-heartedly suggest the possibility of looking again at the CAP. For example, the British chancellor of the exchequer wrote a letter to colleagues stating that it was 'unacceptable, that at a time of significant food price inflation, Europe continues to apply very high import tariffs to many agricultural commodities'.[17] However, the French agriculture minister predictably took the opposite line:

'The solution to the crisis is not, first of all, through free trade.' He argued with typical Gallic logic that rising food prices proved the need to retain the CAP, with its massive payments to French farmers, as a cornerstone of Europe's food security.

Protected against rising prices by her generous EU salary, CAP subsidies for her own farm and even more generous pension, the European agriculture commissioner didn't seem overly concerned by the problem of food price inflation, claiming that food prices would fall again: 'Prices are likely to fluctuate in the medium term around a level that is higher than what we have seen in recent decades. But we do not think that the record levels reached in recent months are likely to persist.'[18] Nevertheless, the EU did make one small concession to hard-pressed consumers by proposing to end the policy of set-aside (the arrangement whereby farmers were paid not to grow any food products on around 10 per cent of their land). If implemented, this could slightly increase food production in the EU over the next couple of years. However, its effect would be limited by the fact that many farmers are now subsidised to grow crops for biofuels on their set-aside land. So even if set-aside payments were stopped, the biofuel subsidies would mean that farmers would be unlikely to switch the land back to food production.

IMPOVERISHING THE IMPOVERISHED

We are reasonably wealthy in Europe, so we can perhaps afford the absurdity of wasting up to €58 billion a year on lavish subsidies to many of Europe's wealthiest landowners and agri-businesses and tens of billions more on the unnecessarily high food prices to consumers that result from the CAP. But the CAP's most pernicious effects are actually most painfully felt in the poorest countries of the Third World, far away from our comfortable lives.

Agriculture represents less than 2 per cent of Europe's economic output, but it accounts for between 80 and 90 per cent of the wealth of many poorer countries, and the only way these countries can drag themselves out of poverty is through their farmers being able to sell their agricultural produce for a reasonable price to their own citizens and on world markets. Currently around 950 million people in the world suffer from hunger, most of them in Africa. Oxfam has estimated that if Africa could increase its share of world trade by just 1 per cent it would earn enough to lift 128 million people out of extreme poverty, as long, of course, as the money was not siphoned off into offshore bank accounts by the continent's many kleptocratic leaders.[19] However, the CAP prevents these poorest countries trading their way out of poverty in three ways. First, subsidies to European farmers still encourage them to over-produce commodities like cotton, sugar, wheat and tobacco, thus stifling demand for imports from the Third World. Second, high import duties put on products from poorer countries often make them uncompetitive compared to sub-sidised food produced in Europe, thus preventing Third World farmers from exporting to Europe. Import duties on food products are often ten times the level of duties on things like clothes and cars. Finally, the EU pays European farmers billions in subsidies to export their excess production so they can dump it into Third World markets at less than it costs local subsistence farmers to produce.

Although the EU claims that it is trying to support the development of farming in the Third World, it has made little attempt to reduce food-dumping. In fact, pressure from EU farmers to get more of our money has frequently led to an increase in dumping. At the start of 2008, for example, the EU reintroduced generous export subsidies, which led to large-scale dumping of pork in Africa.

The effect across the Third World has been devastating. Import duties and €700 million of subsidies given to Greek and Spanish cotton producers prevent countries like Chad, Mali and Togo from selling their crops to Europe. The CAP also gives European producers (mostly large corporations) of expensive beet sugar over €700 million a year of our money, while imposing import tariffs of over 200 per cent on the less expensive cane sugar, to protect uneconomic European sugar businesses. This makes it almost impossible for countries like Mozambique – where three-quarters of the population live in poverty – to export to Europe. It also leads to over-production within the EU, which has consequently resulted in the dumping of millions of tons of excess European sugar on world markets, driving down the prices that poorer countries can get. A World Trade Organisation panel found that the EU, having agreed to sell only about 1.3 million tons of subsidised sugar on world markets, had actually sold about 6 million tons, almost five times the agreed amount.

The situation is similar with milk, beef and many other agricultural products. After the Asian tsunami an EU politician asked the Thai government how the EU could help rebuild the Thai fishing industry. He was told that Thailand did not need any EU money; instead it wanted a reduction in the tariffs imposed on Thai fish sold to the EU. However, this would have been opposed by French and Spanish fishermen, and so Thailand ended up getting nothing. Even more ludicrously, because we cause so much misery in the Third World through protecting our farmers, we are faced with the additional costs of mass economic migration from poorer countries whose development we prevent, and at the same time we have to give them more in aid to try to limit the starvation and disease that result from their inability to earn money from producing their own food and from trade. It has been estimated that for every dollar we give poorer countries in aid, we take away $2 because of the CAP's unfair trading.[20]

Our politicians are so generous with our money that they spend about €2 per day in subsidies for every cow in Europe, when more than half of Africa's population have to live on less than €1 a day.

Germany and Britain, both major contributors to the CAP, seem to be the only two countries where politicians have dared to talk tough on the damage the CAP causes. The leader of Germany's Green Party has demanded: 'The European Commission must stop as soon as possible all subsidies, including export credits to agriculture.'[21] When he was prime minister, Tony Blair said: 'We need more open trade and opening up of markets in general and an end to trade-distorting subsidies which are the greatest problem that developing countries face.'[22] His chancellor and successor as prime minister, Gordon Brown, was equally unequivocal in his condemnation of the CAP: 'If we are to make poverty history . . . let us seek to make the excesses of the CAP history.'[23] However, when faced by the intransigence of the French and the PIGS, both men decided to cave in and sacrifice the welfare of millions of Third World poor. This capitulation will cost EU taxpayers hundreds of billions that perhaps we can afford, but it will cost the poor billions that they do not have and never will have. As the EU politicians and bureaucrats crowd into expensive Brussels restaurants to toast their success in maintaining the status quo on the CAP, hundreds of thousands will die in the Third World. We EU citizens seem happy to salve our consciences by protesting about globalisation and going to concerts to 'make poverty history', while allowing billions of our taxes to be used to prevent the poor from selling the food they can grow and trading their way out of poverty.

PLUS ÇA CHANGE . . .

The CAP could have been wound down and eventually scrapped after the EU became a large net exporter of food by the 1970s. However, our generosity to our farmers has created a huge, politically powerful group of people who have become dependent on the continuing flow of our money for their economic well-being. In one of its many reviews of CAP spending, the EU admitted that 'subsidising production on a large scale and buying up surpluses in the interests of food security are now largely a thing of the past'.[24] Yet it never seems to have occurred to our leaders that the CAP might have outlived its usefulness.

The EU constantly claims that it is reforming the CAP. Two factors seem to have pushed the EU into tinkering with the way CAP subsidies are paid. By 1992 the embarrassing sight of ever-increasing food surpluses while Third World poverty showed no signs of decreasing combined with pressure from the World Trade Organisation to reduce subsidies in order to promote fairer trade caused the EU to start making a series of gradual reforms to the CAP. However, the EU did not consider reducing the amount paid to farmers. Instead, it just changed the way the money was dished out, introducing something it called 'decoupling'. This partially broke the link between subsidies and the quantities of food being produced, so farmers were now paid some of their EU money under the Single Payment Scheme (SPS) just for having farms, with no need to produce very much. These SPS payments were based on how much each farm had been paid historically, so that most farmers continued to receive as much as they had before the so-called reforms.

This did not make enough of a dent in the shameful food surpluses, so the EU introduced set-aside, a system whereby farmers were paid not to grow anything at all on parts of their land. Naturally, many farmers kept on growing as much as possible on the more fertile bits of their farms to get the maximum amount in subsidies, while eagerly grabbing whatever extra cash they could by just 'setting aside' those areas of their land where it was almost impossible to grow anything anyway.

Moreover, at the same time as the EU bureaucrats used billions of our money to encourage farmers to reduce the amount of crops grown, the EU has also insisted on greater use of biofuels (fuel made from crops). This rush to biofuels has predictably led to an increased need for some of the very crops whose production the EU has been trying to limit. This mind-boggling short-sightedness, coupled with rising demand for food from the growing economies of China and India, has led to worldwide shortages of some foods and major increases in prices for consumers.

Originally the main aim of the CAP was to establish a healthy European farming industry: 'The focus of EU policy is to get food producers – of all forms of food from crops and livestock to fruit and vegetables, or wine – to be able to stand on their own feet on EU and world markets.' Yet in spite of this claim, most EU farmers are very far from standing 'on their own feet' and still get between a third and a half of their income directly from taxpayers, compared to just 16 per cent for farmers in the US and around 5 per cent for farmers in Australia. And although just 5 per cent of the EU's population now works in farming and just 1.6 per cent of the EU's economic output comes from agriculture, aid to agriculture still comfortably absorbs almost half the EU's budget. The EU boasts that CAP payments have 'dropped from a peak of nearly 70 per cent of the EU budget in the 1970s to 34 per cent over the 2007–13 period' and that part of this 'drop' is due to 'cost savings from reforms'.

However, CAP spending has never decreased. All that has happened is that other items of EU expenditure have increased even more rapidly than CAP spending. Moreover the supposed 'drop' of CAP spending from 46 per cent of the EU budget in 2006 to 32 per cent over the seven years between 2007 and 2013 has actually been achieved by just renaming about €14.6 billion a year (over 10 per cent of the EU budget) 'rural development' payments instead of CAP payments. So the money will still go to farmers, meaning that until 2013 and probably well beyond, agriculture will continue to get at least 43 per cent of the money we give to the EU.

A good example of how so-called EU 'reforms' to the CAP can actually lead to ever more of our money going to farmers can be seen in the way the EU seems to be approaching the problem of supporting its milk producers. At the moment dairy farmers have to observe strict quotas on the amount they produce. By 2013 the EU is planning to move from giving subsidies linked to production to the single payment scheme, by which money is handed out regardless of how much milk is produced. However, before introducing single payments for dairy farmers, the EU wants to raise or even remove their milk quotas. This would allow EU farmers to increase the amount of milk produced, leading to a larger surplus to be dumped on world markets at cheap, taxpayer-subsidised prices. It would also mean that dairy farmers' new single payments would be based on how much they earned under the more generous quotas, considerably boosting farmers' incomes. Bad for the Third World, bad for EU taxpayers, but very good indeed for EU dairy farmers and also good for the eurocrats, who would be able to claim that they had 'reformed', 'streamlined' and 'modernised' the system of payments to dairy farmers.

In 2007–8, in return for Britain giving up part of its budget rebate, the EU Commission committed itself to carrying out what it called a 'health check' of the EU's agricultural policy. However, CAP-loathers didn't need to get excited. The Commission explained that the health check 'does not imply that the policy is sick'. The aim was just 'an effort to streamline and modernise the policy still further'.[25] Interestingly, the EU decided not to publish the amounts given to each farmer and agri-business until after the health check was completed. So the problem of 85 per cent of CAP money going to a few rich recipients was not considered as part of the review of the CAP's effectiveness.

The agriculture commissioner claimed that the health check would free farmers to 'meet growing demand and respond quickly to what the market is telling them'.[26] However, years ago France and Germany stitched up a deal to maintain CAP spending at its current level until 2013, so all the health check has done is shift a small amount of money out of direct subsidies and into rural payments. Moreover, at the end of 2008 France presented a paper to the Commission calling for the maintenance of the core principles of the CAP possibly up to 2050. These core principles included 'community preference' (protecting EU farming products against imports), 'market stabilisation' (giving subsidies for food production and guaranteeing minimum prices for food should market prices fall) and 'maintaining regional cohesion' (eurospeak for continuing to pour further billions into farmers' pockets). So we can expect the CAP to continue in much the same form for probably the next 30 to 40 years. As usual, the winners will be the aristocracy, the owners of larger farms and agri-businesses. The losers will be European taxpayers, European consumers and, of course, farmers in emerging economies who will be prevented from selling their food in EU markets and be financially ruined when the EU dumps its subsidised excess production into their markets.

Chapter 13

DESTROYING THE ENVIRONMENT

THE EU LEADS THE WAY

In the Treaty of Rome, the basis for the development of the EU, there is no specific legal provision that allows the EU Commission to formulate a common policy on the environment, but this has not prevented the eurocrats from making a huge power-grab to give Brussels almost absolute control over European environmental lawmaking. From 1973 the Commission started issuing a series of five-year environmental action plans in order 'to protect and improve the quality of the environment'.[1] In the 1970s, when the Commission first seized control over environmental action in the EU, global warming hadn't really been identified. In fact, most scientists were predicting that the world was heading into a new mini ice age. For example, in an article about 'global cooling' in 1974 after a series of dreadful winters one of the world's leading meteorologists explained: 'I don't believe that the world's present population is sustainable if there are more than three years like 1972 in a row.'[2] So apart from producing a lot of hot air, EU environmental policy focused on things like improving water quality, reducing waste and cleaning up the air in cities, and it made some real progress in forcing member states to tackle excessive pollution throughout Europe.

In recent years, as scientists seem to have changed their minds and have now decided that instead of fearing an ice age we should actually be afraid of global warming, the eurocrats have enthusiastically taken up the cause of combating the threat of climate change. In a typical announcement the Commission proclaimed: 'Climate change is already happening and represents one of the greatest environmental, social and economic threats facing the planet. The European Union is committed to working constructively for a global agreement to control climate change, and is leading the way by taking ambitious actions of its own.'[3]

The EU was one of the main sponsors of the 1997 Kyoto Protocol, and in 2000 the Commission launched its European Climate Change Programme. In spite of the EU's fine words, many environmental groups were less than impressed by the amount of progress actually made. In 2006 a group of ten organisations wrote a report in which they criticised the Barroso Commission, claiming that 'the Barroso Commission struggled to uphold its predecessor's modest ambitions'.[4] The report attacked the Commission for being too focused on supporting economic growth and not paying sufficient attention to environmental issues: 'We conclude that this Commission made a poor start, paying lip-service to or marginalising the environment agenda.' In a pleasingly short turn of phrase, unusual for environmentalists, at one point in the report they wrote: 'The Action Plan was short on action.' The document went on to suggest that under the Barroso Commission there had even been some backsliding on environmental initiatives: 'All the strategies were timid, several lacked clear targets and the most important ones even proposed weakening existing obligations and commitments.' And it noted that leadership 'has also been in short supply in Brussels'. However, following a series of United Nations climate change studies and Britain's Stern Review, things started to move a bit faster in Brussels.

EU environmental policy seemed to take a major leap forward in early 2007 when, with their economies all looking unusually healthy, EU countries boldly agreed to adopt ambitious binding targets to reduce CO_2 emissions by 2020.

These were dubbed the '20/20/20' targets and committed EU states to a 20 per cent reduction of emissions below 1990 levels, an increase in the proportion of power generated by renewable sources to 20 per cent and a mandated 10 per cent of fuel used by motor vehicles to be from biofuel sources, all by the year 2020. Some outside Brussels tried to sound a note of caution by pointing out the probable huge cost of the 20/20/20 plan for consumers and industry, but the Commission claimed that at only €60 billion to €100 billion a year, this was a cost well worth paying. In a publication entitled 'Combating Climate Change: The EU Leads the Way' the Commission wrote: 'The costs of this action will be very limited and in any case much less than the cost of the damage that climate change will cause if we take no action.' With their big salaries, expense accounts and taxpayer-guaranteed pensions, our euroleaders were so fired up with their new climate change crusade that some started talking about a 60 per cent or even an 80 per cent reduction in emissions by 2050. In fact, there seemed to be no limit to the price our masters were willing for the rest of us to pay so they could save the planet from our shameful energy profligacy. The Commission admitted that 'combating climate change is likely to mean significant adjustments to our life-styles'. But one could be forgiven for suspecting that it would not be the commissioners' lifestyles that would be hardest hit by their efforts for us to achieve their unrealistically ambitious goals.

EU ENVIRONMENTAL HOOLIGANISM IN ACTION

Many of us would probably support the EU getting involved in coordinating international action against global warming. After all, international problems usually need international solutions, and 27 countries acting together will be more influential than if each individual country pursued different policies. However, if we are to give responsibility for dealing with climate change to

EU bureaucrats and politicians, they need to prove that they can exercise this responsibility effectively and for our benefit. Unfortunately, the evidence so far is not exactly reassuring.

When they first started tinkering with environmental protection, the eurocrats notched up a few significant successes. Over the years the Commission introduced legislation concerning water pollution, atmospheric pollution, noise levels, the safety of dangerous substances, waste disposal, recycling and nature protection. All of these forced member countries to make considerable improvements that would probably not have happened without EU intervention. However, when the eurocrats started trying to manage environmental issues themselves, as sure as day follows night, disaster seemed to follow each new EU initiative. Moreover, each EU initiative seemed to take the same predictable course. There appear to be three main phases when the EU launches one of its schemes to supposedly improve the environment:

- *Phase 1 – The stupid idea*: An environmental problem is identified, and the desk-bound Brussels bureaucrats come up with a solution that requires massive amounts of administration, that is hugely expensive, that is almost impossible to enforce and that positively encourages widespread fraud, cheating and deceit.
- *Phase 2 – The ghastly consequences*: When the solution is implemented the results turn out to be the opposite of those intended, and massive environmental damage ensues. Although non-EU countries find effective alternative solutions to the problem being dealt with, the eurocrats stubbornly ignore these examples of intelligent and effective action and persist with their impractical policies, further harming the environment they are supposedly trying to protect.
- *Phase 3 – We're never wrong*: Despite all the evidence that their policies are giving horribly negative results, the

eurocrats responsible deny anything is amiss. Unable to admit they got things terribly wrong in the first place, they delay taking any corrective action. The environment suffers, the eurocrats carry on receiving their big salaries and pensions, and we ordinary people end up paying the price for this recidivist bureaucratic bungling.

There are several examples of these three phases of EU environmental destruction in action, but here we'll just look at three major disasters to demonstrate how this sad and familiar process inevitably occurs almost every time the EU girds up its environmental loins.

Example 1: Flat out of fish

The catastrophe of the Common Fisheries Policy (CFP) is a well-known story and one that eurosceptics like to use whenever they're in the mood for a bit of EU-bashing, so most people are probably now depressingly familiar with the unhappy details of this failed policy. However, a couple of recent internal EU documents, which have not yet been widely distributed, shed some new light on the CFP and possibly make it worthwhile for us to look again at this particular ecological disaster.

The EU shamelessly continues to claim that the CFP achieves its aims: 'The Common Fisheries Policy is the EU's instrument for managing fisheries: harvesting the right amount of fish, of the right size and in the right way.'[5] However, almost anyone with any knowledge of the CFP knows that the EU's assertions about the CFP are blatantly untrue. Finally, in September 2008, a note from Joe Borg, the commissioner for fisheries and maritime affairs, to the other commissioners revealed that the EU had known for many years that the CFP was having catastrophic effects on both EU fish stocks and the economics of the European fishing industry.

The development and implementation of the CFP provide

an excellent example of the three phases of EU environmental hooliganism.

Phase 1 – The stupid idea. Aware that the EU fishing fleet was too large and that fish stocks were being rapidly depleted, the EU launched the CFP, thereby allowing Brussels to become actively involved in trying to manage the EU's fishing industry. At first this was part of the Common Agricultural Policy; then in 1983 it was placed under its own commissioner. The main thrust of the CFP was to encourage reductions in fishing fleet sizes and to impose quotas, called Total Allowable Catches (TACs), on countries, which were then allocated to individual boats. Often a boat's TAC would be for only one or two species. Unfortunately, the whole principle of TACs was ludicrous because European fish aren't aware that eurocrats expect them to swim in shoals of just one species. Most of our fish stocks are mixed, so that a boat will tend to catch a range of different types of fish. However, it would be a criminal offence for a boat to return to port with any fish not included in its TAC. This means that many boats are forced to discard much of their catch, leading to about a million tonnes of good, edible fish being thrown back dead into EU waters each year.

Other side-effects of the CFP that were predictable yet apparently unexpected by the Brussels bureaucrats are the huge cost of policing the policy and the high levels of fraud. For example, Britain spends about £30 million a year controlling an industry landing only £600 million of fish. In contrast, Spain, which has the largest fishing fleet in the EU, is renowned for its relaxed, inexpensive approach to fisheries control. Many members of the Spanish fisheries control department work in Madrid, which is the Spanish city that is furthest from the sea, and those staff who are actually based somewhere near the sea tend to have the same enviably short and very relaxed working day enjoyed by other Spanish public-sector employees and so are seldom around when boats either leave or return to port.

Another way the Spanish circumvented their quotas was by buying fishing licences (with quotas attached) from other countries, especially Britain. Alarmed by a Spanish armada decimating its fish stocks, the UK passed a law trying to stop this quota-hopping. However, the Spanish appealed to the eternally biased European Court of Justice, which, putting the Common Market before common sense, judged in favour of the Spanish, thus encouraging further devastation of the fish population.

Phase 2 – The ghastly consequences. Commissioner Borg's note graphically and helpfully describes the CFP's many failures: '80 per cent of our stocks are fished so heavily – above maximum sustainable yield – that the yield is reduced. This compares to the global average of 25 per cent.'[6] He also explains how this over-fishing inevitably leads to a depletion of fish stocks: 'The productivity of fisheries is reduced because fish are caught before they are allowed to grow and in many cases before they have reproduced.' One particularly striking example the commissioner gives concerns cod:

> North Sea cod, for instance, can live for more than 20 years and will at that time have a weight of more than 20 kg. Presently the average age of cod which are caught in the North Sea is 1.6 years with a mean weight of less than one kilo . . . North Sea cod in general need to be more than four years old before it is mature and can take part in spawning. Presently 93 per cent of fish caught are immature.[7]

Another major problem highlighted by the commissioner is that the policy of reducing quotas to theoretically preserve fish stocks can actually have the opposite effect. Because they are allowed to land only a certain tonnage of fish, in order to maximise their earnings boats are discarding huge quantities of even the smaller fish included in their TAC quotas in order to try to replace them by bigger, more valuable fish. This means that tighter quotas are leading to higher levels of discards, thus further depleting stocks. In March 2007 a communication from the Commission to the council and the European parliament revealed that the Commission has been aware of the problems of discards (by-catches) and has been trying to find a way of reducing them since 2002, but without success. Commenting on its own feeble efforts over five years, the Commission writes: 'Most fisheries remain unaffected and the impact on overall by-catches is negligible.'

Phase 3 – We're never wrong. Other countries – Canada, the USA, Norway and New Zealand, for example – have found ways of successfully managing their fish stocks. Some, like Canada, have even hugely increased their stocks and thus the economic viability of their fishing industries. They have taken actions like forbidding discards, controlling days at sea rather than TACs and encouraging technical innovations that reduce the environmental damage caused by over-fishing. The eurocrats have successfully ignored all these examples of how to run a workable fishing policy and instead have chosen to persist with the catastrophic CFP in spite of all the evidence, and their own admissions in their internal documents, that it is a demonstrable economically and environmentally damaging failure.

Example 2: The emissions trading scandal

The EU seems quite proud of its Emissions Trading Scheme (EU ETS): 'The cornerstone of the EU's strategy for fighting climate change is the EU emissions trading scheme.'[8] The eurocrats claim that the EU ETS is 'an innovative mechanism' and that 'the scheme creates a permanent incentive for participating companies to minimise emissions as far as possible'. There are only two small problems with these claims. First, the EU ETS is not innovative at all; it is just copied from a US scheme to reduce sulphur dioxide emissions that was successfully run in the 1990s. Second, for at least its first seven years of operation the EU ETS will keep hundreds or more probably thousands of bureaucrats impressively busy, but it will not have any effect at all on the level of CO_2 emissions.

The idea of an emissions trading scheme as a way of reducing harmful gases is quite sound, just as having a fisheries policy is not only desirable but necessary. The problem with the EU ETS, as with the CFP, was the dreadful way the eurocrats designed and implemented their fateful policies and then their absolute refusal to admit they could ever make mistakes.

In the late 1980s the US had been looking for a way of reducing sulphur dioxide emissions from power stations because the gas contributed to acid rain. To encourage power companies to find innovative ways of reducing emissions, the 1990 Clean Air Act Amendments were passed, creating a 'cap and trade' system whereby power plants were issued a number of permits to emit sulphur dioxide. The total number of permits was capped at a level that was below the volume of the gas being emitted, and the cap was reduced each year. Companies then had to reduce emissions or buy permits (trade) from other companies that had succeeded in reducing their emissions. As the volume of permits reduced, the price rose, thus increasing the incentives for companies to find ways of bringing down their own emissions. The scheme worked and emissions fell 22 per cent below mandated levels.

Phase 1 – The stupid idea. It was this US scheme that the EU copied and launched in 2005. However, the US policy covered only around 250 companies that were already heavily regulated, and so it was relatively easy to administer. In the EU almost 11,000 separate sites were covered by the EU ETS, and most of these were in countries that had absolutely no intention of allowing the EU to impose new costs on their main energy generators and industrial companies. Things went off the rails right from the start. Instead of being auctioned, permits were handed out free to almost all the installations involved. Because the permits were free there was absolutely no incentive to reduce emissions. Moreover, although EU countries emitted about 2,012 million tonnes of CO_2 at the time, permits were issued for 2,152 million tonnes. So instead of capping emissions as the successful US system had done, the EU ETS perversely allowed an increase of around 140 million tonnes a year, almost 7 per cent.

Phase 2 – The ghastly consequences. In the first year of operation of the EU ETS, CO_2 emissions actually rose by 1.1 per cent, and in the second year by a further 0.78 per cent. The environment commissioner, Stavros Dimas, said: 'Emissions trading is yielding results. Studies show that emissions would most likely have been higher without the EU ETS.'[9] Some countries, like Britain, were actually stupid enough to play by the rules and under-allocated permits, forcing British power generators, industrial companies and even hospitals to pay hundreds of millions buying permits from other countries, including Germany and France, which had massively over-allocated permits to their companies. But by mid-2006, when it was realised that too many permits had been issued, the price of a permit to emit one tonne of CO_2 fell from around €33 to less than €1, providing little incentive to anyone to reduce emissions.

In the period 2007–13 a couple of countries agreed to slightly reduce their massive over-allocations, and the price of permits has now risen to around €25 per tonne of CO_2. This should theoretically have given some new impetus to the scheme. However, EU countries continued to run rings round the unworldly and incompetent eurocrats. The EU ETS allows EU countries to avoid reducing their own emissions by 'importing' credits from outside the EU. They can do this by paying to support supposed CO_2 reduction schemes in the Third World under what is called the Clean Development Mechanism (CDM). Almost all the EU countries have given themselves import levels that comfortably exceed any cuts they would have to make in their own emissions to meet EU targets. Laughably, those countries that did decrease their CO_2 caps for 2007–13 have used the import trick actually to increase their overall CO_2 levels. Germany, for example, 'yielded' to pressure from the Commission to reduce its CO_2 cap by 28.9 million tonnes a year for 2007–13 but extracted as compensation an increase in its import allowance of 32.8 million tonnes a year, about 13 per cent more than it had given up.

Moreover, as could be expected, most of these 'import' projects have turned out to be shams and in many cases are blatantly fraudulent. Incredibly, some have even been extremely damaging to the environment. For example, at least half did not give any real reduction in emissions as the projects, ostensibly aimed at reducing CO_2, had already been planned and would have happened anyway. In the case of Third World hydroelectric schemes the figure was 96 per cent. It was also found that in India companies were deliberately producing the environmentally harmful refrigeration gas HFC-23 so that they could use the EU ETS to get money to install scrubbers to clean the gas. It was estimated that Indian companies had received €4.6 billion in EU ETS money for an investment of less than €100 million. Worryingly, if, as is likely, some of the HFC-23 is released into the atmosphere by inefficient and poorly enforced scrubbing in Indian plants, just one tonne of HFC-23 will do as much damage to the environment as 11,700 tonnes of CO_2.

It was a similar story in China, which has been another major beneficiary of EU ETS cash and which was found to be earning at least €2 billion a year without any real controls to ensure that this money was ever being reinvested in projects that cut CO_2 emissions. A spokesman from the World Wildlife Fund warned: 'Instead of paying to reduce global greenhouse gas emissions, poor quality CDM projects mean that we pay to increase emissions. In a carbon-constrained world, this insanity cannot continue.'[10]

As with the CFP, the costs of administration of the pointless and ineffective EU ETS were huge. In the UK alone they were estimated at £62 million a year; for the whole of the EU they are probably well over £600 million per year.

Phase 3 – We're never wrong. By 2009 possibly €2 billion or more had been wasted on administering the scheme, billions more had been handed over to more than dubious Third World projects and virtually nothing at all had been achieved. Moreover, the scheme will continue working, or rather not working, in its existing form until 2013. The current intention is that the cap on emissions will be reduced by 1.74 per cent a year from 2013 onwards. In addition, it is envisaged that companies will have to buy some credits rather than getting them free. But in view of the near 7 per cent over-allocation granted in 2005, this means that it will be 2017 – around 12 years since the start of the EU ETS – before the scheme could start to make any significant contribution to reducing CO_2 emissions. This is a less than impressive effort from the eurocrats, especially when we remember that the US scheme was operating successfully within two years of its launch and had delivered huge reductions within just five years.

In reality, the many loopholes in importing credits from the Third World and other ways of cheating the scheme will probably mean that the EU ETS never has any effect on EU CO_2 emissions at all. The EU seems unsure whether to acknowledge failure or claim success. The spokeswoman for the environment commissioner once admitted how pointless the whole thing was: 'Unfortunately, the emissions trade doesn't work very well but we can't change anything anymore.'[11] However, in its PR the EU still trumpets the admirable effectiveness of its emissions reduction policy: 'The "cap" or limit on the total number of allowances creates the scarcity needed for the market to function.' And, even though emissions have increased, it claims that the EU ETS is reducing emissions:

'Emission trading helps to ensure that emission cuts are achieved at least cost.'[12]

Example 3: The great biofuels blunder

No review of EU environmental policy would be complete without looking at the way the eurocrats have caused massive environmental damage and immense human suffering through their incompetent attempts to reduce CO_2 emissions by partially substituting biofuels for fossil fuels (petrol and diesel) in EU transport.

Phase 1 – The stupid idea. Since at least 2002 (and probably earlier) the Commission has been keen to enforce a minimum share of biofuels in all motoring fuels sold in the EU. At first it proposed a target of 2 per cent by 2005, rising to 5.75 per cent by 2010. Right from the beginning there were warnings that the environmental credentials of biofuels were questionable. Four of the many concerns raised were that at least 10 per cent of the EU's arable land would be needed for biofuel production to meet EU targets, thus reducing food production; that biofuel was not a good substitute for fossil fuel because you had to use large quantities of fossil fuel to produce biofuel; that biofuel production encouraged intensive farming, which damaged soil and depleted water resources; and that the use of nitrogen fertiliser to produce crops for biofuels had a potential factor for global warming about 270 times higher than the CO_2 the biofuels were intended to reduce. One 2002 report on the EU's biofuels proposal concluded: 'The proposal does not make much sense, neither from an economic, an energy, nor an ecological point of view.'[13] However, anxious to demonstrate what it called 'Europe's global leadership in tackling climate change', as part of its 20/20/20 environmental goals in 2007 the Commission imposed a mandatory target of 10 per cent of biofuels in transport fuel by 2020.

Phase 2 – The ghastly consequences. The EU's love affair with biofuels since 2002 seems to have had at least three worrying effects: a massive increase in biofuel production, leading to a diversion of land and crops from food production and extensive deforestation in countries like Indonesia and Malaysia; a burst of speculation in food on commodity exchanges as poor harvests and increased demand due to US and EU biofuels targets led to huge profits for speculators; and an explosion in food prices, which increased by 12 per cent in 2006, 24 per cent in 2007 and over 50 per cent in 2008. There were food riots in several countries, and the UN Food and Agriculture Organisation (FAO) estimated that an extra 75 million people worldwide have been pushed into hunger and poverty due to the rapid rise in the cost of food.

Naturally, the EU has denied that its biofuels policy had any significant effect on food prices. The agriculture commissioner explained: 'As regards the 10 per cent target by 2020, the Commission impact assessment of the EU biofuel policy shows that its achievement should not cause major strain in the food sector.'[14] This sanguine view of the well-fed Brussels bureaucrats was not shared by many experts outside the Brussels bubble. Two international bodies calculated that biofuels were responsible for up to 60 per cent of food price rises, while the World Bank estimated that up to 75 per cent of the increase in food prices was due to biofuels. The UN's FAO cautioned: 'Policy measures driving the rush to liquid biofuels, such as mandated mixing of biofuels with fossil fuels . . . have high economic, social and environmental costs and should be reviewed.'[15] A policy adviser at Oxfam said: 'Political leaders seem intent on suppressing and ignoring the strong evidence that biofuels are a major factor in recent food price rises.'[16] The UN's special rapporteur on the right to food was more direct when he commented that biofuels could only bring 'more hunger to the poor people of the world' and that they were a 'crime against humanity'.

As food prices were rocketing, new research into biofuels cast further doubt on their environmental benefits. One university study showed that biofuels from crops, so-called 'first generation' biofuels, consumed 29 per cent more energy than the biofuels yielded. Another report found that cultivating crops to produce biofuels released huge quantities of CO_2 from the soil. A UN analysis concluded that the use of biofuels 'did not necessarily contribute as much to reducing greenhouse gas emissions as was previously assumed'. And a study from an environmental protection agency said that biofuels 'create many more ecological problems than they will solve, including deforestation, increase in greenhouse gas emissions, requirements for land that does not exist, enhanced food insecurity, creation of more poverty, increased soil degradation, decreased biodiversity and accelerated depletion of natural resources'.[17]

Phase 3 – We're never wrong. By 2008 the Commission was faced with growing international concern and criticism about the environmental and human costs of its biofuels policy. There was even an EU internal report, which was leaked but never published, that undermined the case for biofuels. At first the Commission refused to change its stance. However, as the evidence against biofuels became incontrovertible, the eurocrats tried to find a way out of the corner into which they had painted themselves. At a conference of EU environment ministers in July 2008 our leaders emerged to claim that everybody had mis-understood the various EU directives that led to the 10 per cent target for replacing fossil fuels for transport. They now said that the Commission had never stipulated that biofuels should be used and what it had really meant was that the 10 per cent target should be made up from fuels from 'renewable sources', which could include some biofuels but might also include other things.

The French minister for the environment tried to clarify the apparent confusion: 'The member states realised that the Commission's plan specifies that 10 per cent of transport needs must come from renewable energy, not 10 per cent from biofuels.'[18]

In fact, the main directive concerning biofuels, Directive 2003/30/EC, was titled 'The promotion of the use of biofuels or other renewable fuels for transport'. So there was some justification for the politicians' convenient new explanation for the biofuels disaster. However, in the directive the word 'biofuels' appears at least 52 times in four pages (over 12 times a page), whereas the word 'renewable' is used just six times in the whole text. Moreover, although Commission spokespeople now briefed journalists that fuel from renewable sources could include hydrogen and 'green' electricity, a Commission document contradicted the politicians' and the Commission's new slant on the story by clearly stating that biofuels were the only viable form of renewable fuel: 'Biofuels from agricultural crops are currently the only available large-scale substitute for petrol and diesel fuel in transport.'[19] Furthermore, a 2007 EU directive reiterated that biofuels were the basis for EU policy when it mandated 'a 10 per cent binding minimum target to be achieved by all member states for the share of biofuels in overall EU transport petrol and diesel consumption by 2020'.[20]

By the end of 2008 the Commission was desperately back-pedalling and trying to cobble together a new directive that would both maintain the 10 per cent target while at the same time imposing new rules to supposedly ensure that in future biofuels came from what the Commission called 'sustainable sources'. As eurocrats and politicians jumped around like cats on a hot tin roof trying to avoid using the now tainted word 'biofuels', a Commission report was more than clear that our eurobosses were still hooked on biofuels: 'The share of biofuels in overall transport petrol and diesel consumption is to reach 10 per cent. This confirms the EU leadership in internalising the adverse effects of CO_2 emissions at the global level.'[21]

This confusion about what the Commission had really meant allowed one commissioner to claim that the Commission was sticking to its target: 'There is no intention from the Commission to change its 10 per cent target.'[22] Yet at the same time Stavros Dimas seemed to be admitting that the whole biofuels policy was turning into a bit of a nightmare: 'The development of the use of biofuels in the EU raises a number of environmental and social risks, including the conversion of high-carbon stock or high-biodiversity land for cultivation and greater competition with food uses for land and feedstocks.'[23] All this left Commissioner Dimas trying to explain how the Commission was taking action to combat the negative effects of biofuels: 'In view of this, the Commission's proposal for a directive on the promotion of renewable energy sources includes a sustainability scheme for biofuels.'

Amusingly and apparently without even the slightest hint of embarrassment, self-knowledge or irony, Stavros Dimas concluded his statement by comparing the Commission's biofuels policy to the Common Fisheries Policy: 'A parallel to the Common Fisheries Policy is possibly relevant.'[24] However, if the latest version of the EU biofuels policy continues to resemble the ecologically disastrous fisheries policy, we can expect continued environmental destruction, continued high food prices and continued mass starvation throughout the Third World thanks to the EU's questionable biofuels targets – and all because the well-paid, well-fed eurocrats stubbornly and persistently refuse to correct even the most obvious mistakes that they make.

Chapter 14

WASTING AWAY

SPENDING OTHER PEOPLE'S MONEY

All bureaucracies waste money. Most bureaucrats throughout the developed world have guaranteed jobs for life, promotion and salary increases based on years of service rather than ability, early retirement, secure, inflation-linked pensions and a relatively stress-free work life. Public-sector managers are seldom fired for incompetence or dishonesty. Should any scandal leak out into the press, those implicated are often just moved, promoted out of trouble and, in the case of senior civil servants, allowed to retire early with honour and often honours. In Britain civil service bosses are routinely knighted and often ennobled, no matter how incompetently they have run their departments. Bureaucrats have easy access to taxpayers' money but are rarely held to account for ensuring that it is spent wisely and responsibly. They live in a different world from the rest of us and have little understanding of the unfortunate fact that money has to be earned before it can be used. So it is not surprising that they spend our money as if there were no limits to taxpayers' generosity.

Like all bureaucracies, the EU wastes much of the money that it takes from us. But the EU's budget of around €134 billion a year is quite small compared to the amounts spent by the national governments of the larger member states, so perhaps we shouldn't be concerned that our EU money is either being wasted by the incompetent or siphoned off by the devious and the undeserving. But there is possibly a difference between national governments' financial profligacy and the EU's. In individual countries changes of government, the occasional attention of the press and politicians' sensitivity to their reputations mean that those intent on emptying the public purse are forever having to find new and more original ways to squander our money or to enrich themselves at the expense of ordinary people. However in the EU the same scandals and scams have been going on for decades without anybody feeling any need to do anything about what is happening. Probably up to a third of the €127 billion spent on the Common Agricultural Policy, regional funds and other EU schemes disappears into the wrong bank accounts because of administrative ineptitude, clever manipulation of loopholes in EU regulations or just good old-fashioned fraud and corruption. For over 40 years this has repeatedly been shown to be the case, yet there has never been any serious attempt by the EU to control its financial incontinence. It is perhaps this fact – that most EU waste can be measured in decades rather than just years – that more than anything else distinguishes it from the many ways that money is squandered by bureaucrats in the member countries.

We've already reviewed the widespread and uninterrupted pillaging of the money that the EU hands out to often already-wealthy farmers, businesspeople and crooks lucky enough to profit from the eurocrats' largesse with our hard-earned cash. So here we'll look at how the EU squanders money that is more directly under its own managerial control.

THE COSTS OF PERPETUAL MOTION

One of the longest-running financial obscenities perpetrated by the EU is the monthly migration of the European parliament from its impressive fortress in Brussels to its equally imposing citadel in Strasbourg. Like so many EU scandals, this one has been going on for so long that the basic facts are now no doubt wearyingly well known. However, this story is still relevant because of the way it reveals the shameless hypocrisy of the EU institutions and the utter contempt displayed by eurocrats and MEPs for the people who pay for their uniquely privileged lifestyle. Moreover, in 2008 there were a couple of new twists to this tale that more than ever highlighted the economic and environmental absurdity of the European parliament maintaining ludicrously expensive bases in two different European countries.

Just to summarise the background: for about the last 30 years the European parliament has worked for three weeks every month in Brussels, but has had to hold its main legislative meetings – its plenary sessions – 12 times a year in Strasbourg. This means that all the MEPs together with at least 2,000 staff and thousands more civil servants and other hangers-on have to travel about 352 kilometres (220 miles) accompanied by a fleet of at least 15 lorries carrying almost 4,000 boxes of papers and office equipment. After just a few days in Strasbourg the whole travelling circus decamps again and returns to Brussels. The French claim that Strasbourg, lying on the oft-disputed French–German border, is a key symbol of reconciliation between the two former enemies, and therefore it is important that the parliament should meet there. However, there is no logical reason for this enforced monthly migration other than to satisfy French vanity and, more importantly, unnecessarily put huge quantities of our money into the welcoming pockets of the parasitic Strasbourg business community.

The cost of this farce has now risen above €200 million a year, and over the last quarter century must have wasted at least €3 billion in travel, hotel, food and other costs, of which over €2 billion has gone straight into the pockets of the city's lucky hoteliers and restauranteurs. In 2006 it emerged that the Strasbourgeois were not content with the flood of euromoney propping up their city's economy. They had also been skimming off somewhere between €1 million and €4 million a year by artificially increasing the rent paid by the parliament for its buildings. The two main buildings were owned by a Dutch pension fund, but rather than renting the buildings directly to the European parliament, the Dutch company had rented them to the Strasbourg city council, which had then sublet them to the parliament at a greatly inflated rent. Estimates of how much of our money was spirited away using this scam vary from €80 million to €150 million. One MEP, responsible for budgets, claimed that the parliament had been fooled by the city council for about a quarter of a century: 'I am very surprised. We knew nothing about it. We have been taken for a ride.'[1] And a vice-president of the parliament explained: 'It is clear that the city of Strasbourg has been siphoning off €1 million a year.'[2]

A sceptic might view such histrionic protestations of astonished innocence as straining credulity and wonder if it had really never occurred to the parliament's budget committee in over 25 years to compare what they were being charged per square metre of office space with what other organisations were paying.

The Strasbourg stupidity is not only expensive, it is also ecologically damaging. It is estimated that the unnecessary travel between Brussels and Strasbourg produces around 20,000 tonnes of CO_2 each year – the equivalent of 13,000 round-trip flights between any European capital and New York.[3] The European parliament recently proudly announced that it was going to 'reduce its carbon footprint by 30 per cent' by spending considerable quantities of our money making its buildings more energy efficient.[4] In developing this expensive new plan, it doesn't seem to have occurred to our euroleaders that they could reduce their carbon footprint by a lot more and also save an awful lot of our money by dropping the Strasbourg stupidity altogether.

When questioned about why they waste so much of our money on this pointless perpetual motion, most MEPs claim that they are not responsible, as any change has to be agreed by the Commission and the member states and then enshrined in a treaty. Although this is strictly true, it rather ignores the fact that for years a tiny minority of MEPs have tried to have this useless travelling circus stopped and they have always been opposed by a huge majority of MEPs who have fought bitterly to maintain the status quo. In early 2006 a proposed amendment by some MEPs to discuss the Strasbourg question was defeated by a huge majority of MEPs. Later that year a petition started by a Swedish MEP collected more than a million names demanding a halt to the Strasbourg sessions. This was handed to the EU president and was immediately ignored by the eurocrats. Again in 2008 the parliament voted over-whelmingly to block the request just to allow a debate on whether the parliament should continue to meet in Strasbourg. One MEP commented on the parliament's continuing refusal to act: 'I find it rather nonsensical that parliament has so long been incapable of addressing this issue and putting pressure on the council to put an end to this flying circus.'[5]

Feeling growing public pressure to stop their wasteful journeys to Strasbourg, the parliament had the bright idea of buying the two main buildings in Strasbourg where MEPs met, even though these two buildings were completely superfluous. The MEPs claimed that this would be more economical than renting the buildings – their real reason was that once the parliament owned the buildings, it would be more difficult for critics to suggest that they shouldn't use them, and so the travelling farce could continue uninterrupted. Between 1998 and 2006 about €440 million of our money was paid to the buildings' owners. In addition, it is said that a €29 million payment was made to the Strasbourg city council as compensation for the city not being able to hoover up so much of our money any more.

In July 2008 French president Nicolas Sarkozy instituted a special fast TGV train service to ferry MEPs and their staff between Brussels and Strasbourg. This train costs us about €200,000 a journey, runs only for the plenary sessions and cannot be used by ordinary members of the public, whose taxes pay for it. They have to fly or stick to the old slow train. However, despite the taxpayers generously providing this expensive new service for the ruling euro-elite, not all the train's users were happy. Some complained that although the old train was slow, because it left Brussels at 07.00 it reached Strasbourg by about midday in time for lunch. The new service left Brussels at 09.37 and would not reach Strasbourg till 13.36 – this meant that it would, according to one EU internal staff memo, 'deprive colleagues of their midday break and the possibility of a proper lunch'. Another worry for the eurocrats was that using the new train would hit them where it most hurt – in their pockets. By travelling second class on the old train, EU staff could make a considerable profit because their flat-rate travel allowance was more than sufficient to pay for a first class ticket. However, the price of a ticket on the new, faster train was considerably higher and would eat up most of the eurocrats' travel allowance.

On 7 August 2008 French attempts to maintain their expensive but pointless Strasbourg meetings suffered a blow. A 200 square metre piece of the main Strasbourg building's roof, weighing about 10 tonnes, collapsed. Normally in France it is impossible to get anything done in August because the French view their four-week August summer holiday as sacrosanct. However, the terrifying thought of losing millions if the parliament had to cancel its wasteful Strasbourg sessions seemed to galvanise the city authorities, who splashed out at least €6 million of our money to try to get the roof fixed before the parliament returned in September. As might be expected, they failed and the first two plenary sessions of autumn 2008 had to be held in Brussels. Even the normally supine europress couldn't help noticing that about €4 million had just been saved by avoiding a couple of futile trips to Strasbourg. This financial saving for EU taxpayers led to some criticism, particularly in the German and British press, of the ever more costly and preposterous Strasbourg folly. But as the French have managed to get the principle of 12 plenary sessions a year being held in Strasbourg enshrined in an EU treaty, the arrangement can be changed only with the unanimous agreement of all EU members. Naturally, there is one country that would never agree to such a change. So the French just shrug off other countries' concerns.

It is likely that at some point in the future, maybe within 10 to 20 years and after the MEPs have wasted another €2 billion or more of our money and after unnecessary travel has produced over 200,000 tonnes of CO_2, the French will eventually accept dropping the Strasbourg exercise in utter futility. Now there is talk of trying to buy the French off by offering to site a new European institute of technology and maybe also a new European research council in Strasbourg in return for the French allowing the parliament to stay permanently in Brussels. But one thing is certain: we European taxpayers will have to pay a heavy price to buy French agreement. Although this Strasbourg shuffle only squanders just over €200 million a year, its symbolic importance may be greater than its economic and environmental waste. Our self-serving, hypocritical MEPs cannot claim any credibility when they grab more of our money for themselves and lecture us about the perils of global warming as long as they continue with this economic and environmental insult to voters' intelligence.

PIGS IN SPACE

Most people would probably agree that the European Airbus project has been a success. No single European country had the resources to compete against US aircraft manufacturers, but working together the European countries involved have managed to build an aviation giant that for many years has given Boeing a run for its money. The Eurofighter may not have been such a triumph as the Airbus civilian planes – it was years late and vastly over its original budget – but it's quite an impressive piece of kit, and those who fly it speak highly of its capabilities, particularly its speed and manoeuvrability. Airbus and the Eurofighter do, however, have one thing in common: although they were European projects, they had nothing at all to do with the EU. They were run by companies cooperating across borders without any involvement at all from EU institutions. On the occasions that the EU has decided to leap into the world of large-scale technological project management, the results have invariably been disastrous for EU taxpayers.

The EU is currently drowning in its own incompetence as it tries to get a project called Galileo off the ground and into space. Galileo is planned to be a global satellite navigation system, consisting of 30 satellites in orbit around the Earth at an altitude of some 23,000 kilometres. It is designed as an improvement on the US military's GPS system and is intended to make Europe independent of the US system, as the EU Commission is concerned that the US 'military authorities can stop or degrade the signal at any time'.[6]

Started in earnest in 2000, Galileo should have been up and orbiting by 2007. Unfortunately, the project has already eaten quite a lot of our money and still won't be taking off for at least another five years, but it is interesting as an example of how the EU has a tendency to launch vanity projects (usually to try to overtake the US) without any proper commercial or technical analysis; of how eurocrats justify these projects with fantasy figures, supposedly independent reports and their ever faithful Eurobarometer surveys; of how EU taxpayers always end up paying the hugely over-budget final costs; and of how such projects are delayed by so many years that they have become technically and commercially obsolete long before they are completed.

When Galileo was given the go-ahead in 2000 the Commission was feeling pretty convinced about the necessity of the project, calling it 'a prerequisite for the EU's independence in the field of satellite navigation'. There was also confidence about the amount of public money that would be used: 'Financing based on public subsidies (€1.1 billion) will be indispensable for the development and validation phase. This has already been scheduled. There will be no need to seek additional public funding.'[7]

A year later the Commission announced that 'a private consortium, appointed by the Commission and led by PricewaterhouseCoopers, carried out an independent study on the economic perspectives offered by Galileo'. The report unsurprisingly concluded that 'Galileo is economically justified' and claimed that it would give a return of 4.6 times the initial investment. Normally, if a project has such a high financial return, you would expect to see private-sector companies banging loudly on your door and clambering eagerly in through the windows to get a share of the lucrative action. So there would be no need to spend any taxpayers' money at all. In fact, taxpayers could just sit back and watch private companies do all the work and take all the risk. Yet, curiously, the Commission used the fact that Galileo would supposedly be hugely profitable to conclude that we taxpayers should foot much of the bill: 'The cost-benefit analysis shows a strong case for public-sector commitment to the project.'[8]

In 2005 a first test satellite was launched. But in 2006 we were told that the operational start date would be 2011, not 2007 after all. However, the Commission assured us that there was no need for us to be concerned about the four-year delay because: 'Galileo will be more advanced, more efficient and more reliable than the current US Global Positioning System.' That was hardly surprising given that the US system was based on older technology and had already been successfully functioning for over a decade. What the Commission omitted to mention was that the US was well advanced with a technical upgrade to its system that would be at least as good as Galileo and would probably be in place long before Galileo ever saw the light of day.

The hugely supportive 'independent' report had also done some more work on the economics of the project and foresaw quite extraordinary opportunities for Galileo to make buckets of money: 'The satellite navigation market, in which Galileo will play an important role, has been forecast to be €400 billions by 2025.' In making this statement, the Commission overlooked a few small details like the fact that Russia was already in the market and new, lower cost competitors, like China and possibly India, were also keen to enter. Moreover, the US provided access to its GPS system free, whereas Galileo intended charging for most of its services. As one executive close to the project explained just a couple of months after the Commission's report claimed that Galileo could earn billions selling its services: 'There is a doubt over the revenues. Why sell Pepsi-Cola when you can get Coca-Cola free?'[9] Another admitted: 'The market is just not there. We were too optimistic. GPS is fine for most purposes.'[10] But the Commission was not to be deterred from its giant leap into space by such mundane, common-sense considerations.

By mid-2007 things were going more than wobbly: the cost to EU taxpayers had more than tripled; the operational date had slipped to 2014 (giving a delay of seven years, just seven years after Galileo's start); private-sector financing for the whole project was collapsing as the various companies involved squabbled over the division of the work; and the second test satellite lay in pieces in the factory as the engineers couldn't get it to work. Realising that the project was on its last legs, the Commission desperately looked around for some way of saving its moribund scheme. What the eurocrats needed was some way of convincing member states' governments to allow them to throw billions of euros of our money at bailing out their disaster. As ever, the Commission could rely on Eurobarometer to ride to its rescue. Quickly the Commission conducted one of its ever helpful Eurobarometer surveys, which naturally concluded: 'Europeans support EU setting up its own navigation system.' This particular survey was such an excellent and entertaining example of how Eurobarometer can get the right answer, even to a question that most people didn't understand, that it deserves more than a brief mention.

About 79 per cent of those questioned for Eurobarometer had never used any satellite navigation tools themselves. Nevertheless, the survey found that: 'There is overwhelming support for an independent European system (80 per cent).' This convenient answer was achieved by the people conducting the survey first reading a short text extolling all the benefits of a satellite navigation system and then trying to frighten people by suggesting that Europe couldn't rely on US, Russian or Chinese systems (see Figure 1) before asking whether Europe should have its own satellite navigation system.[11]

The Commission also claimed that we citizens urgently wanted the project to move ahead: 'Overall 63 per cent of respondents consider that the EU should secure the necessary funds to complete the Galileo project as soon as possible.'[12] Great play was made by the Commission of the fact that we apparently

Figure1 Eurobarometer questions are not always clearly objective

Q.4 INTRO
Before I ask the next question, let me explain you a few things about navigation systems (READ OUT SLOWLY, REPEAT IF NECESSARY)

Navigations systems are used by an increasing number of applications, such as for example car navigation, shipping, aviation, in agriculture to monitor the use of chemicals. The US owns and controls GPS , which is primarily for military use, but also provided for civilian use, however without quality of service guarantees. Russia and China are working on setting up their alternative navigation systems.

Q4a According to your opinion, should Europe set up its own navigation system, or should Europe rely on American, Russian or Chinese systems? DO NOT READ OUT. ONE ANSWER ALLOWED

- The EU should set up its independent system.........................1
- There is no need for an independent system............................2
- DK/NA...9

**Figure 2 How to get people to say Galileo should
be completed 'as soon as possible'**

Q.6 Galileo is the name of the positioning system the European Union has
started to develop seven years ago

Currently, it seems that in order to complete the Galileo system additional
public funding is necessary (about €2.4 billion, which is the cost of about
400 km motorway). What do you prefer?

READ OUT. ONE ANSWER ALLOWED

- The EU should secure the necessary funds in order
  to complete Galileo as soon as possible 1
- The EU should not secure extra funds, even if it means that
  the project will be significantly delayed or even that it fails 2
- DK/NA 9

wanted Galileo to be completed 'as soon as possible'. But given
the emotive wording of the question (see Figure 2) and the
limited choice of answers, it's hardly surprising that people said
the project should be completed. Moreover, the words 'as soon
as possible' were already in one of the only two possible answers.

In this question the Commission claimed that only €2.4
billion were required to complete the project and that this was
equivalent to 400 kilometres of motorway. One suspects that
had the question explained that the total cost of the project to
taxpayers might be as much as €14 billion and that this was
equivalent to over 250 fully equipped hospitals rather than
something boring like 400 kilometres of motorway, then the
eurocrats might have got a somewhat different and extremely
unwelcome answer. They might even have got some rather
colourful suggestions about where they could put their satellite
navigation system – and 'in space' would not have been one
of them.

By late 2007 the idea of using private-sector money for the
project was dead in the water. However, given the massive (80
per cent positive) level of public support for the project
helpfully revealed by Eurobarometer, the Commission felt

confident enough to put forward a proposal to member states providing 'for the deployment phase of Galileo to be funded entirely from the Community budget to ensure that the project continues'. The Commission vice-president Jacques Barrot now claimed to have new figures to justify the unjustifiable: 'I am still convinced that Europe needs Galileo. Today I have come up with all the facts and figures to enable the European parliament and Ministers to take the necessary decisions on the programme and its funding by the end of the year.'[13]

Not everyone was quite as enthusiastic, however. Just eight weeks after Barrot's defence of the project, the British House of Commons Transport Select Committee published a report calling Galileo 'a textbook example of how not to run a major infrastructure project'.[14] On the subject of Jacques Barrot's 'facts and figures' the committee noted: 'In our view, the benefit projections put forward by the European Commission through-out the lifetime of the Galileo project appear fanciful.' The committee went on to express its concerns that Galileo was just a 'vanity' project with no real commercial basis: 'We feel that Galileo's status as a flagship *grand projet* is clouding the judge-ment of some in relation to its true, realistic and proven merits.' The committee suggested that the programme should be scaled back or even cancelled altogether: 'It is entirely conceivable that the best cost-benefit at this stage might be to scrap the programme entirely.' Commenting on the technical viability and expense of Galileo, one of the committee members explained in an interview: 'This is not one pig flying in orbit, this is a herd of pigs with gold trotters, platinum tails and diamond eyes.'[15]

But there are some certainties in this turbulent world. One of these is that no politician will have the courage to end the sad life of this ill-fated exercise in EU extravagance. Galileo will be allowed to continue and will gobble up around €14 billion of our money because the EU claims that abandoning this prestige project 'would harm the image of the EU'.

At present the Commission has to go cap in hand to the member states to get the cash to bail out projects like Galileo. This allows national authorities, such as the British House of Commons Transport Select Committee, occasionally to try to find out how well our EU money is being used and to make embarrassing judgements about eurocrats' devastating incompetence and profligacy. But in the Lisbon Treaty the EU grants itself new powers and money to run its own research and space programmes. This means that in future, member countries will have almost no powers to assess the value and management of major EU projects nor to control their costs. So once Lisbon goes through, we can expect many more prestige projects to be launched using considerable quantities of our cash. Unfortunately, most of them will probably 'do a Galileo' without us having any real idea of how much of our money is being poured away by eurocratic mismanagement.

THE LAND OF LOST OPPORTUNITIES

Wasting money is an inevitable consequence of allowing self-serving bureaucracies power that greatly exceeds their managerial abilities, and it is in no way confined to the EU. What are possibly more important for European citizens are the huge opportunities that have been missed because the EU has knowingly spent our cash on the wrong things.

In the late 1990s the Prodi Commission realised that the EU faced some serious economic challenges. Internally, an ageing population was leading to a reduction in the size of the workforce at the same time as increasing public spending on things like pensions and healthcare. Externally, competition from the US, China and India was putting pressure on European industry, leading to increasing unemployment, particularly among those with lower skills. In spring 2000 the Commission and European leaders signed up to what was called the 'Lisbon Agenda'. This had nothing at all to do with the later, much reviled Lisbon

Treaty, which replaced the rejected constitution. The Lisbon
Agenda was an EU action plan intended to turn the EU into 'the
most competitive and dynamic knowledge-based economy' in the
world by 2010. This would be achieved by closing 'the economic
gap between the EU and the US'. As part of the Lisbon Agenda
EU leaders boldly promised to boost EU economic growth by
such measures as increasing labour market flexibility, stimulating
innovation, encouraging more people to become entrepreneurs
and investing more in research and development. Ironically, in
the year the Lisbon Agenda was launched the EU's growth rate
was actually slightly ahead of its great rival the US. However,
hardly had the leaders returned home to implement their fine
intentions than the EU's growth rate collapsed. So for the next
half decade, as Lisbon policies were supposedly revolutionising
Europe's economic performance, the EU languished behind the
US with a growth rate that was humiliatingly less than half of that
achieved by their dastardly American competitors (see Figure 3).

Moreover, immediately after Lisbon, unemployment in the
EU shot up, and it wasn't till well into 2006 that it reached pre-
Lisbon levels.

Figure 3 After Lisbon, EU growth fell well behind the US

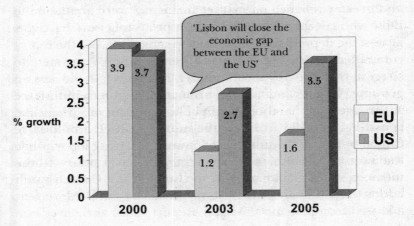

By 2002 the Lisbon Agenda was going nowhere. In July 2002 Prodi commissioned a study from a group headed by Belgian economist André Sapir to suggest ways to kick-start European economic growth. After a year of no doubt serious cogitation, the group published its report, 'An Agenda for a Growing Europe: Making the EU Economic System Deliver'. The report found that, in spite of the fine rhetoric from Lisbon, 'the EU system has failed to deliver a satisfactory growth performance'. It went on to contrast the EU's performance with that of the EU prior to Lisbon and with that of the US: 'This underperformance is striking because it contrasts not only with expectations but also with past EU performance and recent US accomplishment.' The report warned that 'the current combination of low growth and higher public expenditure is not sustainable, and will become less so in future'.

The recommendations made by the report were eminently sensible. Some, such as 'higher investment in both R&D and higher education', would probably have met with general agreement. But unfortunately a few of the proposed actions had the potential to upset some of the most powerful self-interest groups lucratively riding on the EU gravy train. Suggestions such as 'greater mobility of employees within and across firms and greater reliance on market financing' were anathema to those who saw the EU as a fortress for protecting workers' rights against the depredations of unbridled capitalism. But the report committed an extreme form of heresy when it seemed to suggest that the EU's competitive future might lie less in growing potatoes and more in promoting high-tech industries. The suggestion that there might be 'a major cut in agricultural spending' in order to invest the money in R&D would have caused horror to the immensely powerful farming lobby, while the idea of 'devolution of spending for rural policy to the member states' could be seen to threaten the Commission's efforts to continually increase its own central control. Moreover, a letter accompanying the Sapir Report could also have been seen as being critical of EU leaders for being all talk and no trousers: 'Growth must become Europe's number one economic priority – not only in the declarations of its leaders, but first and foremost in their actions.'[16]

A year later Prodi returned to Italian domestic politics, and Barroso took over. The Lisbon Agenda had still not got much beyond fine words, and so Barroso commissioned a study led by the former Dutch prime minister Wim Kok to look at pretty much the same things as the Sapir group had studied. In November 2004 this group concluded that progress on delivering the Lisbon Agenda had been less than impressive: 'Lisbon's disappointing delivery is due to an overloaded agenda, poor coordination and conflicting priorities and lack of determined political action.' Following the Kok report, the Commission relaunched the Lisbon Agenda in 2005 with a document called 'Working together for Growth and Jobs: A New Start for the Lisbon Strategy'. Whatever the value or otherwise of this new effort, the head of Barroso's cabinet seemed to get a bit tongue-tied when it came to having to explain the importance of this latest attempt to breathe some life into Lisbon: 'The new Lisbon is very distinct from the old Lisbon. Of course, they have a lot in common but it is quite different and sometimes the fact that we continue to use the word "Lisbon" is confusing and not always helpful.'[17]

One particular problem identified in the first Lisbon Agenda was that at less than 2 per cent of GDP, EU investment in R&D was lagging far behind the USA's. Lisbon set a target of 3 per cent. However, by 2008, eight years after signing up to the Lisbon Agenda, the EU's level of R&D spending was still stagnating at the pre-Lisbon level.

By 2006 things were beginning to look a little brighter. Several of the major EU economies passed a series of measures aimed at getting people off welfare and back to work, and economic growth soared to 2.9 per cent in 2007. Then came the crash of 2008, and as EU economies struggle to limit the economic carnage of the 2008–9 recession, some might wish they hadn't wasted the first five years of the Lisbon Agenda doing just about nothing at all to improve their economic competitiveness. Incidentally, at the end of 2008 the EU budget commissioner announced the results of a public consultation on the future of the EU budget. This showed a 'broad consensus' of more than 300 organisations that EU spending should be less focused on 'policies of the past' (like the Common Agricultural Policy) and more directed at the 'policies of tomorrow', such as research, innovation and competitiveness.[18] More than five years after the Sapir Report and eight years after the Lisbon Agenda was agreed, little seemed to have changed.

PART 4

WHAT NOW? THE NEED FOR FUNDAMENTAL REFORM

Chapter 15

PUT PRAGMATISM BEFORE POLITICS

WHAT HAVE WE LEARNED?

We've now had just over 50 years of the European Union in its various forms – the Common Market, the EEC, the EC and now the EU – so we are in a fairly good position to judge what it can do well and where it fails. We know that the EU has served as a zone of political and economic stability that has managed to spread democracy and prosperity to countries that have emerged from dictatorship or communism. Moreover, it has had some success in creating a single borderless market that has certainly improved the economic prospects of most of its members. However, people are becoming increasingly aware that EU institutions are bureaucratic rather than democratic; that eurocrats seems obsessed with increasing their own power through over-regulation, land-grabs and propaganda; that Brussels has become the centre of massive administrative incompetence; and that the ruling elite has nothing but contempt for the opinions of European citizens.

Even many europhiles will admit that the EU is far from perfect. However their solution always seems to be more, more, more, more – they claim that if the EU is given more power, more money, more media coverage and produces more regulation, then it will better meet the aspirations of its citizens. More power includes having its own military forces, its own diplomatic service, its own police, its own courts and its own symbols of nationhood – flag, motto and anthem. More money means allowing the EU to raise its own taxes so it can break free from member states being able to limit its already excessive budget. The EU is constantly trying to get more media coverage by expensively befriending media organisations and journalists and by setting up new TV, radio, internet and other channels in order to 'explain' to citizens all the benefits the EU brings them. And the EU seems to be rushing into trying to regulate in areas like healthcare, education, social protection, immigration, transport, energy and even sport. As for EU citizens, once the self-amending Lisbon Treaty is passed, their governments will have ceded so much power to Brussels that what they want or don't want will become largely irrelevant.

The eurosceptics, of course, view this ever-expanding, over-bureaucratic, undemocratic monster with something approaching horror. They fear the loss of national sovereignty, the destruction of democratic processes, economic stagnation due to over-regulation and the inevitable further spread of corruption as more money and power pass into the grasping hands of an increasingly self-serving, arrogant and unaccountable elite.

DO WHAT FITS

Much of the public debate about whether and how to reform the EU has become muddied by the tendency of those involved to base their arguments on political theories and rather meaningless labels, which are usually just disguising their own self-interest. Anyone who can be bothered to take an interest in EU affairs is subjected to a cacophony of the europhiles and europhobes endlessly arguing about what form the EU should take – the 'philes pushing the ideas of a sovereign state or a constitutional union or a USE (United States of Europe) or a federal state and the 'phobes rooting for a federation of independent states or a Europe of democracies or simply a European free trade area. There are many other groups also trying to steer the EU bandwagon in a direction that suits their political, ideological or financial interests. People on the left want to use the EU to create a fortress Europe to protect European workers' rights against the predations of globalisation and unfettered competition from lower cost countries. The various environmental pressure groups see the EU as a way of dragging member states kicking and screaming into their dream of a sustainable low-carbon economy. Many large companies have become masters at siphoning off EU taxpayers' money and at bending EU regulations to wipe out smaller rivals in order to gain competitive advantages for their products and services. And all those lucratively riding on the EU bandwagon know that more power and money for the EU mean increasing their own importance and influence and improving their personal career and financial prospects.

But there may be a more practical way of trying to work out how best to move the EU forwards so that it serves its citizens, rather than just the interests of those it feeds and those who shout the loudest. This is by forgetting politics, ideology and self-interest for a moment and instead looking at the reality of what the EU has achieved and could achieve. If we do this we can identify where, in an imperfect world, the EU could benefit the majority of its subjects and where it is likely to harm our interests.

One way of viewing how we should organise the EU is to split its activities into four main groups (see Figure 1). There are some areas where the EU has provided tangible benefits, so it should be encouraged to focus on these. Second, there are other things that the EU currently does badly but that it is in a better position to carry out than individual countries, and here it should be pressured into improving its performance. Third, there are areas where the EU performs poorly either because of bureaucratic incompetence or because these can be most effectively and appropriately managed by member states, so these should obviously be taken away from the EU and handed back to individual countries. Finally, there are areas into which the EU is trying to expand but in which it should not have any role – here its expansion should be stopped.

Figure I The EU should concentrate on activities it can do best and stop doing what countries are more suited to do

Keep at EU level	
Focus Where the EU can benefit us • Encourage democracy & stability • Name/ shame bad public services	**Improve** What the EU does very badly • European Parliament • The single market • Regulation
Do in countries	
Take away What the EU shouldn't be doing • CAP and fisheries • Propaganda • Financial/fraud control	**Stop** Unnecessary EU scope-creep • The superstate • The euro-army • Healthcare and education • Asylum and immigration • Tax policy and social security

Were we writing a trendy management book, we would call this approach the 'doing what FITS' model, FITS being, of course, an acronym for Focus, Improve, Take away, Stop. But we're not, so we won't.

One of the basic principles of the FITS model is that we propose that activities should be carried out where they are practically, economically and democratically most effectively performed, rather than allocated between the EU and countries according to either theoretical political principles or the power of those pursuing their own selfish purposes. Another principle is that the closer the spending of money is to those who are supplying that money – that is, EU taxpayers – the less likely that money is to be wasted on incompetent management, complex, unworkable programmes, worthless, grandiose schemes, corruption and theft. This approach is based on practicality and pragmatism rather than on the political dogmatism, pursuit of power and personal profits of the 'philes and the 'phobes. Below we give some examples of how we can use this way of thinking pragmatically to design the most appropriate future form of the EU and decide what activities should and should not be performed by the European institutions.

FOCUS ON WHAT THE EU COULD DO BEST

Promote democracy and stability

Until the accession of Bulgaria and Romania, the EU has managed to extend membership to, and reinforce democracy in, countries that might otherwise have become failed states. Moreover on joining, most of these countries have seen a rapid improvement in their economic prospects from being given EU money and from access to the internal market and also in their democratic processes from their cooperation with other EU countries. So the EU should be encouraged to continue its role as an anchor for countries that wish to move away from poverty and political instability. However, this beneficial process seems to have broken down because the accession of Romania and Bulgaria was rushed through for political purposes, while ignoring the reality that both countries were not ready for membership because they were more like corrupt mafia enterprises than properly functioning states. Thus, as soon as they had access to EU money, both quickly went about weakening their laws and diminishing the power of their judiciaries in order to enable the ruling criminals and their political puppets to continue plundering our money with little fear of being stopped and without any fear of punishment. Unfortunately for us EU taxpayers, our political masters in Brussels have not had the courage to deal with this problem, and so our money will continue to flow into the pockets of the wealthy minority in these two countries, mostly bypassing those whom it is intended to help.

The Bulgarian and Romanian experience has shown that there are limits to the type of countries that should be allowed to join the EU. So the EU cannot just continue to grow by almost indiscriminately offering membership to ever more countries in the naïve hope that they will behave modestly and honestly and not just enthusiastically set about stealing as much of our cash as they can fit into their bank accounts. There are probably a couple of countries that are not as rotten as Bulgaria and Romania and that could be admitted to the club. However, the EU needs a way of encouraging democracy and development in some others without letting them run wild with our chequebooks. At the same time, particularly with eastern European countries, the EU needs to find the right balance between its wish to act as an instrument of democratisation and the political imperative of not being seen to threaten Russia's strategic interests.

The expansion of the EU should be stopped at somewhere between 27 and 30 members. Because of their deep-rooted corruption, Bulgaria and Romania have given the EU financial and democratic indigestion, and not only has the EU been unable to absorb them successfully, they have actually both regressed as soon as they got access to our money. In future, instead of inviting possibly unsuitable countries like Turkey, Serbia, the Ukraine and Georgia to join, the EU should focus its political efforts on developing EFTA-style trading blocs on the EU's borders. One could be in the east and include countries like Russia, the Ukraine, Georgia and a few of the Stans. The other should look towards the Muslim countries like Turkey and the North African states. In both regions the EU should encourage countries to form their own trading alliances on the Common Market model and offer these groups privileged partner status with the EU in return for their strengthening democracy, reducing corruption and fostering economic progress for the majority – not just a privileged minority – of their citizens.

'Name and shame' to improve public services

The EU could also play an invaluable role in pressuring member states' governments into improving the quality and cost-effectiveness of public services such as transport, crime reduction, job creation, healthcare and education.

The EU has become expert at collecting and crunching statistics, and now that Eurostat managers are not engaged in funnelling our money into often bogus companies run by family and friends, they are busy producing masses of statistics comparing economics, health, education and lifestyles in all the EU member countries. Whether you wish to know employment rates by age and sex, income inequality, levels of criminality, mortality rates, criminal re-offending, the extent of cannabis use, deaths by neoplasms or whatever – Eurostat can probably supply it in more detail than you could ever wish to have.

This access to the comparative performance of countries' economies, education systems, healthcare, criminal justice and so on gives the EU a unique ability to identify the countries that perform well in particular areas and provides a basis to investigate the reasons for the differences between the high and low performers. Unfortunately, the EU has usually just tried to use this information as an excuse for setting itself up as an expert and then extending its own power into areas that are completely outside its remit and far beyond the eurocrats' managerial competence – healthcare, education, traffic management, sport and criminal justice, for example. However, if the EU could restrict itself to just providing information on performance levels and best practice ideas to help countries improve their own performance, it would provide a stimulus for national governments to improve the service they deliver to their own citizens. Moreover, by showing the service levels being achieved by high-performing countries and naming and shaming poor-performing countries, the EU could take away individual governments' excuses for delivering low-quality or overly expensive public services to their people and force them into action.

IMPROVE WHAT THE EU DOES BADLY

Put democracy into the European parliament

Whenever people criticise the EU for its lack of democracy, the automatic response is for our rulers to claim that as the power of the European parliament is increasing, the EU is becoming more democratic. Trying to make the EU more democratic by having a European parliament consisting of elected politicians was an experiment worth trying, but 30 years after the parliament's formation it is abundantly clear that the experiment has been an abysmal failure. We have not created a democratic body capable of making sure that the EU works in the interests of European citizens. Instead, we have built a largely impotent hot-air factory full of greedy hypocrites spouting vacuous noble sentiments while brazenly trying every trick and fiddle they can think of to fill their own pockets with our money. Moreover, our MEPs have repeatedly demonstrated their highly rewarded disdain for the wishes of their voters. So we need another approach if we are to restore some degree of democratic legitimacy to the work of the EU.

One solution would be to scrap the position of full-time MEPs. Having an assembly filled with full-time European parliamentarians hasn't given us much democracy for the last 30 years, so we can confidently predict it never will. The main reason for the parliament's failure is that its members are so well-paid, so pampered and so unaccountable that they have lost all touch with both ordinary voters and even the interests of the countries from which they come. Their only allegiance is to the eurocracy that has provided them with such an easy and lucrative lifestyle and, of course, to their own financial well-being.

Instead, the European parliament should ideally consist of politicians from national parliaments seconded to the European parliament for one week a month, and they should be chosen in the same proportion as political parties are represented in their national parliaments. Their job should be to scrutinise and vote on legislation proposed by the Commission. In this way, we can get rid of the Strasbourg buildings, scrap the expensive and unnecessary European elections and considerably reduce the cost of our politicians as we would no longer have to pay for over 700 MEPs. Moreover, by using politicians from national parliaments to also work at the European parliament, we would have a new class of politicians who would be known to their electorates and who would have some accountability to their own national parliaments and to their voters, quite unlike most MEPs who see themselves as being a privileged elite seemingly above criticism, above normal morality and of course above the law.

Sort out the single market

Although the euro-elite are pantingly eager to drag us all into their United States of Europe paradise, they seem to have forgotten that the original focus of the European Union was to create a single market. At the moment, the single market is far from working effectively. Many countries are still illegally providing state aid to their main industries. The Italian government, for example, managed to shift the dreadful Alitalia into the hands of private investors without the airline having to repay state loans that the EU had already judged to be illegal, and France is notorious for shovelling its taxpayers' money into propping up its main industries. Moreover, when it comes to utility services such as energy, water supplies and telecommunications, key member states like France, Germany and Spain fiercely protect their domestic suppliers while encouraging them to aggressively acquire utility companies in countries like Britain and the Netherlands, which have opened up their markets to competition. This has allowed these companies to push up prices in their foreign acquisitions, giving them four to five times more profit than they can get in their more regulated home markets. So before trying to herd us all into its superstate, perhaps the EU's many bureaucrats could devote some of their efforts to sorting out the single market by stamping out the most flagrant abuses.

Theoretically the European Court of Justice (ECJ) is responsible for taking action on complaints about practices that distort the single market. However, the ECJ usually takes over two years to reach its decisions, it has been discredited by its repeated failure to deliver objective judgements and many countries just ignore it when it suits their interests to do so. Given the hopelessly politically biased nature of ECJ judgements, it should be radically reformed to act as a legal entity enforcing existing EU law rather than continuing as a political body pursuing further integration. Or else the ECJ should be scrapped and new mechanisms found for allowing individual countries to retaliate against restrictive practices by other members – for example, countries like Britain should be permitted to declare their utilities like energy and water as strategic national resources and thus force French, German and Spanish owners to sell British utility firms back to British-controlled companies.

Effective regulation – turn activity into results

It is now clear that the EU's approach to regulation is leading nowhere. Its attempts to codify almost every aspect of our lives have just resulted in an ever-increasing mountain of red tape that provokes nothing but derision and contempt from most EU citizens. Moreover, as we have seen, the EU's attempts to control its own regulatory diarrhoea have been farcical. It is now time to change the whole philosophy of EU regulation from a prescriptive model, where everything must be regulated, to a preventive approach, where the EU focuses only on the minimum of regulation required to protect its citizens from physical or financial harm.

Moreover, we need to start limiting the total number of laws coming from the EU. One method for starting to control regulation would be to impose a 'replacement principle' on the EU Commission. This means that for every new regulation or directive the EU introduces, it would have to withdraw another regulation or directive so that the overall volume of EU rules doesn't increase. A tougher approach would be to set a target of, say, 5 per cent a year for five years for the Commission. This would mean that each year for the next five years, even while introducing new laws, the Commission would have to reduce the overall number of regulations and directives by 5 per cent a year. As an incentive to perform, each year the Commission failed to achieve this target its administrative budget would be reduced by 5 per cent.

TAKE AWAY WHAT THE EU SHOULDN'T DO

Scrap the CAP

The CAP was designed to deal with a problem that existed in the middle of the last century – food shortages in Europe after the Second World War. That problem was solved at least 30 years ago when Europe started producing excess food, giving us the world's largest butter mountains and wine lakes. Yet the CAP has continued to devour vast quantities of our money for no reason other than to enrich a small section of society. It is now clear that over 80 per cent of the CAP budget goes into the pockets of the wealthiest landowners, farmers and agri-businesses. This mass siphoning of EU taxpayers' money by the already wealthy is a moral obscenity. Moreover, there is no justification for allowing the EU bureaucrats to administer the tens of billions each year that the CAP dishes out. The involvement of eurocrats costs at least £100 million a year in unnecessary administration, increases financial waste and encourages massive fraud.

One of the most obvious measures needed to restore some financial credibility to the EU is to scrap the policy completely. Abandoning the CAP would enable member states' contributions to the EU budget to be reduced by 32 per cent (€42.9 billion). If rural payments were also stopped, another 11 per cent of the EU's budget (€14.6 billion) could be saved. Moreover, EU staff numbers could be reduced by around 1,000 unnecessary people. Member states should be allowed to give as much of their taxpayers' money as they wish to their own farmers and agribusinesses. However, each government would then have to justify to its voters why their taxes were being poured into the pockets of wealthy farmers, companies and landowners rather than being used to build schools and hospitals. In most countries this move to more local and more democratic control of the CAP's tens of billions would inevitably and rapidly lead to a massive decrease in the amount given to agriculture and probably result in a much better targeting of that money to the genuinely needy rather than to the excessively greedy.

Save our fish

We've now had over 20 years of the Common Fisheries Policy (CFP). Publicly the EU claims that the CFP is a huge success, but privately it admits it is a disaster. If you've been paying someone to repair a leak in the roof of your house for over 20 years and it's still leaking, then it's probably time to get a different builder or even to do it yourself. The same goes for the CFP. After 20 years of failure and the virtual destruction of our fish stocks, it's time for a new approach. The idea of trying to preserve fish stocks by allocating Total Allowable Catches (TACs) to countries and boats doesn't work and leads to the ecologically damaging discarding of millions of tons of edible fish, massive cheating to avoid quotas and a deliberate decision by many countries not to bother policing the policy in order to help their own fishing industries. Moreover, the more the EU restricts the TACs, the more dead fish are dumped back into the sea and the more cheating becomes the only way fishermen can earn a living. The whole CFP has become a self-defeating joke.

It's time to abandon the CFP. Fish should no longer be a 'common resource' available to all EU members, and instead countries should be given back exclusive control of their own territorial waters. Then individual countries should have the power to decide who fishes in their waters and how much they can catch. Moreover, in order to preserve fish stocks, countries should abandon TACs for each boat and replace them by each boat being allowed a certain number of days at sea. With their fishing time limited, boats would be encouraged to bring back and sell as much of their catch as they could. This approach would enable fishermen to make a living while also helping fish stocks recover. It is a sign of madness to keep on doing the same thing and expect a different result – to carry on trying to manage fishing with the CFP and its demonstrably failing TACs is insane.

Stop the propaganda

It is now clear that the EU is cynically misusing most of the €2 billion spent on communication and education. Much of the money goes to supporting pro-European propaganda and parasitic pro-European academics and pressure groups, rather than genuinely trying to improve the lives of EU citizens. In order to support its ageing population, the EU needs to remain competitive in international markets through producing high quality, technologically advanced products and services. It's hard to see how almost 800 Jean Monnet professors teaching and writing about European integration and hundreds of thousands of students learning about European integration are going to make any contribution at all to Europe's commercial success. In fact, they are just a huge drain on European taxpayers. Moreover, most EU citizens will never get any benefit from the hundreds of millions being pocketed by a few sycophantically europhiliac organisations.

So it's time to stop this massive waste of our money. The EU's budget for communication and education should be cut by at least 70 per cent and the money returned to member states in the form of reduced contributions to the EU. If member countries want to pour their taxpayers' money into supporting the huge but useless 'European integration' industry, then they should be free to do that. And if member states want to spend hundreds of millions informing their citizens about the benefits of belonging to the EU, again that's their business.

Reduce the EU budget

For 14 years the Court of Auditors has refused to approve the EU's accounts, and for 14 years the Commission has admitted that it is unable to assure us that it knows where around 80 per cent of our EU budget money ends up. The Commission's excuse is that as the money is spent by the member states, it cannot be blamed if the money finds its way into the wrong hands. Yet the Commission is planning to take control of a wide range of new policy areas that will give it much more power, meaning that much more of our money will be spent on the Commission's schemes. This doesn't make sense. Either the Commission should take full responsibility for ensuring that all money spent on its schemes is reliably accounted for, or else the Commission's budget should be drastically reduced to a level where it can get control of the money it uses. In addition to scrapping the CAP and the CFP, we propose that the money spent on things like cohesion and other grants could be cut by at least one-third. This should be matched by a corresponding cut in the number of bureaucrats working in these two areas.

At present the EU is using so much of our money on so many different, complex and largely unworkable programmes that it is hardly surprising that its spending is out of control. A major reduction in spending would allow the EU to move from its current position of financial incontinence to one where it can effectively manage the money that passes through its hands. Then once the EU is able to properly account for all our money, its budget could be gradually increased again. But it is utterly pointless to allow the Commission to continue using so much of our money when it refuses to accept any responsibility for where around 80 per cent of this money goes.

No more self-regulation

The EU has proved that it is quite incapable of policing itself. In spite of 14 years of failed audits, the Commission just shrugs off any criticism of its profligacy by blaming member states and claiming that it is improving its financial control. As for OLAF, it is worse than just an expensive joke, because its ineffectiveness and natural tendency to cover up, rather than expose, fraud actually encourages people to cheat the EU in the knowledge that they will almost certainly never be caught and, even if caught, they probably won't be punished. After so many years of failed self-control, it may be time to look at new ways of trying to make sure that our EU billions are properly spent.

One option might be to disband the Court of Auditors. Instead, each year two or three countries could be given the task of sending in a joint team to oversee and audit EU spending. The countries with this responsibility would change each year or every two years. These teams could be incentivised by allowing the countries carrying out the financial controls and audits to keep and share a percentage (perhaps 30 per cent) of all money recovered from identifying and prosecuting fraud. This approach of having responsibility for financial control rotating between EU countries might also have the advantage that it would set up a kind of competition where countries would be motivated to show they were the most effective at uncovering fraud and recovering wasted money. At the moment, most countries actively work to prevent auditors and OLAF discovering fraud by their citizens because they lose EU funds each time they are shown to have allowed fraud to have taken place. If OLAF is to continue its sad and unproductive existence, it should be made directly accountable to this multinational financial control group and thus made to work for the interests of EU taxpayers rather than in the interest of protecting EU employees and institutions.

Reward whistleblowers to prevent fraud

For years the EU has claimed to be working hard to prevent corruption and fraud. Yet whistleblowers get fired, corrupt officials are protected, and OLAF is largely ineffective. Moreover, the so-called 'whistleblowers' charter' seems to have rendered whistleblowers extinct. This is not surprising, because anyone who contemplates revealing waste or corruption can see that they would only be destroying their own career and livelihood. Unfortunately, the EU does not seem to have looked at ways to provide stronger incentives for whistleblowers to reveal suspected malpractice.

Since the American Civil War the USA has had a law, rejuvenated by Congress in 1986, called the False Claims Act. This allows ordinary citizens with evidence of fraud or corruption against government contracts or programmes to sue, on the government's behalf, in order to recover any money taken illegally. As a reward for their efforts, whistleblowers are given somewhere between 15 per cent and 25 per cent of the money recovered or saved. Just one partner in a US consultancy stood to gain $10 million for revealing how his employer had been cheating the US government over travel expenses. The False Claims Act protects taxpayers' money in two ways. First, it encourages whistleblowers to take action. Second, and perhaps much more importantly, it has a strong deterrent effect – it discourages individuals and companies from defrauding US government funds because they will always know that they run a serious and real risk of being sued by anybody, for example a disgruntled employee, who knows what they are up to. If the EU really was serious about encouraging whistleblowers in order to stamp out fraud, it would find a way to reward them. One solution would be to introduce a European version of the False Claims Act whereby whistleblowers and their lawyers would be able to launch prosecutions on behalf of the EU and take a share of the money that was saved.

STOP THE EU EXPANDING INTO AREAS WHERE IT SHOULDN'T

Where are we going? Not the superstate

One issue that must be clarified is where the EU is actually taking us. Whenever a member country looks as if it is unhappy with a proposed EU treaty, our leaders tend to trot out the line that we may have to move to what they call 'a two-speed Europe'. In a speech to the German Reichstag in 2000 French president Jacques Chirac proposed that France and Germany should set up 'a pioneer group of EU countries leading to rapid integration'.[1] In September 2003, after the Swedes voted not to join the euro, Romano Prodi, who was Commission president at the time, clearly explained how the fast countries shouldn't be held back by the laggards: 'I don't think we can conceive of always going at the speed of the slowest in the convoy.' Just over two months later, in December 2003, when talks on the new EU constitution broke down, Chirac was back with his 'pioneer group': 'This will provide an engine, an example that will allow Europe to go faster, further and better.'[2] He was, of course, backed up by the German chancellor Gerhardt Schroeder: 'If we do not reach a consensus in the foreseeable future, then a two-speed Europe will emerge. This will be the logic of such a final failure.'[3]

In 2007, as the EU constitution went off the rails, Prodi, then Italian prime minister, was back with the two-speed idea: 'At this point a vanguard of countries could . . . be the best way to proceed towards a more integrated union, on condition that the door remains always open to those countries willing to join later.'[4] In an interview two months later Prodi reminded us: 'You cannot go at the speed of the last wagon.'[5] Then, of course, after the Irish rejected the Lisbon Treaty in 2008 those who would decide our destiny were once again talking of 26 countries moving quickly ahead with integration and leaving Ireland out in the cold.

Every time the great and the good talk about 'pioneers', 'vanguards' and 'two speeds', the implied message is that most of the EU countries are intelligent enough and sufficiently politically developed to move rapidly forwards with the great European experiment. But unfortunately, there are occasionally just a few exceptions – countries whose people are so backward and so ignorant about the benefits of European union that they will just have to advance at a slower rate. In fact, when they are supposedly offering us a two-speed Europe our rulers are not offering us a choice at all. They are merely using the concept of moving at two speeds as a means of pressuring all countries to fall in line and not disrupt their European adventure.

However, while telling us that our countries supposedly have a choice when it comes to the speed they move forward towards an ever closer union, our rulers have never dared suggest the idea of a two-destination Europe – of a Europe where some countries opt for full political integration into a single state governed largely from Brussels, while others choose to preserve their independence and maintain only a close, borderless trading relationship with the EU. If our leaders were genuinely interested in gaining democratic legitimacy for their European project, they would allow electors in all EU members to vote on whether they wanted to move to ever closer union or not. But unfortunately this is a choice we can never be offered, because letting us choose our countries' destiny is anathema to our rulers – they know we would not give the answer they want. Over the next many years we will be continually told that the EU is democratic; that it listens to its people; that it is close to voters; that it is working for its citizens and so on. Moreover, each year, or maybe several times a year, we will be fed the results of Eurobarometer surveys that show how deliriously happy we all are with the EU's increasing power over our lives. But we will never be permitted to vote on whether we actually want the single superstate or not. If the EU ever genuinely wanted our support, it would offer us this choice.

The euro-army – no need for battalions of bureaucrats

We already have a full NATO military command structure in Brussels, so there is absolutely no point in the EU expensively trying to duplicate what already exists, largely to satisfy French national *amour-propre*. NATO should remain the western democracies' main way of ensuring a common defence against any major armed threat. However, there is some logic in the EU moving ahead with creating a small but effective rapid intervention force to which each state should contribute around 1,000 personnel. Disappointingly for French ambitions, this force should not seek eventually to become a military entity capable of supplanting NATO. Instead, the role of this rapid intervention force would, as its name makes clear, not be defensive. It should be focused on preventing conflict and restoring peace in failing states, and it should be able to move quickly into areas where the population prefers killing each other to living in peace. The EU force could help separate the combatants, protect civilians and provide humanitarian aid. Previous EU attempts at peacekeeping have tended to be less than effective because of a lack of basics like leadership, trained personnel, motivation and proper equipment, and the French and German contributions to the conflict in Afghanistan have been laughable. The main challenge with setting up this force will be to make it effective and decisive and to prevent it from becoming just a battalion of bureaucrats in battledress armed with PowerPoint presentations who spend all their time sitting in supposedly important strategy and planning meetings in order to avoid anything that looks or smells the least bit risky.

Leave us alone

As for the EU's plans to start regulating our healthcare systems, education, transport, city planning, sport, asylum, immigration, social protection, pensions, work–life balance and many other aspects of our lives – these should stop. As proposed above, there is a role for the EU in providing comparative statistics and indicating which countries perform best and most efficiently in providing public services and which are absolutely abysmal. But there is no reason for the Commission to assume that it should also be legislating in these areas. With immigration and asylum, already crowded countries like Belgium, the Netherlands and Britain should be able to decide how many people and which people from outside the EU are allowed to come to live in their countries. Similarly, with social security payments each country should be able to choose who should receive its taxpayers' money as unemployment benefits and help to pay for housing and child support. Moreover, different countries have differing health, social, transport and educational challenges to deal with – an EU one-size-fits-all mass of regulations dreamed up by desk-bound Brussels bureaucrats will never be the right or effective way to make sure that individual countries meet the needs of their citizens. Unfortunately, this obvious truth is somewhat unpalatable to those whose careers depend on them increasing their authority over us.

WANT TO TRY EU-LITE?

The line of reasoning taken here is, of course, both blasphemous and threatening to all those getting fat from the EU feeding frenzy. After all, here we are proposing a much lighter, low-calorie version of the EU, one where fewer politicians, eurocrats and other hangers-on can gorge themselves on our money. The 2009 EU budget is around €134 billion and about 100,000 people work on a full- or part-time basis administering the EU regulatory production lines. Many more work in the member states to enforce EU rules and regulations. By scrapping the CAP, handing fisheries policy back to the member countries, reducing spending on over-regulation and propaganda and by cutting unnecessary bureaucracy, we could probably shrink the EU budget by well over half to around €50 billion at the most and similarly cut the number of euro-busy-bees down from 45,500 to about 15,000 full-time and from 50,000 to 20,000 part-time people. Of course, if some countries choose to move towards fuller political integration, they would be more than welcome to employ and pay for the 30,000 full-time and further 30,000 part-time bureaucrats that the rest of us would no longer need.

At present the EU is in a vicious spiral where more employees lead to more power-grabbing, which leads to more money being spent, which in turn results in less financial control, more waste and more corruption. By making drastic cuts in the EU's budget and staffing levels we could move from this vicious spiral to a virtuous spiral, where a smaller workforce leads to a better focus on the right regulation, which leads to fewer power-grabs, reduced spending, improved financial control and less waste and corruption. But strong visionary actions require strong visionary leaders. In today's bureaucratic and technocratic Europe, where all our leaders seem to belong to the same privileged club, it seems difficult to imagine any of our rulers wanting to stand up for the interests of the people they are paid to represent.

DON'T KNOW, DON'T CARE?

Now that the EU project has been so successfully hijacked by a parasitical, self-serving, out-of-touch elite, a useful question might be whether it can ever be reformed so that it can properly serve the interests of European citizens. A problem with this question is that in most EU countries it is not even being asked. Increasingly, the ideological gulf in EU member states is not between different political parties, but rather between the rulers and the ruled. Most national politicians throughout Europe feel a greater affinity with members of their own political class than they do with their own citizens, and many may also be eyeing a comfortable place for themselves at the great European self-service banqueting table. So they see no advantage in fighting the lack of democracy and moral decay within all the EU institutions. Moreover, in most member countries there is no eurosceptic press, because much of the media is gorging itself in the trough of EU money and so has little interest in exposing the corruption, waste, fraud and lack of democracy that have permeated almost everything the EU does.

It may be that our lack of outrage about what is happening in the EU is merely a reflection of a Europe-wide trend. Citizens have increasingly handed over responsibility for their lives to an ever-growing ruling political and bureaucratic class. After all, with so many TV channels to watch, so many sporting 'heroes' to follow and so many 'interesting' celebrity lives to distract our attention, who now has time for any serious political analysis or discussion? We seem to have moved into an era where the apathetic are content to be ruled by the ambitious and the avaricious.

There is another possible explanation for the media's and the public's indifference to the EU. Perhaps we have seen so many years of waste, lies and dishonesty from the eurocrats that we feel only contempt for our rulers and are no longer interested in the EU's protestations of being interested in our welfare.

It would be satisfying to claim that everyone knows that the EU is in crisis and needs to be reformed. In fact, the opposite is probably true. Most Europeans are largely unaware of the EU's many shortcomings, and, even if they were more informed, they probably wouldn't care. The recent worldwide financial problems are likely to make more people feel that there is 'safety in numbers' and that they are better off giving more power to EU institutions, as national governments have so demonstrably failed to protect them from economic turmoil. Within the EU, member states that have previously rejected the euro are now changing their minds, and outside the EU there is a queue of countries wanting to join. Even Iceland, which has long stayed away from the EU in order to protect its abundant fishing stocks, now wants to come into the EU's warm embrace to protect it from the chill of potential national bankruptcy. The eurocrats have been quick to exploit the economic uncertainties for their own benefit. Quite forgetting that the EU has been responsible for regulating the financial sector for longer than most of us can remember, the eurocrats are now claiming that only the EU can save people from economic uncertainty. As one euro-politician explained: 'I think we are now in a kind of paradox in Europe, because after the explosion of the financial crisis the European Union has found a new legitimacy for the people.'[6]

LOSING THE BATTLE AGAINST THE BUREAUCRATS?

In the war between those who want an ever larger, centralised EU state and those who want the EU's authority to be controlled, it looks as if those who are pushing for the superstate have the upper hand. On their side they have political power, easy access to the media and widespread public apathy. Moreover, in almost all member states most national politicians see their own personal interests best protected by sticking with their EU peers in supporting the continued growth of the superstate rather than trying to defend national independence against it. Those running the EU project have lost touch with those they are supposed to represent and have succeeded in using the EU to give themselves huge political power and to guarantee themselves a luxury lifestyle and enviable financial security that are beyond the wildest dreams of most European citizens. The hypocritical selfishness of these people will bring discredit on what has so far been achieved by the EU, and the good that could still be done is being put in jeopardy.

In *The Great European Rip-off* we have tried to show the outrageous way the European project has been shamelessly hijacked by the grasping but undeserving euro-elite and why Europe's citizens are justified in their growing cynicism towards EU announcements and actions. We have also tried to propose a calm, rational and, above all, pragmatic way of assessing the EU's strengths and weaknesses and deciding where the EU should exercise its authority for the benefit of its citizens and where it should be forced to show restraint so that political power and money are actually used for effective and constructive purposes.

Unfortunately, the coming battle for power in Europe is going to be anything but calm and rational. The EU plans to steamroller the European project over public doubts and opposition by spending tens of millions of our money on EU-positive information campaigns. The eurocrats are also trying to make only pro-EU political parties eligible for EU funds, thus giving them a huge financial advantage over euro-doubters. In fact, the europhiles seem to be ready to use whatever tactics they can to discredit and destroy anyone who dares voice any criticism of their quest to create a euro-paradise on earth. When Irish businessman Declan Ganley's Libertas group successfully helped move the Irish to a 'No' vote in their 2008 referendum on the Lisbon Treaty, the eurocrats started to suggest that he had been secretly funded by the CIA as part of a plot to undermine the EU. In making this claim, our euroleaders showed a surprising ability to forget their own history – during most of the Cold War, the CIA actually poured millions into the pockets of the europhiles as the US saw a more united, more democratic Europe as a necessary defence against its arch enemy, the Soviet Union.

EU commissioner Margot Wallström gave an excellent summary of the elitist nature of the EU project. As EU commissioner for communications for the period 2004 to 2009, she has been a key player in the final push to get the self-amending and irreversible Lisbon Treaty accepted. Launching yet another EU communications strategy, she seemed to state clearly that the whole EU project has been driven by and for a small elite with little regard for democratic consent: 'This has been a project for a small elite, a political elite. That has worked until now. Has it ever been alive, European Democracy? That is a very good question.'[7] She then went on to admit that to win public consent, EU institutions had to change: 'It's clear that to convince Europeans to the European idea, the institutions have to change. The institutions must lead by example in their ability to reform and to be more transparent and more efficient.' The problem is that the EU institutions have not changed for the better. If anything, they are more bloated, wasteful, corrupt, self-serving and undemocratic than they have ever been.

There was a time when the euro-elite wanted our informed consent to their great project. But now, tired of our doubts and our carping and our 'No' votes, they no longer care what we think. The interesting question is whether we will always be prepared to subserviently accept our euro-leaders' obsession with increasing their own power, profligacy in spending our money, brazen feathering of their own nests and demonstrable contempt for our wishes.

Perhaps we should give the last words to the president of the Czech Republic, Václav Klaus, who took over the rotating presidency of the EU for the six months starting in January

2009. In a conference with MEPs he expressed his concerns about the decline of democracy in the EU:

> I thought . . . that we live in a democracy, but it is post-democracy, really, which rules the EU. You mentioned the European values. The most important value is freedom and democracy. The citizens of the EU member states are concerned about freedom and democracy, above all. But democracy and freedom are losing ground in the EU today. It is necessary to strive for them and fight for them. [8]

NOTES

Introduction
1. Quoted on www.liebreich.com.
2. EU Directorate General for Communication website, 2009.
3. *Better off in Europe*, EU Commission publication.

Chapter 1
1. European parliament DG Information, 10 April 2008.
2. *Daily Telegraph*, 13 April 2005.
3. This entertaining news item can be viewed on http://www.youtube.com/watch?v=xnMtc_QJ4-E.
4. www.ep-reform.eu, 8 August 2007.
5. *Statute for Members of the European Parliament*, 28 September 2005.
6. Quotes from *News of the World*, 17 February 2008 and from www.richardcorbett.org.uk, 12 May 2008.
7. Response by Tom Wise to the *News of the World* article.
8. *The Times*, 27 February 2008.
9. *The Times*, 22 February 2008.
10. Ibid.
11. *Daily Telegraph*, 21 February 2008.
12. *EU Observer*, 26 February 2008.
13. *Daily Telegraph*, 26 February 2008.
14. The website http://www.europatransparent.eu/ europatransparent/2008/06/halbherzige-erm.html claims to give the names of some of the MEPs whose assistants'

payments were included in the audit. We have no way of knowing if these names are accurate.

15. *Daily Telegraph*, 2 June 2008.
16. Ibid.
17. *The Times*, 6 June 2008.
18. *The Times*, 5 June 2008.
19. *EU Observer*, 13 November 2008.
20. *Daily Mail*, 7 June 2008.
21. Ibid.
22. *Daily Mail*, 14 June 2008.
23. *EU Observer*, 13 November 2008.
24. *Sunday Times*, 8 June 2008.
25. Ibid.
26. *Daily Mail*, 14 June 2008.
27. Ibid.
28. *Mirror*, 9 June 2008.
29. www.sir-robertatkins.org, press releases.
30. 'Conservative MEPs' Expenses', 8 July 2008. Discussed in the *Guardian*, 10 July 2008.
31. www.alde.eu, 10 July 2008.
32. www.andrewduffmep.org.uk/news/000162 and *EurActiv*, 14 July 2008.
33. In calculating the expected pay rise from the new Members Statute we have assumed that MEPs' salaries increased by around 3.5% from 2007/8 to 2008/9, as was the case for the UK.
34. News item from the Dutch government, 21 July 2008.

Chapter 2

1. EU website, 2009.
2. *Daily Telegraph*, 11 August 2008.
3. Ibid.
4. 'Comitology Committees Assisting the European Union' and 'EU Register of Expert Groups'.
5. Staff regulations.

6. SGPOE email quoted in the *Brussels Journal*, 18 September 2008.

7. *EU Observer*, 25 September 2008.

8. www.eursoc.com/news/fullstory.php/aid/2562/Roll_Out_The_ Barrot.html.

9. www.baltlantis.com.

10. International News Service, October 2004.

11. Ibid.

12. *The Londonpaper*, 3 October 2008; *Sunday Times*, 5 October 2008; *Daily Mail*, 4 October 2008; *Daily Mail*, 6 October 2008; *Daily Mail*, 14 October 2008.

13. BBC News, 27 October 2004.

14. *Guardian*, 12 October 2004.

15. BBC News, 28 October 2004.

16. 'Investing in our Common Future: The Budget of the European Union EU', EU Commission document.

17. 'The European Union Budget at a Glance' , EU Commission document, 2009.

18. EU Budget, 2008; DEFRA Budget, 2008; Rural Payments Agency Budget, 2008.

19. UK Treasury Budget Report, 2004; 'EU Budget Rebate Briefing', Open Europe, 2005.

20. See Chapter 11, Making Crime Pay.

21. Preparatory notes for EU Council meeting on 4 March 2008.

22. 'Measuring Administrative Costs and Reducing Administrative Burdens in the EU', EU Commission working document.

23. Speech by the Dutch vice-prime minister and finance minister, Gerrit Zalm, to the UK government-sponsored conference 'Advancing Enterprise: Britain in a Global Economy', 26 January 2004; Sir David Arculus, speech to the Financial Services Authority, 4 July 2005.

24. 'European Union Membership – The Benefits', Department of Business, Enterprise and Regulatory Reform, 2009.

Chapter 3

1. Info.hktdc.com/imn/07112304/textiles032.htm.
2. Reuters, 11 June 2007.
3. www.alter-eu.org, 2 May 2008.
4. CBAG Final Report, 2005.
5. Ibid.
6. Press release, 'EU puts Emphasis on Innovation in the Field of Biotechnology', 11 April 2007.
7. 'Lobbying the European Union by Committee', Corporate Europe Observatory briefing paper, July 2007.
8. Corporate Europe Observatory has been particularly effective in exposing the power of lobbyists.
9. CNBC, 27 February 2008; Corporate Europe Observatory, 28 June 2005 and November 2006.
10. Reuters, 7 July 2008.
11. 'Who's Pulling the EU Lobby Strings?', Corporate Watch Newsletter no. 25.
12. *Guardian*, 18 October 2006.
13. Ibid.
14. Ibid.
15. *British Medical Journal*, 6 October 2001.
16. Digene Corporation website, September 2008.
17. *Observer*, 25 January 2004.
18. Ibid.
19. Ibid.
20. *International Herald Tribune*, 27 October 2006.
21. *Daily Telegraph*, 17 August 2007.
22. Alber & Geiger website, 2008.
23. Ibid.
24. *International Herald Tribune*, 27 October 2006.
25. *Le Monde*, 3 September 2008.
26. *Der Spiegel*, 18 June 2008.
27. 'The Evolution of Lobbying in Europe', Dr S. Alber and Dr A. Geiger, 5 August 2007.
28. G Plus website, 2008.

29. With apologies to Pink Floyd.
30. *EU Observer*, 23 June 2008.
31. Ibid.
32. *Guardian*, 30 May 2005.
33. *Wall Street Journal*, 6 February 2006.
34. *International Herald Tribune*, 23 June 2008.
35. Ibid.
36. *Der Spiegel*, 18 June 2008.
37. European Alliance for Access to Safe Medicines website 2009
38. Worst EU Lobbying Awards website December 2008.
39. www.euractiv.com, 3 May 2005 (interview translated from the French).

Chapter 4

1. EU Commission President Jacques Delors, speech to the European parliament, 1988, quoted in *The EU: A Brief History*, Open Europe.
2. *EU Observer*, 15 January 2007.
3. The Maastricht Treaty was actually signed in December 1991, but most texts on the EU date it as being in 1992 because that was when ratification took place.
4. Keith Vaz, Labour Minister for Europe, Biarritz EU Summit 2000, reported in *Daily Telegraph*, 19 June 2001.
5. Preamble to the Treaty of Rome, 25 March 1957.
6. Helmut Kohl, German chancellor, 1992, quoted in *Treaty of Maastricht*, Civitas, November 2005.
7. Romano Prodi, speeches to the European parliament, 13 April 1999 and 13 October 1999.
8. Hans Tietmeyer, president of the Bundesbank, 1991.
9. Wim Duisenberg, former president of the ECB, quoted in *The Euro: A Political Project*, Open Europe.
10. Jean-Claude Trichet, *The European*, 13 December 1998.
11. *The Times*, 27 October 1999.
12. Romano Prodi, address to the European parliament, November 1999.

13. Jean Monnet, founder of the European Movement, 30 April 1952.
14. *The Economist*, 25 September 2004.
15. Quoted in *What is the Point of the European Union?*, Lord Pearson of Rannoch, January 2005.
16. Quoted on www.liebreich.com.
17. R. Leach, *A Concise Encyclopedia of the European Union*, Profile Books, 2004.
18. ECJ press release, 14 October 2008.
19. Roman Herzog and Lüder Gerken, 'Stop the European Court of Justice', *EU Observer*, 10 September 2008.
20. Ibid.
21. Presentation at the European Conference for Investigative Journalists, 22 November 2008.

Chapter 5

1. Laeken Declaration, 15 December 2001.
2. *The Making of Europe's Constitution*, Fabian Society, 2003.
3. Article 2(2).
4. Article 1–18 (ex Article 308 TEC, 235 Rome Treaty).
5. National Forum on Europe, Dublin 30 June 2005.
6. Hans Martin Bury, debate in the Bundestag, *Die Welt*, 25 February 2005.
7. *Suddeutsche Zeitung*, 25 November 2003.
8. Radio debate reported in the *Irish Times* July 2004.
9. Spanish minister for justice, *Independent on Sunday*, 27 February 2005.
10. *Daily Telegraph*, 26 May 2005.
11. Press conference 17 June 2005.
12. Lecture to the London School of Economics, 28 February 2006.
13. Xavier Solana, remarks to the press, Brussels, 30 May 2005.
14. Quoted in Susan George, *We the Peoples of Europe*, Pluto Press, 2008, p.85.
15. Valéry Giscard d'Estaing, Agence France Presse, 12 June 2006.

16. French foreign minister, *Irish Times*, 8 August 2005.
17. French president Nicolas Sarkozy at a meeting of MEPs, *EU Observer*, 14 November 2007.
18. Open Europe comparison of the Constitution and the Lisbon Treaty.
19. *Financial Times*, 19 June 2007; Romano Prodi speech in Lisbon, 2 May 2007; *Irish Independent*, 24 June 2007; *Sunday Telegraph*, 24 June 2007.
20. Speech to the European parliament, 27 June 2007.
21. *Sunday Times*, 21 October 2007.
22. *Daily Mail*, Ireland, 25 June 2007.
23. *Jyllands-Posten*, 25 June 2007.
24. Valéry Giscard d'Estaing, address to the Constitutional Affairs Committee in the European parliament, 17 July 2007.
25. Valéry Giscard d'Estaing, *Independent*, 30 October 2007.
26. Giuliano Amato, vice-chairman of the convention, in a speech to the London School of Economics, 20 February 2007.
27. Giuliano Amato, vice-chairman of the convention, at a meeting of the Centre for European Reform, London, 12 July 2007.
28. *Flandreinfo*, 3 July 2007.
29. Dr Garret FitzGerald, former Irish taoiseach, *Irish Times*, 30 June 2007.
30. *Le Monde*, 14 June 2007; *Sunday Telegraph*, 1 July 2007.
31. Tony Blair, May 2003, quoted on www.liebreich.com.
32. Tony Blair, October 2003, quoted on www.liebreich.com.
33. Tony Blair, speech in the House of Commons, 21 June 2004.
34. Gordon Brown, BBC *Politics Show*, 24 June 2007.
35. Gordon Brown, BBC interview, 24 September 2007.
36. *EU Watch*, May/June 2008.
37. Daniel Cohn-Bendit, leader of the European Greens, *Sunday Times*, 15 June 2008.
38. Axel Schäfer, German Bundestag Committee on European Affairs, *Sunday Times*, 15 June 2008.
39. Nicolas Sarkozy, *Le Soir*, 15 July 2008.
40. *Daily Telegraph*, 10 October 2008.

Chapter 6

1. Joschka Fischer, *Financial Times*, 21 November 2008.
2. Desmond Dinan, *Ever Closer Union*, Palgrave Macmillan, 2005, p.190.
3. Anand Menon, *Europe: The State of the Union*, Atlantic Books, 2008, p.74.
4. *The European Parliament – Working for You*, parliament publication, 2009.
5. Desmond Dinan, op. cit., p.267.
6. Decision of the European parliament, 28 September 2005.
7. *The European Parliament – Working for You*, parliament publication, 2009.

Chapter 7

1. Expo 2008, conference in Zaragoza, Spain.
2. 'Adapting to Climate Change in Europe', EU Commission Green Paper.
3. Ibid.
4. Proposal from the EU Commission to the European parliament on setting emission performance standards for new passenger cars.
5. Green Paper on the future Common European Asylum System (CEAS).
6. *The Times*, 3 December 2008.
7. Article III-271 treaty establishing a constitution for Europe.
8. 'Public Security, Privacy and Technology in Europe: Moving Forward', a document from the Portuguese presidency.
9. Communication from the EU Commission to the European parliament and the council on the implications of the court's judgement of 13 September 2005.
10. 'Towards a New Culture for Urban Mobility', EU Commission Green Paper.
11. Ibid.
12. Ibid.

13. EU Commission proposal for establishing the European Electronic Communications Market Authority.

14. 'Together for Health: A Strategic Approach for the EU 2008–2013', EU Commission White Paper.

15. Ibid.

16. 'Tax Policy in the European Union', EU Commission document.

17. Ibid.

18. 'How the EU's Single Market Benefits You', EU Commission document.

19. Ibid.

20. Ibid.

21. 'Schools for the 21st Century', EU Commission staff working paper.

22. 'A Better Work–Life Balance: Stronger Support for Reconciling Professional, Private and Family Life', communication from the EU Commission to the European parliament, the council and others.

23. Ibid.

24. Ibid.

25. Ibid.

26. 'Basic Orientations for the Sustainability of European Tourism', communication from the EU Commission to the European parliament, the council and others.

27. EU Commission White Paper on sport.

28. Ibid.

29. Ibid.

30. 'The European Research Area: New Perspectives', EU Commission Green Paper.

Chapter 8

1. 'Better Regulation – Simply Explained', EU Commission publication.

2. Ibid.

3. *International Herald Tribune*, 24 September 2005.

4. *Financial Times*, 26 November 1996.
5. Eur-Lex, 2009. Depending on which EU figures you use, you can conclude that there are anywhere between 8,000 and 38,000 EU laws in force. Here we are trying to establish whether the EU is making fewer laws or if legislation is still increasing, so we have taken the number of new laws introduced each year minus the number that have been withdrawn or reached the end of their validity
6. 'Better Regulation – Simply Explained', EU Commission publication.
7. *EU Observer*, 15 November 2006.
8. Communication from the EU Commission to the European parliament, the council and others, COM(2008) 32.
9. *International Herald Tribune*, 24 September 2005; *EU Observer*, 15 November 2006.
10. Annex 3 to list of withdrawals of pending proposals, EU Commission 2008 work plan.
11. *International Herald Tribune*, 24 September 2005.
12. Ibid.
13. *EU Observer*, 23 September 2008.
14. Ibid.
15. Ibid.
16. 'Second Strategic Review of Better Regulation in the European Union', EU Commission, 30 January 2008.
17. 'Better Regulation – Simply Explained', EU Commission publication.
18. *Financial Times*, 7 November 2008.
19. Agence France Presse, 7 October 2008; *EurActiv*, 1 October 2008.
20. www.eubusiness.com, 14 November 2008.
21. Ibid.

Chapter 9

1. EU Budget, Heading 3: Citizenship, Freedom, Security and Justice.

2. EU press release IP/06/1477.
3. 'Communicating Europe in Partnership', DG Communication memo, 3 October 2007.
4. Eurobarometer 288.
5. Agence France Presse, 11 September 2008; EU press release IP/07/280.
6. EU press release IP/07/280.
7. DG Communication work plan, 2008.
8. European Commission, Lifelong Learning Programme.
9. *The Times*, 27 January 2008.
10. 'A People's Europe', Communication from the Commission to the European Parliament.
11. EU website, www.europa.eu, 2009.
12. Ibid.
13. De Clercq Report, 1993.
14. EU press release, 30 September 2008.
15. Annual Work Programme on Grants and Contracts in the Field of Communication for 2008.
16. European parliament press release, 15 October 2008.
17. EU press conference, 30 September 2008.

Chapter 10

1. 'Fight against Fraud', EU website, www.europa.eu.
2. Speech by Siim Kallas to the Investigative Journalists Conference, 21 November 2008.
3. 'Fight against fraud', EU website, www.europa.eu.
4. Protocol (no. 36) on the privileges and immunities of the European Communities (1965), continued in the Constitution Protocol 7 Article 2.
5. Speech by Siim Kallas to the Investigative Journalists Conference, 21 November 2008.
6. *Independent*, 30 June 2004.
7. *Daily Telegraph*, 27 February 2002.
8. *Daily Telegraph*, 26 August 2002.
9. *Daily Telegraph*, 20 July 2002.

10. Ibid.
11. *Accountancy Age*, 6 July 2005.
12. Paul Foot in the *Guardian*, 23 July 2003.
13. *International Herald Tribune*, 23 June 2004.
14. *Daily Telegraph*, 14 October 2004.
15. *Sunday Telegraph*, 20 March 2005.
16. *Daily Telegraph*, 14 March 2005.
17. www.democracymovement.org.uk/mpmyths.html.
18. *Daily Telegraph*, 9 November 2007.
19. BBC *File on Four*, 26 July 2005, transcript.
20. Court of Auditors report on the 2006 EU budget.
21. Ibid.
22. Letter from Neil Kinnock to the *Daily Telegraph*, 21 November 2003.
23. *Washington Post*, 15 August 2004.
24. *Daily Telegraph*, 1 May 2005.
25. BBC News, 19 November 1999.
26. www.dw-world.de/dw/article/0,2144,2425423,00.html.
27. OLAF, 'Fight against Fraud', Annual Report, 6 July 2007, p.20.
28. Speech by Hubert Weber, president of the European Court of Auditors, 12 November 2007.
29. EU press release, 12 September 2007, Memo/07/350.
30. Speech by Siim Kallas, 12 November 2007.
31. BBC News, 13 November 2007.
32. *Daily Telegraph*, 19 April 2007.
33. Speech by Hubert Weber, president of the European Court of Auditors 12 November 2007.
34. BBC *File on Four*, 26 July 2005, transcript.
35. Memorandum to the House of Lords following 18 July 2006 hearing.
36. Court of Auditors, press release, 10 November 2008.
37. *European Voice*, 13 November 2008; speech by Danuta Hübner, 10 November 2008.
38. 'The Court's Opinion Concerning the Reliability of the Accounts 2007', published November 2008.

39. EU Commission Diagnosis, 2008.
40. Annual report of the Court of Auditors, 10 November 2008.
41. European Court of Auditors, press conference 10 November 2008.

Chapter 11

1. 'Fraud Adversely Affecting the Budget of the European Union', Faculty of Law, Zagreb, 17 July 2006.
2. Ibid.
3. The Comptroller and Auditor General Standard Report, HM Revenue & Customs Accounts.
4. Interviews by one of the authors with charity workers in Asia and Africa.
5. Paul Collier *The Bottom Billion*, Oxford University Press, 2008, p. 66 and p.150.
6. OLAF press release, 14 January 2008.
7. Ibid.
8. Ibid.
9. Annual accounts of the European Communities, 2007.
10. Court of Auditors, report on the 2006 EU budget.
11. 'Corruption – The World's Big C', Institute of Economic Affairs.
12. www.farmsubsidy.com, 2008.
13. Court of Auditors, report on the 2006 EU budget.
14. *International Herald Tribune*, 15 October 2008.
15. EU Commission report, January 2007.
16. 'Scathing EU Report Exposes Bulgaria's High-Level Corruption', *Deutsche Welle*, 18 July 2008.
17. *European Voice*, 4–10 September 2008.
18. Radio Free Europe, 27 June 2008.
19. *The Economist*, 3 July 2008.
20. Ibid.
21. *Frankfurter Allgemeine Zeitung*, 14 August 2008.
22. *International Herald Tribune*, 17 March 2008.
23. Preparatory notes for EU Council meeting on 4 March 2008; speech by Commissioner Kovacs, Brussels, 29 March 2007.

24. EU website, www.europa.eu, section on the EU budget.
25. Tempsréel.noulevobs.com/actualités/economie, 23 June 2008.
26. www.tiscali.co.uk/money, 29 May 2007.
27. 'Europe is a Honeypot for VAT Fraud', www.finfacts.ie, August 2006.
28. *Guardian*, 30 November 2007; BBC News Nottinghamshire.
29. *The Herald*, 25 May 2007.
30. www.channelregister.co.uk, 13 August 2008.
31. Ibid.

Chapter 12

1. *The Times*, 23 June 2006.
2. EU website, www.europa.eu.
3. *Metro*, 12 December 2005.
4. EU website, www.europa.eu, 2008.
5. www.farmsubsidy.org.
6. 'Top Recipients for Austrians', www.farmsubsidy.org; *Independent*, 9 November 2007.
7. *Independent*, 9 November 2007.
8. Ibid.
9. *The Times*, 14 December 2005.
10. Figures cover three years from 2002 to 2005; available on www.farmsubsidy.org.
11. *Metro*, 7 November 2005; *Independent*, 9 November 2007; *Financial Times*, 26 July 2008.
12. *Sunday Herald*, 16 September 2007.
13. Ibid.
14. *Sunday Times*, 29 July 2007.
15. *The Times*, 14 December 2005.
16. Official Journal of the European Union, 14 March 2008.
17. *New York Times*, 20 May 2008.
18. Ibid.
19. *New York Times*, 20 May 2008.
20. *The Times*, 22 June 2005.
21. Inter Press Service, 25 April 2008.

22. *Financial Times*, 30 June 2005.
23. Labour Party Conference, 2005.
24. 'Agriculture: Meeting the Needs of Farmers and Consumers', EU Commission, December 2008.
25. EU website, www.europa.eu.
26. 'CAP Health Check Goes a Step Further towards Modernisation and Simplification', www.epha.org, May 2008.

Chapter 13

1. Single European Act, 1986.
2. *Time* Magazine, 24 June 1974.
3. EU website, www.europa.eu, 2009.
4. 'Could Try Harder', report produced by the Green 10, a group of leading environmental NGOs active at EU level.
5. 'Providing Support to the Common Fisheries Policy', DG Joint Research Centre.
6. Note to the College from Commissioner Borg.
7. Ibid.
8. 'Combating Climate Change: The EU Leads the Way', September 2007.
9. EU press release, 23 May 2008.
10. 'Carbon Market Europe', 15 June 2007.
11. *Deutsche Welle*, 5 April 2007.
12. 'Combating Climate Change: The EU Leads the Way', September 2007.
13. 'Biofuels not as Green as They Sound', European Environmental Bureau, May 2002.
14. Parliamentary questions, answer given by Mrs Fischer Boel on behalf of the Commission, 16 September 2008.
15. UN Food and Agriculture Organisation newsroom, 7 October 2008.
16. *Guardian*, 3 July 2008.
17. Environmental Protection Encouragement Agency (EPEA), Hamburg, 2008.
18. *EU Observer*, 7 July 2008.

19. 'Combating Climate Change: The EU Leads the Way', September 2007.
20. Inter Press Service, 28 July 2008.
21. Strategic report on the renewed Lisbon strategy for growth and jobs, European Commission, 2008.
22. *European Voice*, 18 September 2008.
23. Parliamentary questions, answer given by Stavros Dimas on behalf of the Commission, 22 September 2008.
24. Ibid.

Chapter 14

1. *The Times*, 26 April 2006.
2. *The First Post*, 26 April 2006.
3. *Spiegel* online, 10 June 2008.
4. 'EP to Reduce its Carbon Footprint by 30 per cent', European parliament, 29 October 2008.
5. *EU Observer*, 24 October 2008.
6. EU Commission press release, 22 November 2000.
7. Ibid.
8. EU Commission press release, 22 November 2001.
9. *Financial Times*, 15 March 2007.
10. *Financial Times*, 4 May 2007.
11. Eurobarometer survey.
12. EU Commission press release, 5 June 2007.
13. EU Commission press release, 19 September 2007.
14. 'Galileo: Recent Developments', House of Commons Transport Committee, 7 November 2007.
15. *Today*, BBC Radio 4, November 2007.
16. Letter from André Sapir to Romano Prodi, July 2003.
17. 'A European Strategy for Jobs and Growth', House of Lords, 28th Report, 7 March 2006.
18. *European Voice*, 13 November 2008.

Chapter 15

1. BBC News, 27 June 2000.
2. *Sydney Morning Herald*, 15 December 2003.
3. Ibid.
4. *EU Observer*, 22 May 2007.
5. *EurActiv*, 25 July 2007.
6. *Irish Times*, 13 November 2008.
7. EU press conference, Brussels, 13 October 2005.
8. Conference of the presidents of the European Parliament, 5 December 2008.

INDEX